D1010778

Additional Praise for

Jimmy Stewart Is Dead

"The economic crisis has forced us to examine the shortcomings of our financial system. In *Jimmy Stewart Is Dead*, Laurence Kotlikoff argues that trust in the banking system has been broken and that only bold action will restore it. He calls for true transparency and offers thoughtful proposals such as Limited Purpose Banking to help restore trust in the system and to prevent such hardship from occurring again. Every Washington policy maker and public-spirited banker should read this book."
—BILL BRADLEY, former United States Senator

"This book is scarier than anything Stephen King ever wrote, and just as well-written. Distinguished economist Larry Kotlikoff has started a new genre: nonfiction economic horror. Kotlikoff knows what happened and why, and has the courage to point fingers and name names. One cannot turn the final page without the sense that this book may be our country's last hope."
—KEVIN HASSETT, Director of Economic Policy Studies; Senior Fellow, American Enterprise Institute; columnist, *Bloomberg News*

"The only sure way to avoid another Wall Street meltdown and ensure financial institutions act in ways that serve the economy is to separate the utility function of banking, connecting savers to borrowers, from the investment function of the financial market casino. Laurence Kotlikoff's Limited Purpose Banking proposal is an important and timely step forward."
—ROBERT B. REICH, Professor of Public Policy, University of California, Berkeley; former U.S. Secretary of Labor

"Larry Kotlikoff is that rare economist who comes up with the most original ideas when the stage is crowded with pedestrian analyses by other economists. He does it again with the current financial crisis. This is a marvelous book that will repay a careful read, even if you are as smart as Larry Summers and Ben Bernanke."
—JAGDISH BHAGWATI, University Professor of Economics and Law, Columbia University

"This remarkable book from Larry Kotlikoff is an invaluable read for all of us who care about our country's long-term competitiveness. I found it innovative, original thinking with a perspective of great value from a man to whom we should all pay attention."
—ADMIRAL WILLIAM OWENS, Chairman, AEA Holdings Asia;
    former Vice Chairman, Joint Chiefs of Staff

"If Michelin gave out stars to economists, Larry Kotlikoff would get three of them—worthy of a detour. Mixing villains, wit and wisdom, *Jimmy Stewart Is Dead* is a great read with a serious message. Kotlikoff makes a compelling case for regulation that would restructure the banking system to limit banks to their basic functions, and he shows how doing so would allow market forces to make the next financial crisis less likely and less severe. This is a desperately needed antidote to the spate of proposed reforms from the usual pundits that amount to nothing more inspired than a call for more regulation without a recipe for smarter regulation. Iconoclastic but practical, Kotlikoff is one of the most creative economists of his generation and one of its premier policy analysts. It would be folly not to listen to him."
—STEPHEN A. ROSS, Franco Modigliani Professor of
    Financial Economics, MIT

"Informative, infuriating, and insightful. If you think you understand the extent of the malfeasance by Wall Street and by our Federal Government, you are in for a rude shock when you read this book. Larry Kotlikoff understands the scope of the problems we face better than any economist I know; he uses clear, accessible and lively prose; best of all, he offers an innovative and provocative solution to this gargantuan problem. Send copies of this book to your representatives in Washington!"
—EDWARD E. LEAMER, Chauncey J. Medberry Professor of
    Management; Professor of Economics and Professor of Statistics,
    University of California, Los Angeles

"This is provocative and hard-hitting analysis. A leading academic economist takes off the gloves and goes a hard eight rounds with finance-as-we-know-it. The result is a fresh and clear proposal for reducing the risks that arise as people with savings provide funding to people making productive investments in any economy. If we implement Professor Kotlikoff's ideas—or any close approximation—the U.S. can continue to generate entrepreneurship, growth, and jobs, without repeatedly having to bail out our big banks. This is beyond appealing; it is compelling."
—SIMON JOHNSON, Professor of Entrepreneurship, MIT Sloan;
    former Chief Economist, International Monetary Fund

"Larry Kotlikoff has been consistently ahead of the curve in the debate on America's coming fiscal breakdown. Now he turns his attention to the financial crisis that threatens to bring that fiscal breakdown forward to, well, quite possibly this year. I was wholly persuaded by the case he makes for Limited Purpose Banking. It is clearly the best available remedy for the present appalling state of affairs, in which highly leveraged 'too big to fail' institutions can expect taxpayers to pick up the multi-trillion-dollar tab when their gambles go wrong."
—NIALL FERGUSON, William Ziegler Professor of
    Business Administration, Harvard Business School;
    author, *The Ascent of Money*

"Kotlikoff provides a marvelously clear explanation of how today's financial system really works, stripping away all the obscure jargon. At the same time, the book is a passionate and strongly worded indictment of the system and a blueprint for how to fix it from the ground up. Kotlikoff's basic thesis: that today's financial institutions have become taxpayer subsidized casinos increasingly divorced from the basic intermediation activities society expects them to perform—is hard to refute."
—KENNETH ROGOFF, Thomas D. Cabot Professor of Public Policy
    and Professor of Economics, Harvard University;
    former Chief Economist, International Monetary Fund;
    co-author, *This Time Is Different*

"I always make time in my busy schedule to read anything Larry Kotlikoff writes. You should too. Why? He is always insightful in his analysis, provocative in his predictions, and creative in his proposed solutions. In *Jimmy Stewart Is Dead*, Kotlikoff lays open the fundamental fissures in the financial system and presents a radical solution: Limited Purpose Banking, an idea related to proposals during the Great Depression by renowned American economists Frank Knight and Irving Fisher. When I was helping clean up the last American financial crises—the Savings and Loans mess and the Latin American debt fiasco for the big money center banks—I lamented the dearth of creative policy thinking before they struck. Policymakers, investors, taxpayers, and all concerned citizens will find much to mull over in this readily accessible book."

—MICHAEL J. BOSKIN, T.M. Friedman Professor of Economics and
    Senior Fellow, Hoover Institution, Stanford University; former
    Chairman, President's Council of Economic Advisors, 1989–1993

"Laurence Kotlikoff is one of the original thinkers of our time. Even if you don't agree with his specific proposals, Larry's new book—with the provocative title, *Jimmy Stewart Is Dead*—is likely to lead you beyond the conventional ways of dealing with the economic challenges facing our country."

—MURRAY WEIDENBAUM, Edward Mallinckrodt Distinguished
    University Professor and Professor of Economics, Washington
    University, St. Louis; former Chairman, President's Council
    of Economic Advisers

"This book is heaps of fun. But it is entirely serious, and comes at the right time. The profound change—Limited Purpose Banking, which Kotlikoff recommends and that we desperately need—could only be undertaken now that we've seen the full dangers of maintaining the current financial system. Kotlikoff entertains with great energy while instructing using facts made for fiction. To understand the most effective changes we can make to truly fix our financial system, read this book."

—SUSAN WOODWARD, Principal, Sand Hill Econometrics; former Chief
    Economist of the U.S. Securities and Exchange Commission;
    former Chief Economist of the U.S. Department of Housing
    and Urban Development

"Our financial system puts us all at risk. This book shows that it doesn't have to be this way. We can have all the benefits of a modern economy without having crises like the last one. Or, if policy makers don't listen, like the next one. And the next . . . "
—PAUL ROMER, Senior Fellow at Stanford Center for International
    Development (SCID) and Stanford Institute for Economic Policy
    Research (SIEPR), Stanford University

"This book grips like a novel. But, it's no work of fiction. It's our actual financial horror story in which we face ongoing economic torture at the hands of greedy bankers, incompetent regulators, and corrupt politicians. The book is a penetrating and painless (indeed, fun) education as well as a saving grace. It offers the only clear path to economic salvation— forcing banks to do the one and only thing they are here for—financial intermediation."
—CHRISTOPHE CHAMLEY, Professor of Economics, Boston University

"If the Crash caused you to fear for your job, your retirement, and for the future of your children, read this book. You will be led by one of America's most eminent economists through a blow-by-blow account of what happened and why, and there will be times you will feel like running to the window to shout out your outrage and call for change. Kotlikoff's proposal for Limited Purpose Banking calls for the most radical overhaul of banking legislation since the Great Depression."
—URI DADUSH, Senior Associate and Director of International
    Economics, Carnegie Endowment for International Peace;
    former Director of International Trade and
    Director of Economic Policy, World Bank

"Forget narrow banking concepts. Professor Kotlikoff forces us to consider Limited Purpose finance, and does so with humor and enlightenment."
—ROBERT R. BENCH, Senior Fellow at Boston University School
    of Law; former Deputy U.S. Comptroller of Currency

"Larry Kotlikoff has written a fascinating book. It is a must read for everyone who wants to understand the current financial crisis and what we can do about it."
—JOHN C. GOODMAN, President and CEO, National Center
    for Policy Analysis

"Kotlikoff makes a strong case for Limited Purpose Banking as the best protection against the next financial crisis. I worry most about his proposal for replacing all current federal and state financial regulatory agencies with one massive federal financial authority; this authority, I suggest, would increase the scope of regulatory mistakes and the prospect and capability of the federal government to allocate credit for political objectives. I encourage readers of this book to make your own judgment about the regulatory environment that would best complement Limited Purpose Banking."
—WILLIAM A. NISKANEN, Chairman Emeritus of the Cato Institute;
   former Acting Chairman and Member of the President's Council
   of Economic Advisers

"This is a must read for everyone who wants to know not only what went wrong, but how to fix it. Kotlikoff has brilliant answers to the most important questions in economics today."
—ANNA BERNASEK, economic journalist and
   author of *The Economics of Integrity*

"Laurence Kotlikoff has produced an entertaining and insightful analysis of the great credit crisis and the ailments of the U.S. financial system. This sets the stage for some radical proposals to change the structure of the financial intermediation. In his view triage is not enough— what is required is radical reconstructive surgery. Whether you view his recommendations for Limited Purpose Banking as politically viable or not, his analysis goes to the heart of the important flaws that have to be confronted if we are to reduce the likelihood of crises in the future. This book is essential reading for those interested in the perils of financial intermediation in the modern world."
—THOMAS F. COOLEY, Dean and Paganelli-Bull Professor of
   Economics, New York University Stern School of Business

"Kotlikoff understands markets and market makers. And he understands economics. He vividly diagnoses the financial plague, and he argues that, as is, the system is unsafe at any speed. His remarkably simple cure does not rely on a dying breed—honest bankers like Jimmy Stewart (a.k.a. George Bailey), but on limiting banking to its only honest purpose— financial intermediation."
—HERAKLES POLEMARCHAKIS, Professor of Economics,
   University of Warwick

"Larry Kotlikoff provides a poignant, accessible, and engaging account of how distorted incentives, leverage, and risk played a major role in the financial crisis. He also confronts us with a scary account of the government deficits that will come to haunt us or our descendants. Kotlikoff's ideas for how to change the banking system are thought-provoking. This book forces us to step back and think about the basic purpose of financial institutions, and whether there is a better way to organize them."
—ANAT ADMATI, George C.G. Parker Professor of Finance and
    Economics, Graduate School of Business, Stanford University

"Many doubt whether proposed regulatory reforms regarding capital requirements will be effective in reducing the excessive risks taken by banks and other financial institutions. Larry Kotlikoff offers a more fundamental solution called Limited Purpose Banking (LPB), in which banks connect borrowers to lenders and savers to investors without taking on risk. This radical idea, challenging the existing structure of all financial institutions, deserves to be at the center of the post-crisis debate. Economists and practitioners alike will find this a compelling book."
—EYTAN SHESHINSKI, Sir Isaac Wolfson Professor of Public Finance,
    Department of Economics, The Hebrew University

Jimmy Stewart
Is Dead

Jimmy Stewart Is Dead

Ending the World's Ongoing Financial Plague with Limited Purpose Banking

Laurence J. Kotlikoff

WILEY

John Wiley & Sons, Inc.

Published by John Wiley & Sons, Inc., Hoboken, New Jersey.
Published simultaneously in Canada.

For general information on our other products and services or for technical support, please contact our Customer Care Department within the United States at (800) 762-2974, outside the United States at (317) 572-3993 or fax (317) 572-4002.

Wiley also publishes its books in a variety of electronic formats. Some content that appears in print may not be available in electronic books. For more information about Wiley products, visit our web site at www.wiley.com.

Library of Congress Cataloging-in-Publication Data:

Kotlikoff, Laurence J.
  Jimmy Stewart is dead : ending the world's ongoing financial plague with limited purpose banking / Laurence J. Kotlikoff.
    p. cm.
    Includes index.
    ISBN 978-0-470-58155-1 (cloth)
  1. Fiscal policy—United States.   2. Financial crises—United States—History—
21st century.   I. Title.
    HJ2051.K663 2010
    332.0973–dc22   2009041432

Printed in the United States of America.
10   9   8   7   6   5   4   3   2   1

For Miguel, the bravest man I know!

Contents

Foreword

by Jeffrey Sachs

L arry Kotlikoff is a worried man on an urgent mission. He knows that the financial crisis that hit us in 2008 can come back with a vengeance, because our government, so far, is treating the symptoms but not the underlying disease. By the time you finish this book you will be worried too. With brilliance, wit, clarity, and bravery, Kotlikoff explains how our financial system is "virtually designed for hucksters." Yet even more importantly, he shows us how to fix it.

As Kotlikoff makes clear, the litany of faulty incentives and opportunities for fraud in the U.S.'s banking system is distressingly long: "limited liability, fractional reserves, off-balance-sheet bookkeeping, insider-rating, kick-back accounting, sales-driven bonuses, nondisclosure, director sweetheart deals, pension benefit guarantees, and government bailouts." It's a system, in a word, in which bankers make promises they can't keep in order to collect outsized earnings unrelated to real productivity.

What a cast of characters we will meet along the way! Kotlikoff is right to note that most bankers are "fine people doing their best by their clients," but he is also right on the mark to note that the top ranks of bankers "include a remarkably large number of fast-talking con artists, riverboat gamblers, and highway men." And why not? With regulatory loopholes a mile wide, the con artists found ways to abscond with tens, even hundreds of billions of dollars, before the entire economy went over the cliff.

I've taken my own special interest in the bankers' bonuses over the years, as I've witnessed up close how rather pedestrian Wall Street work on restructuring developing country debt could pull in millions of dollars in fees for the bankers. At the start of each calendar year, I've gone slack-jawed at a level of Wall Street year-end bonuses roughly equal to the total worldwide aid given to 800 million Africans.

At a recent dinner with bank executives to discuss African poverty, I surmised the depth of their concern with this heartbreaking issue as they steered the conversation to the relative size of their wine cellars, with several describing their collections as exceeding 30,000 bottles! The typical African could spend his whole life working and never afford a single one of those bottles.

These are signs not merely of moral decadence but of regulatory collapse. Kotlikoff skillfully leads us through the various methods that the banking leaders have developed for taking their slice of the assets. Amazingly, none of the executives who we meet in these pages was technically equipped to understand the deeper risks in which they were placing their firms, and the world economy. But they were very well trained in cutting themselves extremely generous proportions of the action.

If Kotlikoff had stopped at explaining what just hit us, he would have performed a mighty service. Even with the many vivid and entertaining accounts of the great crash in 2008, of who said what to whom on the fateful weekend in September 2008 when Lehman, AIG, and Merrill hit the wall, no previous book comes remotely close to this one in offering a *conceptual* understanding of what has gone wrong. Through ingenious examples and stories, Kotlikoff gently instructs the readers in the core concepts of financial economics: coordination failures, moral hazard, intergenerational accounting, principal–agent problems, Ponzi schemes, and much more.

It is our great fortune, though, that Kotlikoff does not stop there, but proceeds boldly to lay out a novel, powerful, and ingenious set of reforms under the rubric of Limited Purpose Banking. As he explains, the motivation of LPB is to "limit banks to their legitimate purpose— connecting borrowers to lenders and savers to investors—and not let them gamble. But Kotlikoff is no scold. He's not against gambling per se. He's only against others gambling with our money without our knowledge or permission.

This is the protection of LPB. If individuals want a completely safe bank account, their bank deposits will be matched 100 percent by money held by the bank. If they want something riskier, or some form of insurance, then appropriate mutual funds will be available to cater to distinct needs, and set up in ways to avoid systemic risk. In all cases, financial intermediaries will face not 115 different regulatory agencies asleep at the wheel, but a single Federal Financial Authority with a very limited assignment—to ensure that fund managers do not abscond with our assets and immediately, fully, and accurately disclose what each fund is holding. Imagine that—a financial marketplace in which we're actually told what we're buying!

Kotlikoff traces some of the origins of his ideas to proposals for Limited Banking that emerged in the wake of the Great Depression, and which have won the endorsement of leading economists over the decades. He does not shrink from pointing out continued controversies surrounding his ideas, so that the book provides an ideal jumping off point for further serious debate over the ideas.

There are lots of open questions and areas of doubt that require further discussion, notably around the issues of how fast, how far, and in what ways we would need to adopt LPB to reap its benefits. Still, the ideas are powerfully resonant and will find a growing group of adherents.

America is passing through a very difficult economic juncture, with high unemployment and even higher anxieties. Millions of people have seen their financial security lost in the Wall Street tsunami. We feel adrift, with a large majority sensing, correctly, that the country is headed in the wrong direction. Faith in the economic system, the lifeblood of the economy itself, has been badly broken. Kotlikoff knows that each of us bears a responsibility and has a role to play to help repair the damage. With characteristic directness and integrity, he says that every economist has "an obligation . . . to focus on this economic emergency."

Let us thank Kotlikoff for a clear, convincing, and highly original call to action. With this book, he has surely fulfilled his obligation, and much more, to help the world reset its sights on a more stable, fair, and prosperous economy.

JEFFREY SACHS
Director of The Earth Institute,
Quetelet Professor of Sustainable Development,
and Professor of Health Policy and Management
at Columbia University

Preface

'Twas the year the country stood still. Not a car, truck, or bus rode the roads. No one drove to work, no one drove to shop, no one drove to visit. No one drove anywhere. The reason was simple. No one could buy gas. The gas stations had all gone broke.

Their owners had tired of netting pennies on the gallon. They wanted to surge their earnings. The big money, they learned from a bright young MBA, was in securitizing their services. So they started selling GODs—*Gas Options for Drivers.*

Each GOD gave the driver the option to fill her tank for $4 per gallon. Drivers bought GODs religiously. And with gas selling for $3 a gallon, station owners didn't worry.

Then the unthinkable happened. Gas prices skyrocketed to $6.00 a gallon, and drivers began invoking their GODs. Each GOD could save $2 per gallon per tank, and if you didn't need gas, you held up a sign—"Gods for Cash!"

Station owners began cursing the GODs. They now had to buy gas at $6 a gallon and sell it for $4. In short order, the owners went bust. They closed their stations and started looking for jobs in financial services. GODs became worthless. Overnight, there was no gas for the nation's 250 million vehicles, and the economy ground to a halt.

The economic moral is simple. If you want markets to function, don't let critical market makers—intermediaries who connect suppliers (e.g., refineries) and demanders (e.g., motorists) of essential products—gamble with their businesses.

Apply the moral to banks (shorthand for all financial corporations, including insurance companies) and the regulatory prescription is clear. Limit banks to their legitimate purpose—connecting lenders to borrowers and savers to investors—and *don't let them gamble*.

Would that we had heeded this injunction. Instead, we let Wall Street play craps with our financial system, our economy, and our tax dollars. The result—we lost big time. This book describes in plain English and simple terms the big con underlying the big game—the web of interconnected financial, political, and regulatory malfeasance that culminated in financial meltdown and brought us to our economic knees. It's a story with everyone on the take, with a host of villains committing first-, second-, and third-degree economic murder, leaving millions upon millions of victims at home and abroad.

Others have told and are telling this story. They are primarily financial journalists and Wall Street traders. Their insider details are both fascinating and horrifying. But conveying the facts is not the same as assessing their economic meaning. That's primarily the responsibility of economists, of which I am one. We economists are charged with understanding and protecting the economy; we're supposed to spot economic disasters before they arise and recommend solutions.

Unfortunately, we failed in our fiduciary duty. With rare exceptions, those of us manning the watch—the economists hired by the government and the business world—missed what was coming, were shocked when it happened, exacerbated the public's fear, and are now helping resurrect the system that failed so miserably.

The rest of us—academic economists like myself—were perched in ivory towers, too high above deck to see the pervasive financial malfeasance that was underway. We had a clear view had we looked, but we were researching our imaginary world in which people play by the rules. Consequently, we had even less clue that the nation's largest financial companies, aided and abetted by the rating companies, politicians, and regulators, were madly driving our economy straight toward the rocks. They reached their destination. The economy is now firmly on the shoals and in ongoing danger of completely breaking up.

Given that our economy is in DEFCOM 1 or very close to that condition, it's all economic hands on deck. Every economist has an obligation, regardless of her or his area of specialization, to focus on this economic emergency—to understand what really went wrong and to help make sure this never, ever happens again. This book is my attempt to help us escape the rocks, and not just for a quarter, a year, or a decade, but for the long term—the years our children and grandchildren hope to enjoy.

To be clear, my main area of expertise is not finance. It's fiscal affairs, particularly the sustainability of our tax and spending policies and their implications for the next generation. But I've also worked on a range of other issues, including economic growth, saving, international trade, pensions, insurance, health reform, tax reform, Social Security, and personal finance.

Studying a range of economic issues provides a broader perspective for considering the problem at hand. It also helps to be clear of financial conflicts of interest in weighing Main Street's interests against Wall Street's. In my case, my bread isn't buttered by financial companies, but by an independent academic institution, namely Boston University. Unlike my economic brethren working on Wall Street and many of those working in Washington, I don't need to worry that what I say will affect what I earn now or in the future. I'm also free of political constraints. I'm not a registered anything and am beholden to neither political party.[1]

But full disclosure requires full disclosure. Breadth, distance from the Street, and mostly armchair policymaking come at a cost. The more we know about everything, the less we know about anything. In my case, I'm not an expert on all the intricacies *and imperfections* of asset pricing, exchange trading, risk appraisal, dynamic hedging, and securitization. And I can't quote line and verse from banking regulations or tell you precisely how to construct a CDO squared or other exotic derivatives.

Fortunately, for the critical matter at hand—fixing our financial system—seeing the forest is much more important than naming all the trees. My goal then is not just to survey the amazing and disheartening events surrounding our economic shipwreck, but to convey their deeper economic meaning, particularly the extraordinary danger of maintaining the financial status quo, and to propose a solution that follows from the terrible facts.

The right financial fix, called *limited purpose banking*, is remarkably simple and easy to implement.[2] And it can be accomplished without limiting credit, risk taking, insurance, leverage, or any other economically vital financial behavior or service. Most important, limited purpose banking will immediately restore trust in our financial system, which is the sine qua non for reviving the economy and its long-term prospects.

This financial fix is wholly different from the policies pursued to date to rescue the banks and insurance companies. Those policies have administered elixirs when the patient is in cardiac arrest. They've made the patient more comfortable but done nothing to cure his underlying disease. Worse yet, the palliatives are extremely expensive and highly addictive.

The gurus applying these "cures" have a vested interest in preserving the status quo. Their focus is on the next election and, far too often, their next job. What they've ignored is the next generation, which can neither afford their solutions nor tolerate their tinkering. Young, trusting economic lives are at stake, and nothing short of economic open-heart surgery will save the American dream.

Our sad tale, with its hopeful ending, starts with our economic disaster and where it's headed, describes its causes, identifies its architects, and then shows how to fix our financial system for good.

LAURENCE J. KOTLIKOFF

Acknowledgments

This book is the beneficiary of many discussions, some very brief, some extensive, some face to face, and some via phone or email, with the following list of academic, business, and government economists, current and former central bankers, current and former Treasury and Federal Reserve officials, current and former private bankers, U.S. bank examiners, current and former U.S. Senators, business men and women, consultants, former bank and government attorneys, mutual fund managers, hedge fund managers, financial journalists, students, and people (including my 19-year-old and 11-year-old sons) from other walks of life: David Altig, Anat Admati, James Ballentine, Robert Bench, Zvi Bodie, Michael Boskin, Bill Bradley, Beverly Brown, Robert Brown, Scott Burns, David Campbell, Domingo Cavallo, Christophe Chamley, Robert Costrell, John Covell, Uri Dadush, Donald Van Deventer, Douglas Diamond, Michael Dooley, Philip Dybvig, Niall Ferguson, Stanley Fischer, Simon Gilchrist, Kirsten Gillibrand, Robert Glovsky, John Goodman, Jeff Gray, Matt Halperin, Robert Hartman, James Henry, Brian Hinkley, Peter Howitt, Cornelius Hurley, Goda Kalila, Jeffrey Kerrigan, Alexander Kotlikoff, David Kotlikoff, Pentti Kouri, Edward Leamer, Ross Levine, John Liewellyn,

Leo Lindbeck, Dennis Lockhart, Glenn Loury, Gonzalo Sánchez de Lozada, Preston McAfee, Bob McTeer, Perry Mehrling, Robert Merton, Alistair Milne, William Niskanen, Paul Pfleiderer, Edmund Phelps, Michael Polermeano, James Poterba, Eswar Prasad, Paul Romer, Steven Ross, Jeffrey Sachs, Paul Salmon, Virginia Sapiro, Cathy Shavell, Robert Shavell, Karl Shell, George Shultz, John Silber, Michael Spence, Jonathan Treussard, Elliot Vestner, Luis Viciera, Andrew Weiss, Ivo Welch, and Graham Wilson.

Each of these individuals, particularly Anat Admati, Robert Bench, Zvi Bodie, Christophe Chamley (with whom I co-authored the first draft of *Limited Purpose Banking*), Uri Dadush, Cornelius Hurley, Jeff Kerrigan, Edward Leamer, Ross Levine, Glenn Loury, Perry Mehrling, Paul Pfleiderer, Michael Pomerleano, Eric Roiter, Jeff Sachs, Jonathan Treussard, Edmund Phelps, Steve Ross, Luis Viciera, Andrew Weiss, and Susan Woodward helped me formulate and sharpen my views about our extremely dangerous financial system and how to fix it.

I also benefited greatly from presenting seminars on limited purpose banking at Boston University, Brown University, Columbia University, Cornell University, the Federal Reserve Bank of Atlanta, the Cato Institute, and the Policy Exchange in London.

But the fact that the above list of brilliant and practical minds communicated with me, either directly or indirectly, about my policy views doesn't mean they agree with all or any of them. The opinions expressed here are mine and not necessarily those of my witting or unwitting accomplices.

I thank Boston University for its steadfast support of my research over the past quarter-century.

Miguel Ampudia is a wonderful graduate student of mine who was hit by life much harder and sooner than he deserved. He is recovering from a major accident and would benefit greatly from all our prayers.

Finally, I thank my editors, Laura Walsh and Judy Howarth, and the rest of the Wiley team for believing in this book and helping prepare it with so much care.

L. J. K.

Chapter 1

It's a Horrible Mess

Each financial crisis is different, yet they all feature financial institutions making promises they can't keep. "This is a sure bet." "My strategy beats the market." "This loan is triple A." "Our capital's adequate." "Your money's safe." "Don't worry."

Well, we're worried. The financial market has melted down, and with it trust in a system that routinely borrows short and lends long, guaranteeing repayment yet investing at risk. It's a system virtually designed for hucksters, with limited liability, fractional reserves, off-balance-sheet bookkeeping, insider-rating, kick-back accounting, sales-driven bonuses, nondisclosure, director sweetheart deals, pension benefit guarantees, and government bailouts.

It's a Wonderful Life, the beloved Christmas movie, showed just where this can lead: an otherwise honest banker, George Bailey (played by Jimmy Stewart), confessing to a mob of angry *demand* depositors that, in fact, he'd lied—that Bailey Savings & Loan can't return all their money on demand. Despondent and about to take his life, God sends an angel to save George and his bank just in the nick of time.

1

The movie's ending is happy, but its underlying message is not: Our financial system, as designed, is fantastically fragile, perched atop a pillar of trust that can instantly be undermined. Check that, *was undermined*! For here we sit with our financial pillar in ruins, watching Uncle Sam desperately trying to glue the pieces back together.

It's Not Bailey Savings & Loan

Uncle Sam's strategy—fight each financial fire one by one and rebuild the old system pretty much as was—is deeply misguided. It treats the symptoms, not the disease, and will leave us financially and fiscally weaker.

The financial community has close ties to Sam, marked by massive campaign contributions to both parties, and is working overtime to make sure Sam doesn't rock their boat. Their mantra is "The financial crisis was caused by a housing bubble, spurred by the Federal Reserve's low interest-rate policy and lax regulatory oversight. The system is fundamentally sound and critical to our economy. We haven't seen anything like this in 80 years. Yes, some bad apples took on too much leverage, but trust us. 'We're doing God's work.'[1] We'll make sure it doesn't happen again. We bankers know what we're doing, and our financial judgment is critical for allocating credit and choosing investments."

The notion that bankers know what they are doing or can keep this from happening again is risible given everything we've seen. And the proposition that banking as usual is essential to our economy as opposed to extremely dangerous is predicated on a quaint view of banks that bears little resemblance to today's reality.

Bailey Savings & Loan is not your local bank. Your local bank is Bank of America, Citigroup, JPMorgan Chase, or one of the other ten largest banking conglomerates, whose headquarters are hundreds, if not thousands, of miles away and who have taken over most of the banking business.[2]

And Jimmy Stewart, the honest, warm, kind, and trusting soul, is not your local banker. Jimmy Stewart is dead. Your local banker is some underpaid clerk who's been in place for six months and knows nothing about you, your family, or your business, and frankly could care less. His job is not to apply personal knowledge in deciding to lend you money or call your loan. His task is to plug your credit rating, income, loan request, appraisals, and other data into a computer and tell you what the computer tells him, namely how much you can borrow and at what rate.

Our bankers are desperately attached to the current system for good reason. It lets them socialize risks and privatize profits. Socializing risk means having the public take the hit when things go south. Privatizing profits means earning big fees in normal times when the economy generates positive and high returns on investments.

This is by no means to suggest a conspiracy of bankers, but rather to point out that bankers, like members of other professions, are self-interested and have managed to set up a system that works for them, even if doesn't work for the country. Nor do I imply that bankers, as a group, lack financial judgment, integrity, or a social conscience. Most are fine people doing their best by their clients. But their ranks, particularly their top ranks, include a remarkably large number of fast-talking con artists, riverboat gamblers, and highway men whom you'd never trust with your money, let alone your kids, if you really got to know them.

Both the good-guy and the bad-guy bankers are working within a regulatory system designed in the 1930s for Bailey Savings & Loan, not for today's world of global finance, exotic financial securities, computer-ized electronic trading, and enormous trade volume that George Bailey could not begin to fathom. Today, more trades are conducted on the New York Stock Exchange in a single day than were conducted in all of 1929.[3]

The new technologies have not only increased the speed of financial transactions; they've also reduced the costs. This translates into better terms for those needing to raise money by selling assets (e.g., borrowing or issuing stock) and higher returns for those willing to supply money by buying assets (e.g., lending or purchasing stock). But as the spreads to intermediation got squeezed, many financial players started looking to make money the old-fashioned way—by stealing it.

Some of this theft involved simply pocketing investors' money, with Bernard Madoff and Allen Stanford being prime examples. But most in-volved selling snake oil, including complex bundles of incredibly crappy (to use technical language) mortgages, which were stamped AAA by the principal rating companies—Standard & Poor's, Fitch, and Moody's. The rating companies delivered their "appraisals" in exchange for huge payments and after verifying that these mortgages had been "insured" by AIG, MBIA, or some other malfeasant insurer, which the rating companies had, themselves, rated AAA.

The complexity of these securities, the implicit bribing of rating companies, the deceit of mortgage initiators, the incompetence of regulators, the sales-based compensation of management, the complicity of corporate directors, the collusion of bankers and politicians, and the naiveté of investors—all quickly turned the sale of snake oil into a multi-trillion-dollar industry. The collapse of this industry has exposed our financial system for what it is—fundamentally corrupt, incredibly fragile, and never again to be trusted.

Unfortunately, there is no putting the genie back in the bottle. We can't return to yesteryear and outlaw what has become a $600 trillion market in derivatives.[4] (Yes, you read that right.) We can't eliminate the securitization of loans, bar financial innovation, or expect global bankers to act in loco parentis. We can't ban subprime mortgages, credit default swaps, collateralized mortgage obligations, or other so-called toxic assets. Nor can we limit credit only to those with good ratings, stable jobs, and plenty of collateral.

In short, we're stuck with financial modernity for better and for worse. But, as we've seen, financial modernity goes far beyond what our old financial regulatory and rating system can handle. It's also far beyond what Uncle Sam can handle. His decision to bail out the banking sector, the mortgage industry, the insurance industry, the money market fund industry, the auto industry, the credit card industry, the states, the housing industry, the student loan industry, small business, the RV industry, the rental car industry, the boating industry, the snowmobile industry, and Lord knows who's next invites ongoing gambling at the public expense by any business or entity that can reasonably expect a bailout if push comes to shove.[5] This is a prescription for fiscal insolvency, which could culminate in hyperinflation as the government finds that the only way it can get enough money to cover all its handouts is by printing it.[6]

The printing presses are already running overtime. The monetary base measures the amount of money Uncle Sam prints in order to buy things, whether those things are financial securities, tanks, space ships, or lunch for the president.[7] On January 1, 2008, the monetary base totaled $831 billion. On June 1, 2009, it stood at $1.8 trillion!

Uncle Sam printed more money (just shy of $1 trillion) over those 18 months than was printed in the entire history of the republic.[8] And he's just revving up. The Federal Reserve has pledged to print another 1,750,000,000,000 dollars ($1.75 trillion) during 2009 to lower long-term interest rates and thereby continue to bail out the economy. That translates into more than a quadrupling of the monetary base in two years and could, if banks start lending again, culminate in a quadrupling of the nation's M1 money supply and, ultimately, of prices![9]

The authors of this policy know they are playing with fire—the economy could quickly flip from experiencing today's low inflation or even deflation to hyperinflation. The policy's chief architect, Federal Reserve Chairman Ben Bernanke, is an exceptionally thoughtful, responsible, and cautious person, not to mention an outstanding economist. The fact that he's pulling out the stops to this unprecedented extent speaks volumes for the gravity of the situation.

But throwing money at the problem is no long-term solution. It does nothing to fix the system's underlying problems, which requires tough love, not endless handouts. The right path forward is not exhuming Jimmy Stewart, applying some makeup, and propping him up in the bank window. Given what it's learned and lost in this financial debacle, the public would no longer trust Jimmy Stewart in the flesh, let alone the bone. The right path forward is Limited Purpose Banking.

Talking Turkey with Wall Street

Boys and girls, the party's is over. You have one job and one job only—financial intermediation. If you want to gamble, be our guest. But do so on your own time, in your own home, and on your own dime. As a group, you are not to be trusted. So we're going to let you exercise your significant skills and generally good judgment, but in a way that doesn't threaten our savings, jobs, and families. From here on out you'll have to work within a new financial system, called Limited Purpose Banking, that makes you stick to your legitimate purpose—financial intermediate.

Look around. The one part of your industry still standing is the mutual fund industry, which generally stuck to its knitting—connecting suppliers of and demanders for funds. The

(Continued)

(*Continued*)

reason is simple: mutual fund companies, with a few exceptions, didn't play craps with their company's capital.

Limited Purpose Banking transforms all of the financial corporations in which you work—whether they are called commercial banks, investment banks, hedge funds, insurance companies, private equity funds, venture capital funds, brokerages, credit unions, or something else—into pass-through mutual fund companies.[10]

None of your companies, which we'll just call banks, will ever again be in a position to fail because none of your banks will ever again be allowed to borrow short and lend long and leave the public to pick up the pieces. The public ultimately bears the risk of investment and the public, with your proper help, is going to decide what risks to take and what risks, including systemic financial collapse, to avoid.

All banks will be subject to the same regulation, regardless of their particular line of business. A single federal regulator, the Federal Financial Authority (FFA), will verify, disclose, and supervise the custody and independent rating of all securities held by all mutual funds. This will put an end to the pervasive fraud that now attends your initiation and sale of vast numbers of securities.

Limited Purpose Banking is a real, as opposed to cosmetic, fix of the financial system—one that gets and keeps Uncle Sam off Wall Street's hook. Such a fix is essential not only for healing the financial sector, but for achieving overall economic recovery. By itself, the financial sector accounts for over 20 percent of U.S. GDP.[11] And, like gas stations, its operations are vital to the rest of the economy's performance. But no one is going to rely on financial companies if they can't trust what they are doing and selling. Wall Street has completely and irrevocably squandered the public's trust. And left to its devices, Wall Street will keep chasing the almighty buck no matter the risk to the economy, including a rerun of the Great D.

Economics Diary, Spring 2009: The D Word

"Depression" is a word that no economist likes to say. But today it's on the tips of everyone's tongues, and for good reason. The economy is imploding at a rate we've not seen since the 1930s. Output is dropping at a 6 percent annual rate, exports are off 15 percent, and the financial system is on life support.[12] The one industry doing well is the bread line. Food stamp applications have hit record highs, and one in three of our nation's children are now on this dole.[13]

More than 500,000 workers are losing their jobs each month. Close to one in ten Americans—some 12.5 million people—are now out of work. Housing starts are at 50-year lows, and foreclosures are at all-time highs.[14] Two million families lost their homes last year because they couldn't pay the mortgage.[15] Another 17 million may shortly join their ranks.[16]

Everyone is scared. The jobless are worried sick, and those with jobs are sure they're next on the chopping block. The elderly are in acute shock. Many have seen their retirement assets fall in half and their dreams of a comfortable retirement evaporate.

Our children are feeling our pain and asking us what happened. Our answer is that we don't know. We thought we had well-functioning banking and insurance companies with competent directors, world-class managers, responsible regulators, and incorruptible rating companies. But overnight, we learned it was a sham—that while we were hard at work, much of the financial, regulatory, and rating system was busy producing, whether intentionally or not, trillions of dollars worth of assets we now call "toxic."

One financial giant after another has crashed to the ground. They've either gone broke, been forced to reorganize, had to raise equity at fire-sale prices, been fully or partially nationalized, been bailed out, or changed charters to garner FDIC insurance protection.[17]

Countrywide Financial, Bear Stearns, IndyMac Bank, Fannie Mae, Freddie Mac, Lehman Brothers, Merrill Lynch, AIG, Washington Mutual, Morgan Stanley, Goldman Sachs, JP Morgan Chase, Citigroup, Wachovia, Madoff Securities, Bank of America, and Wells Fargo are the most prominent U.S. financial companies to fully or partially hit the skids. Abroad, Northern Rock (UK), HBOS (UK), Royal

Bank of Scotland (UK), Lloyd's (UK), HSBC (UK), Barclays (UK), Grupo Santander (Spain), Fortis (Netherlands), Hypo Real Estate (Germany), Glitnir (Iceland), Gulf Bank (Kuwait), Svyaz (Russia), UBS (Switzerland), Credit Suisse (Switzerland), and many others have met the same fate.

In the face of this serial financial failure, Uncle Sam, to his credit, swung into full gear to fight the emerging economic war. But his actions, plus the actual or effective collapse of so many major financial players, scared the begeezus out of us. In declaring economic war, Sam never said the "D" word, but made sure we knew that the Great D was a good possibility if we didn't give Wall Street trillions of dollars to fix its mess.

The more we worried, the more we stopped spending. Being frugal became chic and demand for nonessentials, like cars and vacations, dropped like a brick. Suppliers responded by cutting production and employment, which reinforced our fears. A negative feedback loop ensued—just how negative remains to be seen.

In scaring ourselves, we scared the rest of the world, and so the economic contagion spread. Iceland, Russia, Brazil, Dubai, Germany—name the place and see the wreckage. Spain's unemployment rate is now at 17 percent.[18] Japan's exports have fallen in half.[19] Sweden's industrial production is down 9 percent.[20]

Particular sectors and parts of the United States have been absolutely clobbered. New car sales are off 37 percent.[21] General Motors has gone bankrupt, and so has Chrysler.[22] Ford is struggling to stay afloat. Circuit City has short-circuited. Linen n' Things, Mervyn's, and the Sharper Image—all history. Home Depot, Target, the *Boston Globe,* and the *New York Times* are looking shaky. The airlines are registering huge losses and, until recently, were selling fewer tickets than they did way back in 1984.[23] They are now canceling half-filled planes with the frequency of Eastern Airlines. Even Exxon Mobile is facing tough times thanks to a massive decline in the price of oil, which has now rebounded somewhat.[24] Major U.S. companies, including Motorola and Forbes, have stopped matching their workers' 401(k) contributions.[25]

Unemployment has reached 13 percent in Michigan, 12 percent in Oregon and South Carolina, and 11 percent in Rhode Island, California, North Carolina, and Nevada.[26] Las Vegas, where one in every 14 homeowners is being evicted, has a new nickname—Sin City is now Foreclosure City.[27]

In their desperation, people are going for broke (actually, for more broke), by playing the lottery. Lottery sales are up across the nation.[28] But people are buying hope on the cheap. Their trips to the casinos are way down. Atlantic City, which recorded 28 straight years of rising revenues until spring 2009, has seen its revenues plunge.[29] The racetracks are also suffering, but by less. This May's Kentucky Derby's total handle was off only 5 percent.[30]

From their peaks through December 31, 2008, stock markets around the world have melted down, wiping out some $30 trillion in worldwide equity holdings.[31] The S&P 500 fell 42 percent. The London exchange fell 34 percent, the French exchange fell 48 percent, and the German exchange dropped 41 percent. Asia, too, was creamed with the stock markets in Japan, Hong Kong, Australia, Singapore, India, and China plunging 52 percent, 54 percent, 47 percent, 55 percent, 53 percent, and 70 percent, respectively. Brazil's market lost 49 percent. Russia's market dropped 68 percent. Canadian stocks fell by 40 percent, South African stocks fell 35 percent, and Irish stocks fell a whopping 77 percent.

In the United States the leading indicators of the contraction—house prices—are now off 27 percent from their peak.[32] Yet house prices are still heading south, with another 20 percent decline still likely, at least to my mind![33] As it is, U.S. household net wealth has declined by $13 trillion since the second quarter of 2007.[34]

Economics Diary, August 22, 2009

Much can change in four months. The Index of Leading Indicators—an early gauge of economic growth—has risen four months in a row, and house prices are, it seems, beginning to head up. But other data don't look so good. One in eight homeowners with mortgages is now in foreclosure or behind on payments, and one in five is now upside down on the mortgage; that is, the homeowner owes more on the home than the home is worth.[35] New claims for unemployment benefits are running close to 600,000 per week.[36] The unemployment rate in Michigan is now 15 percent. Fourteen states have unemployment rates above 10 percent.[37] And the FDIC just seized Guarantee Financial Group, Inc. This is the 10th largest bank failure in U.S. history and the 105th bank failure since the financial crisis started in the spring of 2007.[38]

Guarantee Financial is a serial bankrupt. It went under during the S&L crisis in 1988, when it was called Guarantee Building & Loan. With federal help, it reopened under its current name, growing its assets to over $18 billion and its Texas- and California-based branches to 150. Starting in 2005, Guarantee plunked down $3.5 billion on triple-A rated, option-adjustable rate mortgages (mortgages that give borrowers the option to decide, each month, how much to pay). Two in five of these mortgages are now delinquent.

Not surprising. The people who took out option ARMs were short on cash and wanted to dramatically lower their payments without dramatically lowering the quality of their housing. They figured their homes would appreciate by the time their payments went up. This would let them either sell the house at a profit or refinance, taking out their newfound equity to cover their now higher payments. At the peak of the housing extravaganza, option ARMs were a very big deal in certain places. They accounted for 40 percent of mortgages in Salinas, California; 25 percent of mortgages in Naples, Florida; 51 percent of mortgages in West Virginia; and 26 percent of mortgages in Wyoming.

Back on September 11, 2006, *BusinessWeek* worried out loud about these mortgages in an article entitled "Nightmare Mortgages." Yet it ultimately blessed them:

> But the Wall Street pros who buy option ARMs are in the business of managing risk, and no one expects widespread losses. They've taken on billions in iffy option ARMs, but the loans are no shakier than the billions in emerging market debt or derivatives they buy and sell all the time. Blowups are factored into the investing decision.[39]

Guarantee Financial is no longer one of the Wall Street pros in the business of managing risks or managing anything else, for that matter. Guarantee Financial is now dead and, hopefully, won't be resurrected with yet another name and another "winning" business strategy. But there are hundreds of dicey banks still operating, meaning we're likely to see hundreds more bank failures in the near term.[40] Even though many bank stocks are on a tear, albeit from extremely low values, banking analysts are giving failing grades to almost 2,000 of the 8,164 FDIC-insured institutions.[41]

These banks aren't formally insolvent in large part because they are using phony accounting to stay afloat. For example, the banks are using a reporting gimmick to report as revenue what the option ARMs would pay were the borrower to refrain from exercising the option not to pay. That is, the borrower may be handing the bank $5,000 this year, but the bank can legally report it's receiving $10,000. For some banks, assets producing such phantom income constitute well over half of their reported assets, where "reported" means carried on their books.[42]

The Treasury's No-Stress Stress Test

The Treasury recently conducted a stress test to determine if the 19 largest banks could make it through the next two years. Many observers were astonished that the Treasury looked out only two years and they felt that it bent over backward to paint a rosy scenario. To pass the Treasury's test, big banks had to be able to withstand a 9 percent loss on the loans they've made without violating their *capital requirements*—their financial cushion against losses in the value of their assets. It appears that losses have already reached this 9 percent level.

If the economy picks up or if banks can generate a bigger cushion by selling more equity (shares of stock), the system will likely get by. But if neither of these things happens, look out. According to economist Michael Pomerleano, one of the world's foremost experts on banking crises, the banks are continuing to make phony calculations based on wishful thinking and could easily be overstating the true value of their assets by $1.5 trillion.[43] This means we could see banks reporting $1.5 trillion in losses in the next year or two. The FDIC insures 8,246 financial institutions with $13.5 trillion in assets and about $1.3 trillion in owner's equity. So a $1.5 trillion write-down would devastate our reeling banking sector.

Economics Diary, August 26, 2009:
The State of the States

The states are going deep into the red. As a group, they are on course to run a $350 billion deficit over the next two fiscal years.[44] Compared with last year, state personal income tax receipts are down 7 percent, state sales tax receipts are down 3 percent, and state corporate income tax receipts are down 15 percent.

Hawaii has put state workers on a three-day-per-month furlough, in effect cutting their pay by 14 percent. Maine, Rhode Island, Maryland, and Michigan have gone further; they've simply closed all nonessential state offices on Fridays. Colorado's doing the same, except on Tuesdays. Altogether, some 20 states are furloughing their workers or closing state offices for part of the week to save money.[45]

There's more. Maine is now taxing candy and ski lift tickets. Kentucky is taxing cell phone ring tones. The Massachusetts legislature wants to raise the state's sales tax by one quarter or introduce casino gambling in some of the seamier parts of the states. My candidate would be the capital building. There's plenty of space, and the politicians can keep an eye on the house take.

Georgia is thinking more creatively and considering a "pole" tax on strip club patrons. Arizona is contemplating running bingo games and bringing in slot machines to increase severely strapped state coffers.[46] Delaware is now running sports betting. Illinois has stopped paying for funerals for the poor. Oklahoma is reducing visiting hours at its museums and historical sites, Wisconsin is raising the cost of elk-hunting licenses, Washington is laying off teachers, New Hampshire is selling state parks, and California is considering taxing its largest cash crop—marijuana.[47]

California just passed a $25 billion package of budget cuts after endless political deadlock. The cuts include furloughing state employees, from DMV workers to U.C. Berkeley professors, long enough to effect a 10 percent salary cut. It's also releasing prisoners early, closing 200 state parks, and printing its own money, called California State IOUs, which promise to pay 3.75 percent tax-free interest.[48]

To date, California has printed 194,000 such IOUs with a face value of $1.03 billion. If California remains underwater, it will need to print more IOUs so that it can come up with the $1.03 billion to cover the initial IOUs. California's IOUs aren't legal tender as far as Uncle Sam is concerned. So don't try sending California IOUs to the IRS to pay your taxes. And good luck depositing your IOUs at the bank. The big banks are saying, "Thanks, but no thanks."[49] But the IOUs do have market value. Investors are offering anywhere from 65 cents to 95 cents on the dollar for IOUs on Craigslist.[50] If California was fully trustworthy, the IOUs would sell for more than one dollar, indeed, for about $1.03 thanks to the interest they bear.

In forcing its creditors to accept IOUs worth at most 95 cents on the dollar, California has, effectively, defaulted on its debt. Yes, California may eventually pay back every dollar it owes, but if it doesn't pay back what it owes when it owes it, it's not paying what it owes. The possibility of receiving a given amount of money three months, six months, one year, and so on from now is not the same as getting that money today for the simple reason that were it received today one could invest it and earn interest for sure over the period.

As the eighth-largest economy in the world, California may feel more entitled to print money than other states. But if California can print money, so can Delaware, Maine, Nebraska, and any other states. Soon we could have 50 state currencies circulating—a nice throwback to the early days of our country when each of the original 13 states had its own banknotes. And if the states print their own money, what's to stop local towns and cities and even individuals from doing the same? Nothing.

During the Great Depression, some $1 billion in new currencies was issued by towns and cities, as well as school boards and wealthy individuals.[51] Most of the IOUs were written on paper. But certain new monies had peculiar "backings." Some were stamped on metal. Others were written on pieces of spruce, some were engraved in leather, some were registered on pieces of discarded tires, and some were printed on fish-skin parchment.

There are big problems with everyone and his mother printing his own money, not the least of which is counterfeiting. During Argentina's financial crisis in the early 2000s, all 23 of its provinces began generating hoards of their own script. This made the Argentine central government nervous about fakes. So the government took the remarkable step of using its own presses to print the provincial currencies. Each province was free to order up as much fresh money as it wanted, and, bingo, it was delivered.

It's the Psychology, Duh!

The worst part of all this is the overhang of anxiety. A world that freaked out once can do so again. And short-term improvements in economic conditions don't guarantee prolonged, stable growth. The

It-That-Should-Not-Be-Named of the 1930s lasted a decade notwith-standing two expansions generating rapid growth. Watching venera-ble, "rock-solid" financial behemoths collapse—one after another—has transformed the "impossible to imagine" into the "sure to happen" and left everyone looking over their shoulder.

British economist John Maynard Keynes referred to collective anx-iety as "animal spirits," which references another word economists are loathe to use—*psychology*. We economists like to think of ourselves as hard scientists even though few share our conceit. And, down deep, we think of psychologists as medicine men. At least we used to. We now realize that psychology is critical to the functioning of our globally inter-connected economy. Indeed, macroeconomists have spent the last two decades developing models with "multiple equilibria" featuring "coor-dination failures" in which confidence, emotion, psyche, feelings—call it what you will—dictate how the economy performs.

Recall Bill Clinton's 1992 campaign slogan, "It's the economy, stupid!" Were he running today, he'd be proclaiming, "It's the psy-chology, duh!" because the collective fear is palpable. The reality of our economy is little changed from December 2007 when the D/R-thing began. We have the same physical and human capital—the same equip-ment, factories, homes, apartment buildings, stores, skills, and people. What's different is the degree to which all these inputs are being used together. Adam Smith's marvelous *invisible hand*, which is supposed to turn self-interest into social well-being, has failed miserably. Self-interest is very narrow-minded and can just as easily coordinate on bad rather than good outcomes (equilibria), persuading us all to sit on our hands.

It's tough selling your products to the unemployed. The bad equi-librium to which we've now switched involves no one hiring because everyone thinks (has coordinated his or her beliefs on the idea) that no one else is hiring and that there won't, therefore, be much demand for goods and services once they are produced. Were everyone to suddenly believe the opposite—that times are good—hiring would kick back in and this alternative belief would become self-fulfilling. This is where President Obama and his hard-working economics team may be help-ing. Their cautious confidence and hyperactivity in announcing new policies to fix the economy may help change economic opinion even if the policies themselves are deeply misguided.

The reason that beliefs matter so much is that we don't have anyone matching demand and supply. Adam Smith isn't sitting in a rowboat in the middle of the lake shouting to Alex and David on opposite shores that now's the time to swim to the middle so that Alex can swap his fish for David's hot dogs and vice versa. It's a long, cold swim, with heavy bundles to tow, and neither Alex nor David wants to jump in the water if the other party isn't going to show up. The lake's quite wide, and neither person can see or hear to the other side. One option is for each to simply eat what he has. But Alex is sick to death of fish, and David hates hot dogs. They'd sure like to get what the other's got, but they'll end up eating what they hate without something *visible*—a huge pep rally by the president or even a sunspot—to coordinate their icy plunge.[52]

When Lexington, Massachusetts, Turns into Camden, New Jersey

Flipping to a bad equilibrium as big companies fail and psyche out the public is the largest cost of bankruptcy, but far from the only one. If we could costlessly move managers, workers, and capital from one concern that goes bust to another that's thriving, having companies die wouldn't be such a big deal. But that's not the case even in our "information age." It still takes time and money to search for a new job, and not everyone can telecommute. Many of the unemployed have to move to a new town, a new state, sometimes a new country, to get back to work.

And getting the buildings and equipment of one company sold and reused by another can take what seems like forever. I grew up in Pennsauken, New Jersey, right next to Camden. My father, Harold, and his two brothers, Tanfield and Albert, owned Camden's first and last department store, called Kotlikoff's. It was started in 1909 by my grandfather Louis.

In the 1970s, all the big department stores, including Sears and Penneys and Lit Brothers, closed their doors. And no one came in to open them. Instead, as you drove through Camden, more and more of its storefronts, as well as its homes, went from inviting to boarded-up. Campbell's Soup is still headquartered in Camden, but most of Camden's manufacturers pulled out of Dodge and simply abandoned their factories. This was neighborhood-effects at their worse, with no new businesses wanting to open up next to others that were boarded up.

Our store held out through 1981, but after three break-ins in one night, my dad and his brothers called it quits.[53] They sold the store to Goodwill for peanuts, but even Goodwill couldn't stay afloat. On my last visit to Camden, Kotlikoff's large, block-long picture windows, which used to house beautiful seasonal displays, were all boarded up.

Today Camden is, well, Camden—possibly America's least desirable place to live. And as I drive through my current hometown, Lexington, Massachusetts, I don't see Camden, but I do see things I never expected to see when my wife and I moved there 20 years ago. Lexington is, of course, a historic town, having hosted the first battle of the Revolutionary War. And its Battle Green, its Minute Man National Park, and its reenactment of the fight each Patriot's Day still attract plenty of tourists. But if you walk the four blocks of Lexington center today, you'll see lots of empty storefronts. The town's main department store has shut down; so has the local bookstore, and the largest restaurant, as well as the major furniture store. But, not to worry, there are about five coffee stores per inhabitant, so if you need to caffeinate yourself, Lexington will do fine.

Given my training, I'm not surprised that stores go out of business. What I find shocking is how long the buildings themselves stay out of business. I can't tell what's happened to the people who used to work in these places, but I can see with my own eyes the ongoing unemployment—coming up to two years now—of the buildings themselves.

Such bankruptcy costs are quite disturbing to academic economists, not because they affect our personal finances, but because these costs mess up our mathematical models. When we assume zero bankruptcy costs, our financial modeling is simple and elegant, and we can generate very strong financial propositions. The most important and dangerous of these is the *Modigliani-Miller Theorem*, derived by Franco Modigliani and Merton Miller in 1958.

Both of these economists have now passed away, and both were brilliant and simply wonderful people. So I certainly don't mean to suggest that they developed their model to cause economic danger or harm. They did so to help economists understand whether leverage matters—whether it makes any difference if companies, including banks, borrow rather than issue equity (sell shares of stock) to raise money to finance their operations.

Modigliani and Miller showed in their beautiful paper that, absent bankruptcy costs, leverage doesn't matter one iota![54] The reason goes back to who is ultimately bearing risk—it's the public, not businesses, for the simple reason that the public owns the businesses. And so, in the Modigliani-Miller model, if a company takes on more risk by borrowing more, its owners will simply offset that risk by borrowing less, leaving their total indebtedness unchanged.

Think about a husband and wife, each with his or her own credit card. If the husband borrows $1,000 more on his card, but the wife borrows $1,000 less on hers, the couple doesn't take on more debt, on net. Assume the husband and wife are cooperating and jointly keeping close track of their overall indebtedness as well as deciding what the level of their spending and overall borrowing should be. In this case, which of the two is more leveraged (has the larger credit card bill) is economically irrelevant; that is, it makes no difference to anything real.

Modigliani was awarded the 1985 Nobel Prize for the Modigliani-Miller Theorem, his work on life-cycle economics, and his many other fundamental contributions to economics. Miller received the prize in 1990, together with Harry Markowitz and William Sharpe, for their independent major breakthroughs in finance, which in Miller's case clearly included the Modigliani-Miller Theory, which we economists simply call MM.

MM is easy to teach, so each year, clear across the world, thousands of bright-eyed economics and finance PhDs as well as MBA students learn a theorem that says "corporate leverage (the ratio of debt-to-equity) doesn't matter." Yes, they are told the extreme and empirically irrelevant assumptions needed to produce this result, but with so much being crammed into their brains, it's easy for students to focus on the delicious intellectual cake and ignore its ingredients. Years later, when these students are working for governments, businesses, and banks, this "not to worry about leverage" message may be the first thing that flashes back when the CEO suggest borrowing some more to fund his "can't lose" brainstorm. The real truth is that business bankruptcy is costly and having large numbers of firms go bankrupt all at once can be incredibly costly if it switches on a bad equilibrium. Hence, the real lesson to be learned from MM is to play it safe. If "business leverage doesn't matter," then zero business leverage is just as good as lots of business leverage. As we'll see, getting the leverage out of the banks, *but not out of the financial system*, is the essence of Limited Purpose Banking. The goal is *not* to keep people from borrowing from and lending to one another and leveraging themselves to their hearts' content. The goal is to keep banks from leveraging, because in so doing they risk going broke and taking the economy down with them, with all the macroeconomic and microeconomic damage that entails.

Economics Diary, August 29, 2009: The Great D or the Great R?

There are signs that the economy is stabilizing. Recent reports show fewer Americans losing their jobs (only one-quarter of a million per month). House prices are no longer plummeting, and output is falling at slower clip. These days, less bad news passes for good news. Let's hope we get some actual good employment news. The stock market, which is an early indicator of future economic performance, is heading north. This is promising, as are the small but positive growth rates being posted in some developing and developed countries.

Americans are resilient and don't stay depressed for long. And post-war recessions have generally lasted for one year, so it's certainly time for a turnaround; this downturn has already clocked 20 months.

But this downturn is big because it's global, because it's wiped out so much wealth as well as so many jobs (15 million Americans are now looking for work) so quickly, because it's taken away our mojo, and because the economy's major source of grease—the financial sector—has ground, if no longer to a halt, at least to a crawl. No one really trusts the banks, least of all the banks themselves, which remain reluctant to lend to one another. No one fully trusts insurance companies, whose reputations have been thoroughly sullied by AIG. No one trusts hedge funds, with more closing shop each week and the rest struggling to retain their investors.[55] No one trusts startups, which have largely given up raising money. No one trusts credit card holders, whose balance limits are being tightened. And no one trusts the financial planners, who missed the financial tsunami like everyone else.

These days, what trust is left reposes primarily in Uncle Sam, who has taken more and more of the nation's financial operations onto his back. Uncle Sam now fully owns the country's largest mortgage businesses (Fannie Mae and Freddie Mac). Uncle Sam is now the major shareholder of two of the nation's largest banks—Citigroup and Bank of America—and virtually the sole owner of the nation's, and indeed the world's, largest insurance company (AIG). The Federal Reserve is now directly lending to large and small business and, indirectly, to households by supporting institutions that are engaged in credit card lending, making car and boat loans, and extending other forms of consumer credit.

From one perspective, this is no big deal. The private sector is too scared to lend to itself or invest in itself, so Uncle Sam is swapping his assets for their assets; that is, he's selling Treasury bills and bonds to the private sector and using the proceeds to purchase the securities that the private sector no longer wants to hold. When things calm down, Uncle Sam can run this process in reverse.

But there are two buts. The first problem is that the government may be paying far too high a price for the assets it's buying and may end up losing money either by holding onto these assets and earning less than was hoped for or by trying to resell them and finding they fetch very little. Since we don't know precisely what assets Sam is buying or what price he's paying for those assets, it's very hard to know.

A second problem is that the government is loathe to sell any more Treasury bills or bonds because doing so is classified as government borrowing even if the money so borrowed is immediately used to buy an asset. This fiscal year's federal deficit (the annual amount of new issuances of Treasuries) is running at $1.8 trillion, or 13 percent of GDP. The outstanding stock of debt is now $11.7 trillion ($38,000 per American) and growing by $14 billion every four days, which is the cost of a new Ford–class U.S. Navy supercarrier.[56] If we weren't running this year's deficit, we could pay for 91 of the world's largest and finest aircraft carriers and anchor them side by side off the coast of any country we'd like to impress. Alternatively, we could increase the living standards of all 800 million people living in sub-Saharan African by 71 percent for an entire year.[57]

With the deficit running at a postwar record high relative to GDP, borrowing even more money is not something Sam is prepared to do. So Sam is having Uncle Ben (as in Ben Bernanke) simply print the money Sam needs to lend or give to the public.

But are we spending more than we can afford? President Obama's initiative to provide health insurance to almost 50 million uninsured Americans (one in six) is starting to sink in the opinion polls, primarily, it appears, because of concerns about its costs. Providing all Americans with a basic health insurance policy is vital, but the idea of borrowing or printing hundreds of billions more each year to pay for this policy isn't sitting well in anyone's gut, including the president's. We already have two government healthcare programs—Medicare and Medicaid—whose spending is completely out of control and has been for decades. Adding yet a third program in the midst of this exorbitantly expensive financial crisis without coming up with any credible means of controlling the spending of the first two is making us all very queasy. As it is, the Office of Management and Budget is projecting a $9 trillion increase in official debt over the next decade.[58] And the cost of the president's healthcare proposal would likely add another $1 trillion to this staggering figure over the same period.[59]

There is a straightforward, efficient, and equitable way to provide universal health insurance and also get our tax and retirement systems in order (as I briefly describe in the afterword), but paying for government programs, even reasonably structured ones, requires a solid tax base, which requires a solid underlying economy, which requires a solid financial system; that is, one that doesn't break down over time due to fundamental flaws in its design.

Systemic Risk Insurance

As suggested by the deficit figures, our government has already laid out huge sums—$2.5 trillion, in fact—in fighting this financial crisis. In real terms, this exceeds all spending done by the federal government throughout World War II!

In addition, the government has simultaneously been engaged in a massive and, potentially, even more expensive policy that entails providing systemic risk insurance to the financial sector—insurance against system-wide financial and economic collapse.[60]

The face value of these systemic risk insurance policies also totals in the trillions. The policies are expressed like this: "If your security doesn't pay what you thought you were owed or if you can't borrow at reasonable rates from the banking system, or if you can't pay what you owe, we, the government, will come to your rescue."

It's very hard to understand how much of what Uncle Sam is doing these days is simply giving away money, providing insurance at a reasonable price (insurance that wouldn't otherwise be available on the market), or doing both these things by providing insurance either for free or at very deep discounts. What we know for sure is that Uncle Sam has already handed out or has publicly committed to hand out, in certain circumstances, more than $12 trillion to the financial sector.[61]

Who's Backstopping the Backstop?

The largest single component of the $12 trillion is the government's decision to insure money market mutual fund shareholders that they would never suffer a loss on their investment. The second-largest component is the Federal Reserve's decision to lend $1.6 trillion to corporations if they have trouble floating their commercial paper. This, too, is a form of insurance—a guarantee that corporations will be able to sell their paper at a price that's equal or above (equivalently, borrow money at an interest rate that's equal or below) what Uncle Sam feels is a reasonable level.

Then there's the joint Treasury and Fed decision to purchase $1.5 trillion of poisonous bonds and mortgage-backed securities from Fannie Mae, Freddie Mac, and Ginnie Mae at what were surely above-market prices.[62]

Of course, if you give big business a cookie, small business and consumers are going to want one too. And with Uncle Sam these days, the message is: "Ask and you shall receive." In this case, small business and consumers are now, collectively, free to borrow up to $900 billion from Uncle Sam to deal with any liquidity problems they face, real or imagined. The Treasury, in conjunction with the FDIC, has committed, via the Public Private Investment Program (PIPP), another $900 billion to implicitly bribe hedge funds to purchase toxic assets at inflated prices from banks.[63]

And let's not forget the Treasury's $700 billion Troubled Asset Relief Program (TARP), the Treasury's $400 billion in actual plus potential pledges of monies to cover Fannie's and Freddie's losses, the Fed's $301 billion guarantee of Citigroup troubled assets, the close to $200 billion spent by the Fed on AIG (with hundreds of billions more likely to come), the $118 billion guarantee of Bank of America's poison securities, the $29 billion spent by the Fed on Bear Stearns' toxic assets, and the $4 billion handed out by the Treasury to backstop the Reserve Primary Money Market Fund.

Again, some of this is direct spending, some is pure insurance, and some is a combo. But to me $12 trillion is a huge red flag screaming, "You can print it, but you can't produce it." This figure, after all, is close to one's year's gross domestic product, that is, the value of all the final goods and services produced in the United States by over 130 million people working over the course of an entire year. So if the U.S. government actually had to quickly come up with $12 trillion in real goods and services as opposed to 12 trillion green pieces of paper marked ONE DOLLAR, it would find itself unable to fulfill its promise to backstop, in real terms, its long and growing list of supplicants.

At the end of the day, Uncle Sam has no backstop for his backstop. His green pieces of paper say, "In God We Trust." None say. "In Sam We Trust." And this is for a good reason. Uncle Sam can't extract manna from heaven. Yes, he can go after our kids and grandkids and make them share our losses, but there are also limits to this expropriation—limits, as we'll see, we've already reached.

The one real advantage the government has in insuring macroeconomic performance is in coordinating the economy's choice of equilibria—or, in noneconomic speak, in keeping us psyched up. The president, in particular, is in a unique position to play the economic cheerleader—to get us all thinking positively and acting upon our good vibes. But pep rallies can go only so far and be held so often. There is, in fact, no assurance that the government's financial guarantees, which are stated in dollars but are meant to be real, can actually be fulfilled.

Trust Doesn't Come Cheap

The financial panic has abated, but could quickly return, given that the public has seen nothing to change its view of private financial institutions. Letting the financial sector engage in business as usual and having the government pretend it can insure us against real losses won't do the trick. People need to have a reason to park their money anywhere near people who, it's now clear, have been selling fake securities for years and have no intention of telling their investors precisely and honestly what they are doing with their money.

Because investors have been burnt so badly, they are more likely, going forward, to be skittish and to quickly sell their financial assets on rumor or small signs of bad news. This spells greater volatility in the financial markets down the road, which, in turn, will reinforce investors' concerns and raise the costs that businesses face in borrowing or raising equity. And such panicked selling can, as we've seen, bring down major financial institutions, which then look to Uncle Sam for life support.

Restoring trust often requires radical surgery, as Johnson & Johnson learned in the fall of 1982 when several of the company's bottles of Tylenol were tampered with, laced with cyanide, and put on store shelves by some miscreant whose identity has yet to be determined.

Seven people died before Johnson & Johnson learned what had happened. The company didn't think twice. It immediately recalled 31 million bottles of Tylenol and destroyed their contents at a cost of $100 million. Johnson & Johnson then rolled out new triple safety seal bottles and, within a short period of time, the company was again a trusted supplier of the product.

Contrast this behavior with the reaction of our financial industry to the public's discovery that large numbers of their products were financially toxic. Not a single troubled financial company went public to fully disclose, with all available details, what assets they held and what liabilities they owed. So the public was left to imagine the worst and ran away from these companies as fast as possible.

Full Nondisclosure

Consider Lehman Brothers, which was founded in 1850 and filed for Chapter 11 on September 14, 2008, in what may be the largest bankruptcy in the history of the world.[64] According to some accounts, the company was in hock to the tune of three-quarters of a trillion dollars when it went under.[65]

A year earlier, Lehman's stock had been valued, not at $0 billion, but at $47 billion, with a share price of $67. So over the year, the public came to understand that what it thought was sitting on Lehman shelves wasn't actually there. Lehman's bottles weren't full of carefully selected assets with substantial protection against downside risk. Instead, the bottles were stuffed, in large part, with claims to highly risky real estate and dicey mortgages—mortgages that were variously referenced by those in the industry as "subprime loans," "Alt-A loans," "no-doc loans," "liar mortgages," and "NINJA mortgages," which stands for a no-income, no-job mortgage applicant.

In making these "investments," Lehman Brothers leveraged itself 31 to 1, meaning that for every dollar of company capital, Lehman borrowed another 30 dollars and then invested the total in these and other high-risk securities.[66] With leverage of this magnitude, all it takes is a 3 percent loss in the value of assets to wipe out the company's capital, which is measured as the difference between the company's assets and its debts. Since Lehman's shares were claims to its capital, the perception that its assets had taken more than a 3 percent hit drove the stock from $18 in early September to essentially zero on September 14.

Stock movements of this magnitude hit most of the financial firms. Goldman Sachs's stock fell by 80 percent between its November 2007 peak and its November 2008 nadir. Goldman shares have since recovered, but, as I write, they are still trading 40 percent below peak. Bank of America saw its share price drop from $40 in October 2008 to $3 in March 2009 and then back to the current $14 value. Citigroup, which traded at $24 per share in October 2008, fell dramatically later in the fall and now stands at $4 a share.

Fannie Mae traded at $70 a share in 2007, but stood at $13 a share on the morning of July 15, 2008. By the end of that day, it had crashed to $7 a share. Today, you can get a share of Fannie for . . . well, I don't want to look because I bought Fannie at $20. Freddie Mac experienced a similar meltdown. Together these firms had borrowed north of $5 trillion and were leveraged 65 to 1![67]

Columbia University finance professor, Charles Calomiris stated in congressional testimony, that these government-sponsored enterprises were primary enablers of the subprime and Alt-A toxic asset industry, buying up half of the $3 trillion total supply of these securities, while failing to tell the public.[68] Their CEOs and other top executives repeatedly ignored warnings from their senior risk managers that the "assets" they were buying held much more than the usual default risk because of systematic fraudulent misrepresentation of the incomes, collateral values, and credit histories of the mortgages.

And why were the warnings ignored? Because the people at the top had no interest in rocking their personal boats just when they were raking in small fortunes and because they were under very strong political pressure to help low-income Americans purchase homes. According to Calomiris, "This commitment to affordable housing was the quid pro quo for government support for the GSEs, which took the form of implicit, but universally recognized guarantees by the government of their liabilities."[69]

Calomiris' testimony may be overly tough on Fannie and Freddie with respect to their "enabling" the toxic mortgage market. First, they came late to the subprime and Alt-A buy-a-thon. Second, they bought only the highest rated subprime mortgage securities, which were easiest to sell. Third, a good portion of their portfolio was invested in shorter maturity subprimes, which are less risky because they are closer to making final payment. And fourth, the Community Reinvestment Act, which encouraged the GSEs to lend to low- and moderate-income households in poor neighborhoods, dates back to 1977.

Share prices move for a reason—the arrival of new information. In the case of the financial sector, the new information was that there was no information—that nobody, including, it appears, the top executives of these companies, knew precisely what assets these companies were holding and the true risks they were accepting.[70] Nor did anyone seem to have even a ballpark estimate for the ultimate downsize associated with their holdings of derivatives.

To its shock and dismay, the public learned that the derivatives market has exploded to the tune of hundreds of trillions of dollars. Indeed, as indicated above, the latest estimate—provided courtesy of a highly reliable source, the Bank of International Settlements—places the size of the global derivatives market at a gargantuan $600 trillion![71] This is over 40 times U.S. GDP.

The public also learned that one of the new derivatives, called credit default swaps, represented a new form of insurance policy sold against corporate bond and mortgage defaults. The size of this market was $45 trillion.[72] The market was very thin and very poorly regulated, with no centralized bookkeeping. Moreover, Credit Default Swap (CDS) policies could be sold to third parties without the original policyholder even learning the identity of the new insurer. All this raised the question of which company held what derivatives in what magnitude and what was the size of their net exposure.

The financial industry is keen on keeping the precise details of its financial holdings private. "Proprietary information" is how they phrase it. Their concern is that explaining their investments will reveal their investing strategy and give away their competitive advantage.[73] This position comes down to saying "trust us" after the industry has shown it merits no trust.

A System with No Firewalls

There is one other critical feature of our once and future horrible financial mess that begs early mention. It's the cascading of financial collapse. Under our financial system, we can have party A hocked to its eyeballs to party B, which is hocked to its eyeballs to party C, which is hocked to its eyeballs to party D, and so on. So when party A defaults, party B can't pay C, so B defaults, and then C can't pay D, and C defaults.

Even if A hasn't borrowed from B, who hasn't borrowed from C, who hasn't borrowed from D, the failure of A can bring about the failure of B, C, and D and so on if A, B, C, D, are viewed as in the same business and, therefore, perceived to be in the same straits. If all these letters stand for drug stores and only A has tainted Tylenol, but B, C, D, and others can't prove to the public they have safe Tylenol, well, B, C, D, and so on aren't going to see too many customers walking through their doors.

Now let's set A equal to Lehman Brothers, B equal to AIG, and C equal to Goldman Sachs, and we start to see how the dominos fell or started to fall before Uncle Sam intervened. When Lehman crashed, it immediately put pressure on AIG. The reason is not that Lehman owed AIG money. The reason is that Mr. Joseph Cassano, a former AIG employee, together with a small band of fellow swindlers, sold tons of credit default swaps to Goldman and other entities. Goldman's purchases alone totaled to $20 billion.[74] These credit default swaps were insurance policies that covered their purchasers against debt defaults by Lehman's and all manner of other U.S. and foreign companies, financial as well as nonfinancial. Were the United States and rest of the world to experience a deep recession, large numbers of these policies would come due all at once and sink their issuer.

Selling insurance against diversifiable risks whose losses you can fully expect to cover is one thing. Selling insurance against aggregate risks you have no ability or intention to cover is something else entirely. It's called fraud.

This is what Cassano did. He effectively sold massive amounts of hurricane insurance against a CAT 5 hitting the Gulf Coast, while praying it would never happen and using the premiums to buy beachfront property. And, wouldn't you know it, a CAT 5 hurricane came roaring in.

When Lehman went down, AIG had to pay up on its Lehman insurance claims. More importantly, AIG was immediately forced to post more collateral on large volumes of its other insurance contracts, which were suddenly understood, even by AIG's co-conspirators (the rating companies), to be much riskier. And AIG wasn't sitting around with a lot of free cash to meet those collateral calls.

By analogy, the collateral deals were provisions in the CAT 5 hurricane contracts stipulating that AIG wouldn't wait until the hurricane actually made landfall, but would pay its customers more and more of their potential claim the closer the storm got to their properties. This gave each purchaser of hurricane insurance the sense that he or she didn't need to worry about AIG's not paying up when the storm hit; AIG would pay up most of what it owed as the storm approached.

Or would it?

When the CAT 5 was spotted right off the coast in the form of Lehman Brothers biting the dust, AIG found itself drowning in obligations to pay off claims on Lehman and meet its collateral calls.

Had AIG simply shut its doors, as opposed to selling itself to the government, it could have set off a run on the entire insurance industry—a point discussed below. It might also have started a run on a number of big banks, like Goldman Sachs. Goldman, some claim, would have lost about $13 billion from AIG's bankruptcy. Goldman says otherwise, asserting that it was fully hedged against AIG's collapse and couldn't have cared less whether the insurance giant lived or died.

Maybe it was hedged, maybe it wasn't. We know that Treasury Secretary and former CEO of Goldman, Hank Paulson, had a dozen conversations with current CEO of Goldman, Lloyd Blankfein, in the week leading up to Lehman's collapse and AIG's takeover, and they surely weren't just whistling Dixie. Paulson may have been simply soliciting Blankfein's financial policy advice, or he may have been trying to understand Goldman's exposure to a run of the same type Bear Stearns had, and now Lehman was experiencing. Or maybe they were discussing the weather.[75]

In any case, Lehman shut its doors on September 15, and AIG was effectively nationalized the next day, at a cost to the taxpayer of $85 billion. The decision to "rescue" AIG was taken on September 15 at a meeting held by the New York Fed to determine AIG's exposure to Lehman's failure. The fact, by the way, that the Fed and the Treasury didn't at that point fully understand this exposure or have a game plan for dealing with it, is, itself, quite telling. After all, this was September 2008, and the financial crisis had arguably been underway for over a year. And Bear Stearns had collapsed back in March.

In his September 14, 2009, *New Yorker* article, "Eight Days that Shook the World," James Stewart reported that Paulson had no idea that AIG was in danger from a collapse of Lehman. When asked two days prior to Lehman's demise if he had been watching AIG, Stewart quotes

Paulson as saying, "Why, what's wrong with AIG?" Paulson thought the New York State Insurance Commission was regulating AIG and handling its "liquidity issues." Not the case. And when Paulson was shown AIG's exposure, his response was chilling: "Oh my God!"

The other interesting thing about the meeting is that one of the attendees was Goldman's Lloyd Blankfein. Interests don't get more conflicted than this. Here, arguably, was Goldman advising the Fed and Treasury on how to have the taxpayer help AIG to help Goldman. This, at least, was the appearance given. And appearances count in a setting where no one knows who's got precisely how much cyanide sitting in what bottles on which shelves.

The bottom line? Trust in financial companies and the folks running them took a holiday. Had AIG gone bankrupt, lenders to Goldman could have expected it to be next, whether or not Goldman publicly claimed that it was hedged. At some point it didn't matter who claimed what or who was or wasn't telling the truth. No one could fully confirm the details of any company's holdings or obligations, and there was evidence aplenty that too many Wall Streeters would sell their mothers for a profit. Thus, if enough lenders thought other lenders had given up on Goldman, Goldman would have gone down as well.

So in saving AIG by swallowing it almost whole, Uncle Sam may also have rescued Goldman and other banks and insurers, at least in the short run. Truth be told, Uncle Sam himself is barely treading water, and the shore is a long way off. He's also having a terribly hard time digesting AIG.

To summarize, party A failed, and this required Sam to rescue party B, or else party C, party D, party E, and so forth would likely have failed as well. Whether Sam should have let party A, Lehman, go down in the first place is a good question. Many commentators have suggested that Paulson let Lehman go under because he couldn't stand Lehman's CEO, Dick Fuld. That's hard to believe since Fuld could easily have been replaced as part of a government rescue mission. The other view is that Paulson wanted to send the Street a message that being leveraged 31 to 1 was rather risky.

We may never know what Paulson's real thinking was at the time, but what we do know is that Lehman's failure put a terrible scare in the marketplace. Now it was no longer a case of shareholders of company

X not knowing if X had tainted painkillers sitting on its shelves. Now it was shareholders of X not knowing if the delivery trucks on their way from company K to X had tainted painkiller on board or whether X itself had, of late, shipped some poison to company H for which X would be liable.

Counterparty risk—the risk that your business partners would damage you by reneging on their debts or that you would damage them and get sued—went through the roof. Party A may be able to repay party B, who is trying to borrow from party C, but if party C doesn't believe party A will repay party B, it won't lend to party B. This freezing of capital markets is precisely what transpired in the days, weeks, and months after Lehman failed, even though Uncle Sam prevented any more major financial bankruptcies.[76]

■   ■   ■

Clearly we need a financial system that is completely transparent to keep us from falling back into our "trust no one" equilibrium. We also need a system with automatic financial firewalls, which also keeps Uncle Sam from catching fire. Limited Purpose Banking satisfies both these requirements.

Chapter 2

The Big Con

Financial Malfeasance, American Style

One of the remarkable features of our financial system is how much power it concentrates in the hands of a small number of players. If these players play by the rules, the financial system can withstand lots of shocks and keep the economy on track. If they don't, they themselves become the shocks and all hell can break lose.

Our financial system is designed to fail for a number of reasons, but the most important is allowing financial miscreants to leverage the American taxpayer to the tune of what has now become trillions of dollars. It's important, therefore, to understand the kind of folk to whom we have been entrusting our personal finances and our nation's economy and to realize that these types of people are not going away.

Nor are they always easy to spot. Some may look smarmy, while others are modest, refined, well-educated, cultured, and charitable. But they all have one thing in common. They are all on the make and all on the take because we've established a system that let them acquire fabulous fortunes by playing "Heads I win, tails you lose." And if we perpetuate that system, they will surely continue to gamble on the public's dime and re-create the type of disaster we are now facing.

Richard Fuld or Elmer Fudd?

"Enough of the f******g losses. Enough." This was the sophisticated strategic advice Dick Fuld, CEO of Lehman Brothers, gave his traders in the weeks and days before his ship went down.[1] These were the words of a man who borrowed close to three-quarters of a trillion dollars in order to buy securities whose risk he clearly didn't understand. These were the words of a man who very rarely, if ever, met with his top traders—people who were routinely placing bets in the tens of millions and sometimes hundreds of millions of dollars. These were the words of a man who handpicked a compliant executive committee with even less ability or interest in assessing the company's risk than he had. These were the words of a man who kept his key employees, his shareholders, government regulators, his chief economist, his chief risk officer, and, most importantly, himself in the dark about his company's exposures. These were the words of a man who received close to $500 million in compensation as CEO for spending years gambling with his company's money and, it turned out, the economy's fortunes. And these were the words of a man whose luck finally turned terribly bad.

Dick Fuld is a poster child for the con job Wall Street's masters of the universe pulled on the country—pretending to be experts in something in which they had no real knowledge and selling financial products to the public, which they knew, or should have known, to be highly defective.

In considering Fuld's practice of internal as well as external nondisclosure, one needs to bear four things in mind. First, had Fuld been the world's most responsible risk manager, as opposed to the world's most irresponsible, he could not possibly have kept track of all of Lehman's positions on his own, given that just the listings of these positions filled up volumes the size of a New York City phone book. Second, pricing and evaluating risk is not the same as knowing how the Street works and where the company's men's room is located. It requires highly specialized knowledge of financial theory, economics, statistics, and mathematics.

Fuld never received such training. He earned a BS (sounds right) in political science from the University of Colorado and an MBA from New York University. In other words, he had no advanced mathematical or financial technical training. Fuld was in no position to understand, at a deep level, the true risk of any given asset or liability, let alone tens of thousands of such assets and liabilities. Nor was he in a position to understand the limitations of the tools being used by his risk analysts. By analogy, Fuld was an MBA running a hospital who thought this entitled him to perform brain surgery. Not surprisingly, he killed his patient.

Third, many, if not most, of the assets Lehman held were highly illiquid, making them particularly hard to price and risk adjust. Fourth, as we now have been very painfully reminded, financial markets are subject to systemic collapse. But these collapses are rare events, leaving us with very little data to use in measuring their likelihood. Statistically speaking, such outcomes lie far out on the probability distribution—way out in the tail. But when they occur, the market places a much larger premium on liquidity, dropping the prices of illiquid assets like lead balloons.

Trying to think about these risks using mathematical models is difficult enough. Trying to evaluate (calibrate) these models using data from short-time series is asking for big trouble. In Lehman's case, the illiquid nature of its assets, the very limited time series data, not to mention its extreme leverage, made the company particularly vulnerable to losses in the event of a systemic meltdown. Hence, it required thinking very precisely about tail risk—something Fuld had no training to do.

In sum, Fuld was rolling loaded dice without knowing their odds. As long as they came up sixes, he was hailed as the investment world's Second Coming. In 2006, *Institutional Investor* magazine named Fuld the Number One Top CEO of Brokerage and Asset Management Companies. In 2007, his bonus equaled $22 million. But one year latter, Fuld received three very different awards. One was bestowed by the *Financial Times*, which granted Fuld its lowest honor—the "Thief Award." The second was granted by CNBC, which named Fuld to the top of its list of "Worst American CEOs of All Times." And the third was presented by *Time* magazine, which included Fuld among its list of the nation's 25 "primary financial villains."[2]

Fuld has his own take on what happened, indicating in his October 6, 2008, congressional testimony that his company was working throughout

2008 on a daily basis with regulators to reduce the risk exposure of Lehman and that the company was destroyed not by his actions, but primarily by those of naked short sellers who were feeding the market with false rumors to enhance their positions.[3]

According to Fuld, "What happened to Lehman Brothers could have happened to any firm on Wall Street, and almost did happen to others. A litany of destabilizing factors: rumors, widening credit default swap spreads, naked short attacks, credit agency downgrades, a loss of confidence by clients and counterparties, and strategic buyers sitting on the sidelines waiting for an assisted deal were not only part of Lehman's story, but an all too familiar tale for many financial institutions."[4]

What Fuld fails to make clear is that he failed to make clear to the public what his company was actually holding and what it actually owed. In not disclosing this information on the web on an asset-by-asset basis, it was his word against the market's word. And the market didn't trust him.

Fuld's laying blame on events and on others is not surprising. What I find interesting and alarming is his statement that "What happened to Lehman Brothers could have happened to any firm on Wall Street." If this is even half true, why would we consider maintaining the system as is?

Playing Bridge as Bear Burned

Bear Stearns' CEO, Jimmy Cayne, also made *CNBC*'s and *Time*'s dishonor rolls. Cayne had even more limited training in the technical tools of his trade than did Dick Fuld. A college dropout, Cayne's preparation for his career in finance consisted of selling copiers, hawking scrap metal, and playing bridge. As luck would have it, bridge turned out to be Cayne's strong suit when he met the employer of his life, Ace Greenberg. Ace was chairman of Bear Stearns' board of directors at the time and instantly fell in love with Jimmy's bridge game. In no time flat, Jimmy was working at Bear as a stockbroker, playing cards with Ace on the side, and plotting his strategy to become head honcho.

Cayne's operational style as CEO differed from Fuld's. Fuld went out of his way to avoid his employees. He was chauffeured to a private entrance at Lehman's headquarters. He then took a private elevator to

Lehman's top floor, and closeted himself there for the day with a small set of self-dealing henchmen. Cayne, in contrast, didn't much bother coming to work, let alone spending the time needed to understand precisely what his company—the nation's fifth-largest investment bank, was doing. Instead, Cayne spent his time playing golf, playing bridge, and, allegedly, smoking dope.[5] These preoccupations arguably left speculators with more knowledge about the company's fundamentals than its CEO possessed.

In March 2008, Bear collapsed in the course of a week on a rumor, whether justified or not, that it was insolvent. Bear's stock price stood at $57 on Monday, March 10. The following Monday, it stood at $2. It would have been zero had the Federal Reserve not persuaded JPMorgan Chase to purchase Bear. At $2 per share, JP Morgan paid less for the company than the appraised value of Bear's New York headquarters building. But since Bear came packaged with unknown liabilities, the Fed had to sweeten the deal by purchasing $29 billion of Bear's most toxic assets.[6] These holdings are now appropriately listed on the Fed's balance sheet as Maiden Lane—a street that kisses the rear end of the New York Federal Reserve.

When Bear was sold in this fire sale, it clearly had lots of worthless assets, which it was carrying (valuing) on its books, not by marking them to market—valuing them using prices the market was actually willing to pay—but by marking the assets to model; that is, using prices that complex mathematical models calibrated with limited data said the market should be willing to pay.

Thus, there was a basis for the market to price Bear below its self-reported book value and to be highly uncertain about Bear's real value. It's not like anyone could jump onto the web and look at each of Bear's assets to see precisely what they were. This was proprietary information, which Bear's management was purportedly safeguarding for its shareholders.

Bear's current and prospective shareholders were, thus, being treated like children. They were being told that they couldn't be told what they owned because they wouldn't understand it and, furthermore, if Bear were to tell them what they owned, Bear would be giving away its magic formula for making them rich. Once other companies learned Bear's trading strategy, they'd copy it and move markets in a way that would close down Bear's ability to buy low and sell high. Bear was saying, "Not to worry. The problem isn't as bad as you might think and please stop asking. If we tell you too much about the problems we encounter, it will just panic you and make things worse. Leave everything in our safe, experienced hands."

During that week that was, Jimmy Cayne might have come forward to calm the market and reassure the kids, in some way or other, that their toys were safe. But Jimmy was busy. He was playing in a bridge tournament in Detroit and couldn't be bothered to call in or check his email as his 85-year-old company with its 15,500 employees gasped its last breath.[7] This took real chutzpah given that Kate Kelly, a *Wall Street Journal* reporter, had written a full-length article back in November discussing how Jimmy had spent much of the prior July playing bridge and being out of touch as Bear's two huge subprime hedge funds went under.

Financial leadership of this kind appears to be highly valuable. Or so Bear Stearns' directors must have believed. After all, they paid Jimmy over $1 billion in cash and securities. But, you know, Jimmy, he needed the money. He had lots of expenses, including routinely paying $1,700 to take a 17-minute helicopter ride from company headquarters to his country club and smoking $150 cigars.

Maybe Jimmy was too stoned to play his trump card, or maybe he had no trump card to play. At some point it didn't matter. When the rumor that Bear was insolvent hit the street and no one at Bear was able to credibly deny it, either because they had no facts to support their case or because the Street didn't trust those at Bear to tell the truth, Bear experienced a classic run on the bank.

Everyone doing business with Bear realized that if everyone else doing business with Bear stopped doing business with Bear much or all of the money they had lent to or parked with Bear in uninsured brokerage accounts would be lost. So Bear's lenders (primarily other banks) yanked their lines of credit, and hedge funds and other depositors withdrew their deposits. Overnight, Bear was out of cash and could no longer operate.

The market also realized that much of the true value of Bear Stearns, whatever it was, was in its people and their synergies, not in its buildings. Were Bear's traders and investment bankers to pick up the phone and move to a different company, Bear's most important asset, its human capital, would be lost. The market also realized that if top Bear's employees saw other top employees leave, they too would leave. That is, the firm could and would, under the right circumstances, run on itself. At some point, Bear's investors thought things had reached that point and collectively said to themselves, "It's time to bail."

Bear's demise sent a shudder down Wall Street and Pennsylvania Avenue. True, Bear hadn't gone bankrupt. But it had gone down the tubes almost from one minute to the next based on rumor and panic. And to echo Richard Fuld, what had just happened to Bear could just as readily happen to other financial giants.

"Trust me. We've been in business for decades. Your funds are safe and our top people are staying." Those words weren't going to cut it anymore, coming as they were from global financial conglomerates run, in large part, by salesmen who had squirmed their way to the top of the gravy train by hook or by crook, but mostly by luck.

Suddenly, the potential for the economy to flip from a very good to a really bad equilibrium was staring everyone in the face. And there was no Jimmy Stewart/George Bailey around to calm everyone down and set things straight. There was George Bush in a daze, Hank Paulson and Ben Bernanke pulling out their remaining hairs, and Jimmy Cayne playing bridge. How quaint and remote Stewart's speech—the one that saved Bailey's Saving & Loan—now sounded.

> You're thinking of this place all wrong. As if I had the money back in a safe. The money's not here. Your money's in Joe's house; that's right next to yours. And in the Kennedy house, and Mrs. Macklin's house, and a hundred others. Why, you're lending them the money to build, and then, they're going to pay it back to you as best they can. Now what are you going to do? Foreclose on them? . . . Now wait . . . now listen . . . now listen to me. I beg of you not to do this thing. . . . Now, we can get through this thing all right. We've got to stick together, though. We've got to have faith in each other.

Google this speech and you'll discover a link to a modern-day reworking of the movie's story line.[8] In the new version, Jimmy Stewart's not dead. But his bank is. Jimmy, you see, didn't save his bank. He absconded with its cash, got caught, and was sent to the slammer for 20 years.

History is fantasizing enough without concocting alternative versions. But my fantasy puts a different Jimmy in jail—the one who drove Bear down the tubes and is now blaming others. In *House of Cards*, William Cohan interviews Cayne. Here's his passing of the buck:

> The audacity of that punk (then New York Fed President, now U.S. Treasury Secretary, Timothy Geithner) in front of the American people announcing he was deciding whether a firm of this stature . . . was good enough to get a loan. Like he was the determining factor, and it's like a flea on his back, floating down underneath the Golden Gate Bridge, getting a hard on, saying, "Raise the bridge." This guy thinks he's got a big dick. He's got nothing except maybe a boyfriend. I'm not a good enemy. I've a very bad enemy. But certain things really—that bothered me plenty. It's just that for some clerk to make a decision based on what, your own personal feeling about whether or not they're a good credit? Who the fuck asked you? You're not an elected officer. You're a clerk. Believe me, you're a clerk. I want to open up on this fucker, that's all I can tell you.

Macho, Macho Men

The point of quoting Fuld's and Cayne's obscenities is not to juice up this book, but to point out that even the best risk analysis in the world isn't going to prevent CEOs who are incredibly arrogant, irrationally overconfident, and loaded to the gills with testosterone from ignoring that analysis and betting the farm to show they have larger *cojones* than their competitors.

Larry McDonald, author of *A Colossal Failure of Common Sense*, relates in detail Fuld's intense animosity toward Pete Peterson and Steven Schwartzman of the Blackstone Group and his perceived need to beat them in the market, by making more deals, earning higher profits, acquiring more real estate, and so on. To quote McDonald,[9]

> Dick Fuld's dark eyes glowed with envy, because Blackstone was owned and run by two old Lehman men: Pete Peterson and Stephen Schwarzman. Peterson, his former boss and effortless superior . . . Schwarzman, another elegant and richly talented banker, a man who had gazed with mere amusement at the pushing and elbowing of Glusksman and his ambitious disciple Fuld.

I'll leave it to others to sort out precisely how much of Wall Street's financial malfeasance was due to machismo, how much to stupidity, how much to greed, and how much to bad luck. But the bottom line is that giving folks like Fuld and Cayne the power to run amok is leaving our system at tremendous risk.[10] And Fuld and Cayne are just the tip of the iceberg when it comes to the host of malfeasants that have been running and ruining Wall Street.

Stan the Man

Stan O'Neal is another member of *Time* magazine's financial rogue parade. O'Neal received a $160 million severance package when he stepped down as CEO of Merrill Lynch, where he spent six years carefully running the company (founded in 1914) into the ground. Merrill, whose symbol is a horned bull and whose motto is "Merrill Lynch is bullish on America" survived lots of bear markets, including the Great Depression, but it didn't survive Stan.

According to Win Smith, former executive VP of Merrill Lynch, Pierce, Fenner & Smith, son of one of the original founders, "He [O'Neal] was a mean person, a disrespectful person, and he drove out thousands of years of experience."

Like other Wall Street "savants," O'Neal loaded up on subprime mortgages—some $41 billion in total, which proved nearly worthless.[11] And like the boards of Lehman, Bear, and all the other failed banks, insurance companies, rating agencies, hedge funds, and government-sponsored enterprises (Fannie and Freddie), the board of directors of Merrill Lynch did nothing to keep Stan O'Neal from gambling with the 83-year-old company. Win minced no words in describing the Merrill board's incompetence: "Shame on them for allowing [O'Neal] to over-leverage the firm and fill the balance sheet with toxic waste to create short-term earnings. Shame on them for not resigning themselves."[12]

By the time O'Neal was invited, with a huge severance package, to get lost, Merrill was on course to lose tens of billions and 61 percent of its market cap. The company was purchased by Bank of America (B of A), whose CEO, Kenneth Lewis, also appears to have had no idea what he was doing. The deal was struck on September 15, 2008, for $50 billion. By January 2009, Merrill had lost tens more billions of dollars and

B of A's market valuation, including its holdings of Merrill, was worth only $45 billion; that is, B of A was worth less than it had spent buying Merrill! Lewis's enormous gamble on Merrill (and Countrywide before that) had failed terribly, and left B of A itself on the brink of bankruptcy.

But Uncle Sam came to the rescue. He pumped in close to $50 billion in B of A and provided the bank with guarantees covering close to $118 billion in potential losses. Lewis didn't escape without penalty; his reputation has been irretrievably tarnished. Yet his wallet is still packed with million-dollar bills. In 2008 alone Lewis was paid over $9 million by B of A in reward for taking his company from profitability to receivership.

Economic Diary, August 11, 2009:
Uncle Sam Sues Uncle Sam

For the public, though, the icing on the outrage cake came when word leaked out that Ken Lewis and the B of A Board had agreed to let Merrill pay its employees $3.6 billion in bonuses for their fine work in 2008, which consisted of losing $27 billion. Since Uncle Sam was putting money into B of A and B of A was paying it out to Merrill for bonuses, Uncle Sam was, effectively, paying those bonuses. The public clamor over this was too much even for the Securities and Exchange Commission, which sued B of A for failing to inform its shareholders of this bonus arrangement.

B of A is now trying to settle the suit with the SEC for $33 million, which is, of course, trivially small compared to the $3.6 billion at stake.[13] Indeed, one of the 39,000 bonuses paid by Merrill was itself larger than $33 million. But whatever B of A ends up paying to the SEC, that is, to Uncle Sam, will come in large part from the bank's largest shareholder, who now happens to be? Yes, you've got it, Uncle Sam.

The practice of federal regulators settling suits against the financial industry for trivially small amounts, relatively speaking, is commonplace. The suits are meant to show the public that the regulators are actually regulating. But they aren't meant to alter behavior. If they were, the regulators would be personally suing the Ken Lewises of the financial world. No, the show must go on, so the show trial must appease the public without inflicting too much damage on companies that are "too big to fail," which means those companies the cost of whose failures would end up back in Uncle Sam's lap. The show trial also needs to entail some show, but no real trial. A real trial would produce too many headlines, which could go on for months, if not years, and damage the business prospects of Uncle Sam's implicit charges.

In the case of this federal government lawsuit against Merrill, that is, against Merrill's owner, B of A; that is, against B of A's owners, which now includes the federal government; the federal judge—Jed Rakoff—needs to approve the $33 million settlement, but he isn't playing ball. He's not letting this fantastic giveaway, which entailed paying 696 Merrill employees bonuses of at least $1 million, to slip quietly away now that it's moved off the front pages. Instead, he's forcing the SEC to publicly disclose who knew what when.

In refusing to approve the settlement, Judge Rakoff asked the following innocent question, in open court, for all to hear: "Do Wall Street people expect to be paid large bonuses in years when their company lost $27 billion?"[14] And when told by the SEC lawyer, David Rosenfeld, that the average bonus across all Merrill employees was only $91,000, the judge responded, "I'm glad you think that $91,000 is not a lot of money. I wish the average American was making $91,000."

During this exchange, B of A's lawyer was whispering advice into Rosenfeld's ear as he was being raked over the coals by the judge. Apparently, he advised Rosenfeld to point out that Uncle Sam's bailout funds hadn't been used to pay the $3.6 billion bonus bonanza. But the judge wasn't buying this malarkey. "Money is money, the last time I checked."

The good judge knows that Uncle Sam is suing Uncle Sam, but he's seeking to impose the only real penalty he can on those who perpetrated this crime, namely publicly embarrassing them. He's also seeking, and rightfully so, to make clear that the SEC is shielding B of A executives and in-house counsel as well as external B of A lawyers from taking responsibility for hiding the $3.6 billion in bonuses from the company's shareholders. Protecting the responsible corporate officers and the company's lawyers in this manner is, in the judge's words, "at war with common sense."[15]

Economics Diary, September 14, 2009:
Judge Rakoff to the SEC: "Drop Dead"

Today, my hero, Judge Rakoff, rejected the proposed $33 million settlement between the SEC and B of A and ordered the SEC to sue B of A's management in public court over its alleged lying to B of A shareholders about the Merrill bonuses.[16] In making his decision, the judge made clear that the real victims in what happened in this case and, by extension, the entire financial collapse, are the shareholders of the banks and insurance companies.

To quote the judge, "It is quite something else for the very management that is accused of having lied to its shareholders to determine how much of those victims' money should be used to make the case against the management go away." As for the proposed settlement, the judge said, "[It] suggests a rather cynical relationship between the parties: the S.E.C. gets to claim that it is exposing wrongdoing on the part of the Bank of America in a high-profile merger; the bank's management gets to claim that they have been coerced into an onerous settlement by overzealous regulators. And all this is done at the expense, not only of the shareholders, but also of the truth."

The really interesting point here is that the trial that the judge is demanding is not about the money. The bonuses have been paid, and they can't, it seems, be taken back. And the B of A management and lawyers who approved the bonuses, but didn't bother to tell B of A shareholders before they were asked to approve the merger, aren't likely to be hit up for $3.6 billion. They have directors' and officers' insurance, so I presume they can't be financially impaired. The real point of the trial is publicly disclosing the process by which top management is effectively stealing from shareholders and the failure of the B of A directors to exercise their fiduciary responsibilities.

The Prince of Redness

Charles Prince, Citigroup's CEO, who took over as chairman of Citigroup in 2007, also bet the ranch on subprime mortgages, with the alleged encouragement of former U.S. Treasury Secretary Robert Rubin.

Prince lost billions of dollars for his bank, putting its stock price below its ATM fee, and leaving it a virtual charge of the U.S. government. To put a precise point on it, we, the people, have now handed Citigroup close to $50 billion and are guaranteeing Citigroup obligations in excess of $300 billion.[17]

But the Prince-Rubin tag team earned lots of personal dividends. Prince received a $38 million severance package and roughly $150 million in pay and other benefits in return for his mistakes. Rubin received over $126 million in pay from the time he joined Citigroup in 1999 to his departure this year.[18] According to the *New York Times,* Rubin cashed out the stock portion of this compensation early on, so that when Citigroup's market value vaporized, Rubin's net worth did not.

Unlike several of the other gentlemen mentioned above, Rubin is soft-spoken, thoughtful, calm, deliberate, and modest—at least this is what comes across in public. But as Secretary of the Treasury, he, together with Lawrence Summers, President Obama's chief economic advisor, and former Senator Phil Gramm, helped repeal the Glass-Steagall Act, which limited the investment options and risk-taking of commercial banks like Citigroup. In killing Glass-Steagall, the threesome got lots of help from Wall Street. The Street spent some $350 million on political contributions and lobbying in the run-up to the vote on the legislation.[19] The new law provided Citigroup with a legal blessing for its expansion into other types of financial services. When Rubin joined Citigroup he pushed it to join its competitors in trading and holding what became toxic mortgage-backed securities, and he managed to misperceive the potential for systemic collapse even though no one in the world was better positioned to see what was coming.

In announcing his departure from Citigroup, Rubin said, "My great regret is that I and so many of us who have been involved in this industry for so long did not recognize the serious possibility of the extreme circumstances that the financial system faces today."

Rubin's take on his role in Citigroup's missteps is that he was not directly involved in the decisions that put the bank at deadly risk. He claims to have had no direct knowledge of the "CDO liquidity puts" that cost Citigroup so dearly. These securities were a type of insurance contract sold by Citigroup to investors in its collateralized debt obligations (CDOs).

CDOs to the Races

We'll return to Bob Rubin in a moment, but let's stop to understand Collateralized Debt Obligations (CDOs). CDOs are claims on the income streams derived from packages of loans, typically mortgages, which are secured with collateral, for example, the home of the mortgagee. Citigroup and other companies sold different CDO *tranches*. *Tranche* means "slice" in French, but in this context it refers to claims to streams of income from the underlying pool of loans where the income streams have different degrees of risk. CDOs were typically sold in five tranches with the higher tranches representing more senior claims; that is, they'd get paid their prespecified monthly payment amounts before the lower tranches were paid their prespecified monthly amounts.

So the top tranche was the safest. Whatever payments were made on the loans, whether the payments represented interest or principal, the funds coming in each month on all the mortgages in the pool were first used to take care of the top-tranched investors (lenders). Any money left over after the top tranche was paid off would be used to pay off the second tranche, and so it would go down the line to the bottom tranche. Since the bottom tranche was at the lowest end of the totem pole, investors in the bottom tranche really got nailed if there were more than the expected number of defaults. Indeed, with a sufficiently large number of defaults, bottom-tranche investors would get wiped out.

In selling tranched CDOs, Citigroup and other companies were, in effect, selling a mutual fund to a set of investors in which the investors agreed in advance to share the pot (the assets purchased by the fund), but in a different manner depending on the returns generated by the pot and on the basis of how they invested. "How they invested" refers here to which tranche they selected when they gave their money to what I'm calling, for reasons you'll see later, a mutual fund.

An example, from a different context—horse racing—helps, I think, make this tranche business easy to see. Fred, Sam, and Sally collectively come up with $3,000 to place bets on four horses recommended by their buddy Joe, a horse trainer. The horses are Princess Bride, Young Guts, Twinkle Toes, and Sure Bet.[20] The four horses have different odds of winning, and, based on Joe's advice, the three friends decide to bet different shares of the $3,000 on the four horses. Given the odds and the bets they placed, Fred, Sam, and Sally know that if Princess Bride wins, the $3,000 bet will end up paying $4,000. If Young Guts wins, it will pay $10,000. If Twinkle Toes wins it will pay $15,000. And if Sure Bet wins it will pay $50,000.

Sally, being a first-time bettor, is very nervous. To ease her anxiety, Fred and Sam agree to pay Sally $4,000 and only $4,000 regardless of which horse wins, *assuming one of the four wins*. This helps allay Sally's fears. Sally, who contributed only $500 to the $3,000 pot, now knows that even if the lowest-paying horse, Princess Bride, wins, she'll still do very well. For Fred and Sam, who put $1,250 each in the pot, this arrangement puts them at more risk. In particular, if Princess Bride wins, they'll get nothing, and if Young Guts wins, they'll also end up with less money than Sally.

Fred is less nervous than Sally, but more nervous than Sam, so Fred and Sam agree that if Young Guts, Twinkle Toes, or Sure Bet wins (so there is money left over after paying Sally), Fred will receive $6,000 and only $6,000. Given this arrangement, Sam is holding the riskiest tranche—he gets nothing if either Prince Bride or Young Guts win. But he'll get $5,000 if Twinkle Toes wins and $40,000 if Sure Bet wins.

Sam likes Twinkle Toes' and Sure Bet's chances and can't wait to spend his winnings. If you think about it, Sam is taking on a lot of default risk here. If both Twinkle Toes and Sure Bet lose, the two horses are, effectively, defaulting on the investment Sam has made in them, and Sam will lose his entire stake.

The one thing left out of the story is that Joe is a horse trainer by night, but a securities trader by day, working for Citigroup. And Joe, who works on commission, offers to sell Fred, Sam, and Sally a very inexpensive Citigroup insurance policy that will give the threesome back their $3,000 if none of their four horses wins.

CDO Liquidity Puts

This, in short, is what Citigroup did. It sold insurance on the cheap against a particular risk. The risk wasn't losing a horse race. The risk was failure to make full payment on CDO tranches.

Why did Citigroup sell this insurance knowing that it might have to pay off and be stuck with huge claims? There are six reasons. First, the macho men and women selling this product were greedy and over-confident. Second, they were being paid on a commission basis. Third, they weren't risking their own savings and homes. Fourth, no regulator was carefully overseeing their behavior. Fifth, the rating companies were saying it was safe to do. But sixth, they had their ace in the hole—their hundred-million-dollar man, Robert Rubin, at their beck and call, ready to pick up the phone and arrange a bailout with his replacement at the Treasury in the event Citigroup faced insurance claims and other losses beyond its means to cover.

Note that Rubin wasn't being paid for his banking expertise or business advice, but for his contacts. Indeed, Rubin was, it appears, intentionally kept in the dark about CDO liquidity puts and, no doubt, about other risky and complex investments because the folks at Citigroup doing these deals didn't want any interference from Rubin or anyone else and also wanted to provide Rubin with full deniability.

As it turned out, the CDO puts cost Citigroup, and ultimately we taxpayers, $25 billion and Rubin was able, probably honestly, to say he never recommended their sale. Indeed, Rubin claims that he didn't know what a CDO put was. As he put it, "Actually, I'm probably close to 20 years beyond which I had a granular knowledge (of financial details). Conceptually I can fully understand what Libor's doing versus three-year swaps. But if you say, 'How do you design a "swaption"?' that goes beyond where I am today."

Rubin, let's recall, headed up Goldman Sachs prior to becoming Treasury Secretary. And he got to the top of Goldman by trading highly complex securities, with full knowledge of how they worked, if not necessarily how to measure their risk. So Rubin didn't know about CDO puts because he didn't want to know and because Citigroup wanted to keep it that way. If and when the time came for Rubin to pick up the phone to call Hank Paulson, his former colleague at Goldman (who had also run that company), and ask for tens of billions of dollars, he didn't want to ask Hank to help him cover up his own mistakes. He wanted to ask Hank to cover up the mistakes of the "kids"—young, rogue traders who, like their former minions at Goldman, had occasion to run amok.

But let me make sure I give Rubin his full due. There is no question that Rubin was able to learn the mechanics of how CDO puts and other complex derivatives being sold by Citigroup worked. What Rubin surely did not understand and could not understand, because he wasn't equipped with the mathematical, financial, or statistical training to do so, was the manner in which these assets were being priced by Citigroup's traders, by which I mean adjusted for risk, as well as incorporated into the overall risk assessment of the company.

Unless you are trained as a hardcore financial quant, you won't know the details of the risk and statistical modeling being used and, consequently, you won't understand all the pitfalls involved. In this respect, Rubin, who had been trained as a lawyer prior to joining Goldman Sachs, was in the same boat as all the heads of the top banks and insurance companies. None had the training needed to really understand what their technical minions were doing or saying. More importantly, if you don't feel on top of a mathematical or statistical technique, you naturally feel intimidated by it and give it more credence and respect than would be the case if you intellectually owned it.

This too represents a big part of the problem with our current financial system. It's technically complex, and the people at the top don't know enough about what's going on to understand that the people who do know enough about what's going on really don't know enough either—that they are using models based on very strong assumptions and data, which has limited power, because of its quantity and nature, to provide real statistical confidence about the nature of the risks materially affecting the company's prospects. So Rubin, Citigroup's hundred-million-dollar man, who, as chairman of Citi's board, had a fiduciary responsibility to understand what the company was doing, was not qualified at a very basic level to do his job. And neither, for that manner, were his counterparts at the other top financial firms.

AIG's Three-Hundred-Million-Dollar Man

Joseph Cassano is the former Chief Financial Officer of AIG's Financial Products unit. Before he was invited to leave AIG in March 2008, Cassano more or less single-handedly destroyed the entire company, which is now almost wholly owned by us. Accomplishing this task took some doing. AIG has over 116,000 employees working in 130 countries.[21] AIG is also heavily involved in a range of noninsurance businesses. For example, it runs one of the world's largest aircraft leasing businesses, purchasing, in the process, more planes from Boeing than any other customer.[22]

Cassano brought AIG to its knees by having the company sell something it didn't have the ability to sell, namely insurance against risks that were uninsurable. In this case, Cassano's bottles of snake oil were Credit Default Swaps. A Credit Default Swap (CDS), as indicated, is another fancy term for an insurance policy that guarantees the payment of a risky income stream. Some of these income streams were monies owed on mortgages, either on standard mortgages or on tranches of CDOs and CMOs (Collateralized Mortgage Obligations based on underlying pools of mortgages). Others were payments due on corporate bonds, car loans, credit card payments, and so on. Regardless, the payments were sure to stop or decline in a severe recession, meaning AIG would have to make good on a huge numbers of policies, which it was in no position to do, as Joe knew all too well.

But Joe and others were sure that day would never come. Indeed, instead of holding the premiums from the sale of the CDS insurance policies in safe assets as a reserve against future claims, AIG doubled down by investing in many of the same securities against whose default it was insuring. This meant that in case its policies needed to be paid, it would find that the assets it had to cover those claims had fallen in value. This is like a flood insurer investing its premiums on homes situated solely in flood plains.

But Joe had no worries. Joe was a confident confidence man. In August 2007, a year before things really blew up, Joe publicly stated, "It is hard for us, without being flippant, to even see a scenario within any kind of realm of reason that would see us losing one dollar in any of those transactions."[23]

As he made these public pronouncements, Joe Cassano proceeded to have his team of 377 cofraudsters sell CDSs by the boatload, generating billions of dollars each year in premiums for AIG, but helping leave the mother ship facing what AIG now says is $1.6 trillion in notional CDS exposure. In return, AIG paid Joe over $300 million.

So why did AIG hire Joe? Well, Joe was no slouch. He had great credentials—credentials that jumped off his resume. For starters, Joe had actually finished college, in this case Brooklyn College. Second, he had majored in political science, which everyone knows provides superb training in actuarial science, stochastic calculus, time-series economet-rics, risk modeling, and the many other, highly specialized mathematical and quantitative skills needed for a career in insurance and banking. Third, Joe had lots of practical experience. He learned the financial ropes at a place called Drexel Burnham Lambert, studying at the feet of Dennis Levine, Ivan Boesky, and Michael Milken. Yes, all three gentle-men went to jail for securities fraud, taking Drexel down with them, but so what?

Sarcasm aside, it appears that the only credential AIG's leadership, including its board of directors, really cared about was Joe's ability to make a quick buck.[24] In turning a blind eye, the board was aided and abetted by two players: the rating companies, which rated as AAA both AIG itself, as well as the CDS securities it sold, and by the Office of Thrift Supervision (OTS), AIG's federal regulator, which was beguiled by the rating companies' appraisals and decided the best way to assess AIG's risk was to ask AIG.[25]

According to C. K. Lee, head of the OTS at the time, "We missed the impact" of the collateral triggers. He said the (credit default) swaps were viewed as "fairly benign products"[26] until they overwhelmed the trillion-dollar company. "We were looking at the underlying instruments and seeing them as low-risk. . . . The judgment the company was making was that there was no big credit risk."[27]

The fact that "hear no evil, see no evil, speak no evil, and recognize no risk" OTS, known as the "dumbest regulator in town," ended up as AIG's regulator was no accident. Hank Greenberg, AIG's egomaniacal CEO, who hired Cassano and laid much of the groundwork for its future demise, went to great lengths to ensure OTS was its watchbunny. In 1999 he purchased a Newport Beach, California, Savings and Loan and, voilà, his entire financial behemoth had a single, new, comatose federal regulator—OTS.[28] Not only that, since OTS had only one insurance specialist on its entire staff, the world's largest insurance company ended up, effectively, with a single human being overseeing all its insurance operations.[29]

OTS was the regulator of choice of other major financial malfeasants. Countrywide Financial, IndyMac Bancorp, and Washington Mutual are examples. All three companies gambled on subprimes and lost their shirts. Washington Mutual's demise represented the largest U.S. bank failure in history.[30]

But shopping for regulators wasn't the only reason these banks ended up in OTS's hands. OTS also went shopping for companies it wanted to regulate. Indeed, it actively encouraged Countrywide Financial to switch from using the Comptroller of the Currency as its regulator to using OTS. What was in this for OTS? Three things—first, the ability to collect higher regulatory fees; second, fulfilling the political and philosophical deregulation goals of those running OTS and the White House; and third, the opportunity to beat a competing regulatory agency.

A good example of regulators courting regulatees is the meeting that Darryl Dochow, an OTS official, held in 2006 with Anthony Mozilo, Countrywide's CEO. According to the *Washington Post,* "Senior executives at Countrywide who participated in the meetings said OTS pitched itself as a more natural, less antagonistic regulator than OCC (Office of the Comptroller of the Currency) and that Mozilo preferred that. Government officials outside OTS who were familiar with the negotiations provided a similar description."

OTS's marriage proposal was quickly accepted by Mozilo, whose firm was heavily involved in marketing ARMs (adjustable-rate mortgages) and other extremely dicey mortgages, whose issuance OTS was encouraging. During these years, Countrywide became the largest home-mortgage provider and made Fortune's list of "Most Admired Companies." Mozilo was named by *Barron's* as "one of the thirty best CEOs in the world," given a lifetime achievement award by American Banker, and paid himself over $200 million dollars for providing Americans with mortgages he knew they couldn't afford.

By the time B of A purchased Countrywide, Mozilo had laid off 11,000 employees and lost four-fifths of his company's market value. Today, Mozilo stands charged by the SEC with securities fraud for misleading investors about the company's loans and engaging in insider trading. Senator Charles Schumer, who sits on the Senate Banking Committee, declared that he'd like to see Mozilo "boiled in oil, figuratively."[31]

The OTS is also in the hot seat. It's the only one of over 100 federal and state financial regulatory bodies that the Obama administration wants to terminate. Many of "the friends of Anthony" are also being investigated. The list here includes Senator Kent Conrad, a member of the Senate Budget Committee and the Senate Finance Committee, and Senator Chris Dodd, who heads up a Senate committee that oversees the mortgage business.[32] Both Conrad and Dodd received at least two "VIP mortgages" each from Countrywide. VIP mortgages were also given to, among others, Henry Cisneros and Alphonso Jackson, former Housing Secretaries, to Franklin Raines, when he was chairman and CEO of Fannie Mae (which, incidentally, was at the time buying billions of dollars of toxic loans from Countrywide), and to Senator John Edwards.[33]

Franklin Delano Raines

Prior to becoming chief honcho at Fannie Mae, Franklin Delano Raines, who was named after President Franklin Roosevelt, looked like he could do no wrong and would put Horatio Alger to shame. Son of a janitor, Raines graduated Harvard College, earned a law degree at Harvard Law School, and attended Oxford University as a Rhodes scholar. He then held top positions in the Carter Administration, spent a decade at Lazard Freres and Co., a prominent Wall Street investment house where he made partner, became Fannie Mae's vice chairman, served in the Clinton Administration as director of the Office of Management and Budget, and reached the pinnacle of Fannie Mae in 1999.

Five years later, Raines "accepted early retirement" from Fannie as the SEC and the Office of Federal Housing Enterprise Oversight began investigating the mortgage giant for accounting "irregularities," which shifted losses in such a way as to raise Raines's already outrageous compensation by an extra $90 million. Fannie was fined $400 million for this miscarriage of corporate accounting. The payment came out of the company's coffers, which means it came out of the pockets of its shareholders (as if they had any knowledge or ability to control the board or Raines). For his part, Raines got away with a couple-million-dollar slap on the wrist.[34] The *Wall Street Journal* rightly called this a "paltry settlement," allowing Raines and his accomplices to "keep the bulk of their riches."[35]

Speculation with Other People's Money

It's easy to focus on the outrageous egos, astronomical earnings, colossal mistakes, and malfeasance of people like Fuld, Cayne, O'Neal, Prince, Rubin, Cassano, Mozilo, and Raines. But the critical takeaways from these examples are that power is extremely concentrated at the very top in modern American financial companies, that decisions are being made as much on emotion and ego as careful business planning, that the folks at the top are so rich as to face no real financial loss for themselves or their families if they role the wrong dice for their companies, that board after board of directors did nothing to oversee the decisions of their ultimate paymasters, and that the correlation between performance and compensation was negative.

In 2008 the highest paid CEO was Motorola's Sanjay Jha, who bagged $104.4 million while helping deliver a negative 71 percent return for his investors. American Express's Kenneth Chenault earned $42.8 million for delivering a negative 63 percent return. Citigroup's Vikram Pandit earned $38.2 million, while his shareholders earned −73 percent. And the list goes on. In total, 73 U.S. CEOs earned more than $10 million in 2008, notwithstanding the fact that 67 of these CEOs generated negative income, and in most cases, substantially negative income, for their shareholders.[36]

Had Fuld, Cayne, O'Neal, Prince, Rubin, Mozilo, Raines, and others known that their mansions, swimming pools, Porsches, airplanes, yachts, villas, and other necessities of life were on the line, they would never in a million years have taken the risks with their companies that they took. They made sure they worked for companies with limited liability and with plenty of directors' and officers' insurance, so they could not be personally sued or, if so sued, could not be financially hurt.

Most important, they made sure they had lifelines in Washington they could call for help if things got bad. Nor did the folks in Washington need to be former Wall Street employees. All a new young government staffer or bureaucrat needed to see was Robert Rubin earning $100 million, not for playing what he'd call "global strategist," but for being a "fixer," and they'd know that if they played nice with Wall Street and developed good contacts on the Hill and with the administration, they too would be able to move to New York, Boston, San Francisco, Chicago, or some other financial center and cash in on their influence.

Or they could look at Lawrence Summers, President Obama's current chief economic advisor. Prior to joining the administration and subsequent to his "resigning" as president of Harvard at the behest of a majority of Harvard's faculty, Summers received $5 million for working just one a day a week for D. E. Shaw, one of Wall Street's largest hedge funds. Again, connections, rather than financial acumen, seem to have been at play in setting pay. Summers was U.S. Treasury Secretary prior to being named president of Harvard University (thanks, by the way, to the support of Robert Rubin, who was serving on Harvard's executive governing board). Summers, too, was in a position to make urgent calls to top members of the previous administration. And there was also the option value that Summers would join the new administration and be able to "impartially" help D. E. Shaw and other hedge funds in the future. Funny enough, the Geithner–Summers plan for ridding banks of their toxic assets, the Public-Private Investment Fund (PPIF) described below, includes a starring role for large hedge funds.

If D. E. Shaw was paying Summers to advise on financial matters, they were likely wasting their money. When it comes to making financial deals, Summers' skills aren't exactly impeccable. Harvard lost well over $1 billion of its endowments thanks to interest rate swaps Summers had the university purchase while he was running the show. And Summers was, apparently, still pushing "AAA-rated" CDO tranches on D. E. Shaw's customers in the aftermath of Bear's collapse. These securities lost most of their value.[37]

Summers and his replacement, Drew Faust, also failed to hedge the university against major declines in the market even though the university's budget draws heavily on endowment income. Harvard has now lost roughly 30 percent of its endowment and is facing tough times, freezing faculty salaries, cutting programs, and eliminating hot breakfasts for the undergraduates.

But the critical lesson from the above examples of financial failures is not that Wall Street routinely lets influence peddlers play craps with its own chips, but that Wall Street lets influence peddlers play craps with our chips, where the "our" refers to us, not only as investors, but also as workers and taxpayers. The worst part is that Wall Street is doing this on a daily basis without our knowledge, let alone our consent.

FDR expressed deep concern about this practice in his inaugural address on March 4, 1933: "There must be an end to speculation with other people's money."[38] "Other people's money" refers to the general public's livelihood, tax obligations, and investment returns. Roosevelt was not condemning risk taking per se or investment management per se. What he was condemning was a system that gambled with the economy's performance, the financial market's stability, and the nation's fiscal solvency.

It's the Leveraging, Not the Leverage

Is this placing too much blame on Wall Street and too little on Main Street? After all, every crime needs a victim. Lots of commentators on the financial crisis are blaming the public for excessive leverage—for taking on too much debt, particularly too much mortgage debt to purchase homes they were sure would appreciate. And, no question, millions of Americans did borrow far beyond their means to repay.

But every borrower needs a lender, so if millions of Americans were borrowing too much, this implies that millions of other Americans were lending too much. Borrowing is viewed as a bad thing, while lending is a form of investing, which is viewed as a good thing. So if we had more Americans doing more bad financial things (borrowing), we also had more Americans doing more good financial things (investing).

Now, it's true that China and other countries have been lending money to us personally as well as to our government, but our national saving rate, while a pitifully small 1 percent, is still positive. So, on balance, we Americans, as a group, haven't been borrowing from abroad to consume more than we make. We may have borrowed abroad as a group to invest in risky assets, but even this isn't clear. There is no government agency that measures the overall riskiness of the nation's portfolio and compares that risk with the historical record. That is, the country may be collectively borrowing from abroad to invest in risky assets both at home and abroad, but the real question is whether this behavior entails more collective risk taking today than was the case in the past.

It's easy to look at part of the national ledger and say, "It's the leverage, Stupid" that brought the economy down. And clearly, certain companies that failed, including Lehman and Bear, were leveraged to extreme degrees. But our society has always had gambling and gamblers. We can be sure that someone will be sitting at the craps tables in Las Vegas at 3 am every night trying her best to lose her life's savings. The real problem with Bear and Lehman and other companies leveraging (which meant that other Americans were de-leveraging) is that when they lost their bets they took so many others down with them.

Let's ignore the rest of the world for a moment, to think more clearly about leverage. The first thing to say is that an isolated economy cannot, as a whole, be leveraged for the simple reason that it can't borrow abroad. Think about Robinson Crusoe. Robinson can't borrow from people on a neighboring island because there is no such island. And he can't borrow from someone on his island because as much as he searches its meadows, trees, beaches, and hills, he can't locate a single person and, therefore, he can't find a single lender.

So, ignoring the rest of the world, an economy can't borrow to take on more risk or lend to take on less risk. It simply holds the risk with which it's endowed. Whatever storms are going to wash over Robinson's island, they are going to hit him full force. The real issue of leverage, then, is not whether our country as a whole became more leveraged, for which there is, again, no evidence. The real issue is who within our country became more leveraged and who became less leveraged and how the failure of those who were more leveraged affected those who were less leveraged.

To make things more concrete, let's suppose Robinson's not alone, but shares the island 50–50 with Sue and that ten coconuts fall from the trees each day on each person's half of the island. One day Robinson takes 10 coconuts, five of which he borrows from Sue, and breaks them open and plants them, sure that they will sprout 30 coconuts the next day. Sue's sure that the investment will be eaten by the island's giant coconut worms. So she charges Robinson 100 percent interest. Both Robinson and Sue eat five coconuts today. Tomorrow, if Robinson is right, he'll eat 30 (10 new ones plus 30 sprouted ones less 10 paid back to Sue). If he's wrong, he'll eat none (the 10 new ones he gets care of his trees being used to repay Sue). Either way, Sue gets to eat 20 tomorrow.

This leveraged investment by Robinson presents only upside risk for the economy. If Robinson's right, he and Sue will be able to grow coconuts and expand their incomes and the economy's total output. If he's wrong, the economy will still keep on producing 20 coconuts every day. So Robinson hasn't placed the economy in jeopardy. Nor has he placed Sue at risk. She consumes five for sure today and 20 for sure tomorrow.

What Robinson's done by borrowing is to place himself at greater risk. Had he just planted his own five, he'd consume five for sure today and either 25 tomorrow or 10 tomorrow. But by borrowing, he still consumes five for sure today, but either 30 or zero tomorrow.

Clearly, if we measure leverage in the economy by the total net amount borrowed, the total degree of leverage is zero. Robinson's net borrowing is plus five and Sue's is negative five, so on this measure their economy has zero leverage. A more useful macroeconomic definition of leverage in this setting would be the economy's overall risk exposure, which has increased, even though it's all upside risk. That is, the economy's output goes from being 20 for sure tomorrow to either 20 or 50. A micro definition would consider how the variability of tomorrow's living standard has changed for Robinson and Sue. Here, there's clearly more variability. Sue has none (she consumes 20 either way). But Robinson, who consumes either zero or 30, faces more variability.

But, while I hope this example is helping clarify that leverage is an easy word to say but a hard thing to measure, I don't think this example gets at the real concern about leverage raised by our financial crisis. Here's an example that does:

Suppose Robinson borrows five coconuts from Sue, promising to pay her back 10 as before, but instead of planting the 10 coconuts (his five plus her five), he uses them to lure a big sea crocodile onto the island, which Robinson is sure he can capture and cook. But he's wrong, and once the croc is on the island, the croc devours Robinson and Sue, washing them down with coconut milk.

So Robinson leveraged up Sue—put her at risk—without her having any idea this was happening. This is the key problem with our financial system. It's not that Robinson was leveraged. If he wants to take risks with his own lunch or his own life, that's his own business. It's Robinson's deceitful leveraging of Sue that's the problem. And Sue is us. We're stuck in a system that's not just built for hucksters to pick a pocket or two. It's built for hucksters to wreak complete economic havoc on an ongoing basis and do so with high probability of huge personal financial gain.

Stealing Other People's Money

Were FDR around today, he'd be appalled not just by Wall Street's speculating with other people's money, but by their simply stealing it. Yes, this is a terribly strong word, but how else would you describe the following, all of which have been the subject of publicly disclosed government investigations leading to huge fines?[39]

- Bear Stearns paid millions to settle federal charges of illegal loan collection practices.
- Bank of America deceived investors by selling risky auction-rate securities as perfectly safe.
- Ditto UBS, Merrill Lynch, Morgan Stanley, and Wachovia.
- GMAC Bank and other student loan companies engaged in deceptive advertising.
- IndyMac Bank routinely issued liar loans until it went broke.
- Countrywide engaged in deceitful lending. Its former CEO is under indictment.
- JPMorgan Chase, Citigroup, and CIBC paid billions to settle securities fraud charges.
- S & P, Moody's, and Fitch took billions in exchange for rating toxics triple-A.
- HSBC and Citigroup used structured investment vehicles to conceal risky mortgage holdings.
- Freddie Mac failed to fully disclose its portfolio losses.
- AIG hid huge losses on its credit default swaps.
- Lehman Brothers failed to come clean about its real estate losses.
- Lehman, Morgan, Citigroup, and Merrill competed to develop abusive tax-evasion schemes.
- B of A settled with the SEC for withholding news of huge Merrill bonuses from shareholders.

This is a trivially small sample of the financial cheating that is going on as part of what has become routine business practice. The SEC is "settling" close to 700 cases of financial fraud each year.[40] Google "SEC settlements" and peruse the 50-plus pages that come up to get a quick sense of the magnitude of the problem. The settlements tend to be slaps on the wrists, with the median settlement totaling only $1 million.[41] The fraud includes all of the above, plus insider trading, late trading, market timing, "misstatements" of financial statements, investor management fraud, misrepresentations of investment products, accounting fraud, and, of course, Ponzi schemes.

Madoff's Ponzi Scheme

No description of financial thievery American style would be complete without including Bernard Madoff's $65 billion Ponzi scheme. Interestingly, Madoff was ruined by the subprime, toxic-asset crisis not because he was investing in these securities—he wasn't investing in any securities—but because when the crisis hit, Madoff's investors started getting nervous about all their investments and started to withdraw more funds from Madoff than they invested with him. Madoff had little or no cash on hand and no assets to sell to use to cover major withdrawals. He depended on inflows to his fund exceeding outflows so he could keep pretending to investors that he was actually making steady, above-market returns on their investments.

Even though Madoff wasn't engaged in Wall Street's standard method of fleecing the public—borrowing short, lending long, taking huge fees, and cutting out before anyone's the wiser—he was engaged in massive nondisclosure, which is one of the fundamental problems bedeviling our financial system. So thinking carefully about what Madoff did and why he wasn't caught can tell us a lot about what needs to be fixed, financially speaking.

The Essence of Ponzi Schemes

The fact that Bernard Madoff described his enterprise as a "Ponzi scheme" to the arresting officers and the judge, who sentenced him to life in prison, is not, in and of itself, evidence that it was a chain letter. Indeed, Madoff is the last person anyone should believe about financial matters. The man is a pathological liar.

So let me play devil's advocate and ask what precisely it was that Madoff did that constitutes a Ponzi scheme and whether what he did is different from what other supposedly honest entities, including Citigroup, GE Capital, Uncle Sam, and pension funds (federal, state, local, and corporate) are doing on a routine basis.

Let's start with the fact that Madoff used new investor money (new contributions) to pay off old investors (cover withdrawals). This fact per se is not evidence of anything untoward. Every mutual fund in the country, and there are over 10,000 of them, does precisely this. The same holds true for each of our nation's pension plans, private and public, including Social Security. They all use contributions to cover withdrawals. This practice is called "managing cash flow."

Next consider Madoff's failure to mark his participants' holdings, to the extent that there were any at any particular point in time, to market. Does this constitute evidence per se of a Ponzi scheme? Again, the answer is no. Essentially all financial institutions, nonfinancial corporations, and governments hold and value assets, many if not most of which they fail to mark to market because there is either: (a) no market in these assets, or (b) the market in these assets is viewed as too thin to be reliable.

Citigroup, Bank of America, and other large and small banks throughout the country are collectively sitting on trillions of dollars in "toxic" assets, which they still, today, aren't valuing at market. These assets include plain vanilla mortgages that are in arrears, exotic mortgage-backed securities that have unique properties, and credit default swaps, not to mention real estate holdings (including millions of foreclosed homes) for which there are no ready buyers.

These banks are making up the valuations of these assets based on their own arbitrary assessments. Every major company in the country is doing much the same when it reports its earnings, which includes its own assessment of capital gains and losses on its often highly illiquid assets and liabilities. Even some mutual funds are in this boat. TIAA-CREF has two funds that are routinely valued on a nonmarked-to-market basis. These are the TIAA fund itself, the return on which appears to be based on a hidden formula that pools risks across cohorts, and the CREF

Real Estate Fund, which is valued, in large part, based on rough and out-of-date appraisals.

Social Security and state and local pension plans, including teachers' retirement plans, are also playing this game. In devising their annual assessments of their financial conditions, these systems/plans are valuing their liabilities using procedures that have little connection to market valuation. For example, Social Security's trustees specify a path of nominal interest rates as well as inflation rates, which are used to discount protected future benefits payments and tax receipts to form what Social Security calls its *open group liability*. This procedure makes no attempt to adjust for the risk of these inflows and outflows or even to connect its interest rate assumptions to prevailing market rates.

Most teachers' pension plans use very high interest rates to discount their future net payments. And since these plans are generally underfunded, meaning the "measured" present value of their benefits exceeds the market value of fungible assets on hand, the use of higher than appropriate discount rates leads to statements of financial condition that are grossly misleading, looking much better than is actually the case.

Now if everyone is using new contributions to cover withdrawals and if everyone is making up, to a large extent, their net asset values, what is it that Madoff did differently that makes his enterprise a Ponzi scheme?

The answer is twofold. First, Madoff was exclusively using new contributions to: (a) meet withdrawals by his existing clients, (b) satisfy his personal avarice, and, it must be said, (c) make charitable contributions. He was running a chain letter, pure and simple, by which I mean he was paying (rather than earning) above-market returns to entice new contributions to continue to be able to pay above-market returns. Because money is fungible (a dollar's a dollar), honest financial companies may literally take Peter's money and use it to pay Paul, but they'll make sure to have invested an amount of money equal to Peter's money in the assets they said they'd purchase on Peter's behalf.

Second, Madoff used a valuation scheme that was so clearly different from the market's valuation of his holdings that it constituted prima facie evidence of fraud. To be specific, Madoff allegedly told his investors their assets were worth $65 billion, but, at the time of his arrest, he had less than $1 billion in marketable securities. Note that Madoff could have claimed that the present value of his future trading profits would cover the remaining $64 billion, but he made no such claim. Nor did he claim he had suffered huge trading losses over the years and had lost in the market all but $1 billion of what he felt was an appropriate collective asset valuation of $65 billion given the future excess returns he was going to provide his clients. Instead, Madoff spoke the words "Ponzi scheme." In so doing, he no doubt made absolutely sure he'd spend his remaining years in jail.

Economics' Take on Ponzi Schemes

For its part, economics places no moral stigma on the words "Ponzi scheme." Indeed, there is a significant economics literature concerned with the question of whether Ponzi schemes—chain letters—are preferred investments for everyone.

How could a Ponzi scheme work for everyone? Here's an example. Suppose the population grows at 5 percent year in and year out forever, so that each age group is 5 percent larger in size than the next-oldest age group. Also assume that the economy's return to investing in real assets, on a safe basis, is only 2 percent per year.

Then if I or you or anyone else invests in the real asset, we'll earn a 2 percent annual return, whereas if we invest in the Ponzi scheme, we'll earn a 5 percent annual return. The Ponzi scheme would entail everyone at the beginning of the year taking a fixed amount, say $1,000, and giving it en masse to the cohort that is one year older. Since the cohort that is one year older is 5 percent smaller in size, each member of that one-year older cohort gets $1,050. A year later, each person who contributed $1,000 receives $1,050 from the cohort that's one year younger. This beats getting $1,020 from investing for a year in the real asset.

Can this go on forever? Yes, provided the economy's population always grows at 5 percent. Indeed, we don't need population growth to make a Ponzi scheme work and beat regular investing. If the economy's population growth is zero, but each cohort experiences a growth of 5 percent each year in its labor productivity, we can also generate the same welfare improvement from running a Ponzi scheme.

For economists, then, the issue is not whether Ponzi schemes are morally good or bad. The issue is whether the conditions for their use are actually satisfied. Here, the evidence appears clear; the conditions are not satisfied, particularly when one takes into account that neither population nor productivity growth nor real asset returns are sure things.

Moreover, it's one thing for a government that will be around, potentially forever, to try to make a Ponzi scheme work for society over time. It's another for a private party that may find itself unable to continue running the scheme and that has no ability to compel participation even if such participation were in everyone's interest.

Had Mr. Madoff been forthcoming from the start and claimed to be running a Ponzi scheme, he would have had few takers because of concern that the scheme would quickly run out of "investors." Instead, Madoff lied about what he was doing, claiming that he was investing, when, in fact, he was exclusively robbing Peter to pay Paul as well as himself.

Don't Show Me the Money

In conducting his Ponzi scam, Madoff was assisted by one Frank DiPascali, his Chief Financial Officer. DiPascali had even less formal education than Jimmy Cayne did. He didn't flunk out of college. He simply never went. But it doesn't take a college degree to lie and cheat with the best on the Street, even to the tune of $65 billion. As DiPascali stated in rendering his guilty plea, "I represented to hundreds, if not thousands of clients that trades took place. . . . It was all fake. It was all fictitious. I knew no trades were happening."[42]

DiPascali spent 33 years working for Madoff. He was recruited by Madoff's secretary and "worked" his way up to a hefty annual compensation, large enough to purchase a 61-foot fishing boat, a mansion, and a fleet of pricey cars. At one point, according to his resume, DiPascali served as chairman of the NASDAQ stock market options committee, notwithstanding the fact that the NASDAQ never had such a committee.

But the main reason that Madoff made off with so many people's money was not thanks to the brilliant help of a high school grad who thought he could lie on his resume and never get caught, nor was it due to Madoff's evil genius, but rather it was due to our securities laws, which permitted Madoff to self-custody the "assets" he was "investing" for his clients. Had Madoff been required to use an independent third-party custodian to hold the assets (as every mutual fund must do), that third-party custodian would duly have reported to the SEC that there were no assets corresponding to Madoff's reported holdings.

Actually, the SEC was repeatedly warned by financial analysts starting in 1992 that Madoff was engaged in fraudulent practices.[43] One of these warnings included a detailed 1999 letter accusing Madoff of running a Ponzi scheme. Yet the SEC failed to investigate. The investigation would have had to have been an "extraordinary investigation" because Madoff was formally running a hedge fund, and hedge funds are not formally regulated by the SEC. And to initiate an extraordinary investigation, the SEC would probably have needed more evidence than was included in the warning letters. The bottom line, though, is that the SEC never once walked into Madoff's shop to utter these four simple words: "Show me the assets."

Madoff, himself, in a jailhouse interview, pointed out that the SEC never checked his asset holdings with parties supposedly holding his assets and conducting his fictitious trades. "If you're looking at a Ponzi scheme, it's the first thing you do," he said.[44]

Instead of looking at the basics, the SEC was completely bamboozled by Madoff, who was considered a titan of the securities industry for helping set up NASDAQ, the first electronic stock exchange. According to the SEC's independent investigation, "Unseasoned investigators from the Securities and Exchange Commission were alternately intimidated and enthralled by a name-dropping, yarn-spinning Bernard L. Madoff as he dodged questions about his financial house of cards."[45]

According to the *New York Times,* "The report details six substantive complaints against Mr. Madoff received by the agency, which were followed by three investigations and two examinations. Yet the agency never verified Mr. Madoff's trading through a third party. Time and again, it was noted that the volume of his purported options trades were implausible. When the enforcement staff received a report showing that Mr. Madoff indeed had no options positions on a certain date, the agency simply did not take any further steps." In fact, the string of lapses was capped by a staff lawyer receiving the highest performance rating from the agency, in part for her "ability to understand and analyze the complex issues of the Madoff investigation."[46]

Madoff served as chairman of the board of directors of the National Association of Securities Directors and held other high-profile positions in the securities industry. Not only did the SEC trust Madoff, but it consulted him on a routine basis about its regulatory policy. Madoff even intimated to the SEC investigators that he was likely to be appointed the next SEC chairman!

Far from spotting the largest securities fraud in world history, the SEC pronounced Madoff's shop clean as a whistle (a fact he proceeded to advertise) and let him spend additional years destroying the financial and emotional lives of thousands of his clients. The SEC is now being sued by Madoff's victims, and rightfully so. But if Madoff's victims win, we the taxpayer will get to pay for Madoff's mess as well as Bear's, Lehman's, AIG's, Fannie's, Freddie's, Citigroup's, Countrywide's, Washington Mutual's, Merrill's, B of A's, Wachovia's, Wells Fargo's, Financial Guarantee's, and those of a host of others.

The fact that the SEC and all our other federal and state financial policemen couldn't shoot straight when financial crimes were happening right under their noses should give us considerable pause about trusting these Keystone Kops to protect us in the future. Former SEC chairman Arthur Levitt has this to say about the government's ability to detect and prevent securities fraud: "The SEC going back to its formation, and the Justice Department going back to its formation, are never adequate to crime at its time. . . . A very skillful criminal can almost always outfox the regulator or the overseer." Levitt knows whereof he speaks. As SEC chairman, he knew and respected Madoff and routinely sought his advice.

For his part, Christopher Cox, chairman of the SEC at the time Madoff was arrested, stated, "I am gravely concerned by the [SEC's] apparent multiple failures over at least a decade to thoroughly investigate these allegations or at any point to seek formal authority to pursue them."

For the thousands of victims of Madoff, this is pouring salt into wounds. But it's also a telling comment from an SEC chairman who had a genuinely impressive record of accomplishment prior to the Madoff scandal. What it suggests is that Cox, who was appointed to head the SEC in June 2005, knew nothing of the repeated allegations made to the SEC about Madoff's operations. This, in turn, means that decisions about investigations are being made by regulatory subordinates based on their own judgments—judgments that we now know are not reliable.

The Real Crime in a Ponzi Scheme

To return to the key point, the real crime with a Ponzi scheme is not that chain letters per se always violate economic feasibility or notions of morality. They do neither. The real crime is that people running Ponzi schemes don't admit that they are running chain letters. Their accounting isn't honest. They don't show that the present value (the value today—i.e., the value in the present) of what each contributor will take out exceeds the present value of what each contributor will put in, where the discounting is done at market rates of return appropriate to the risk of the return being advertised. The people running Ponzi schemes don't show this, because they can't. Chain letters that make all participants better off, while feasible in theory, aren't possible in practice given the economy we know and record in our data.

In Madoff's case, he wasn't telling investors that the present value of their safe, above-market future returns would be covered by the contributions of new investors, and that the new investors would receive above-market returns from subsequent new investors, and so on. If he had, his gig would have been up immediately. Instead, he told his investors that their streams of future withdrawals would come from safe, above-market returns that he would earn based on his proprietary investing strategy. For investors in his fund—virtually all of whom knew very little about finance, but were aware that there were financial wizards out there, like Peter Lynch of Fidelity and David Swenson of Yale, who had the Midas touch—what Madoff promised and reaffirmed in monthly statements seemed completely on the up-and-up.

Is the U.S. Banking System a Ponzi Scheme?

On February 2, 2009, the *New York Times* ran a front-page story detailing how a major bank (not named) was valuing a mortgage-backed security it owns. The security represented a proportionate claim to the receipt of all payments from 9,000 second mortgages packaged together into a single financial instrument. The *Times* reported that the market price of the security was 38 percent of par value, but that the bank was using a valuation equal to 98 percent of par. The *Times* also indicated that Standard & Poor's valued the security at between 53 cents and 87 cents of par value. The bank justified its valuation based on the argument that the market was temporarily depressed and would come back over time and that the current market was too thin to be reliable—this despite the fact that a quarter of the 9,000 loans were delinquent

This is one gigantic discrepancy. The bank, in effect, is telling the public that it will be receiving 2.6 (98 divided by 38) times more income from this security than the market price indicates will be the case.

The *New York Times* did not report this case as an exception to the rule. It reported it as the rule, suggesting that large parts of the banking industry have failed to book their losses on their mortgage-backed securities and were, consequently, grossly overstating a key component of their future profits.

How does this differ from running a Ponzi scheme, which, recall, entails doing two things: (a) paying (rather than earning) above-market returns to entice new contributions to continue to pay (rather than earn) above-market returns in order to entice . . . and (b) using a valuation scheme that is so clearly different from the market's valuation as to constitute prima facie evidence of fraud.[47] The industry seems to clearly meet the second criterion. It's engaging in false/misleading/economically heroic accounting, if not to the degree of Madoff. Madoff's overvaluation was 65 to 1, whereas, in the *New York Times* example, the bank's overvaluation was only 2.6 to 1.

The industry also seems to meet the first criterion. Madoff was, at the end, telling his investors that for every dollar the market would say he could earn for his investors, he'd be able to earn $65. The bank in the *Times* story was telling its investors that for every dollar the market says it can earn on these securities for its investors, the bank would earn $2.6. In making these implicit statements, both parties are enticing new contributions with misleading statements about the returns earned by prior investors. And each party can be said to have paid above-market returns. In Madoff's case he announced, and paid out to those who asked for their money, a stream of returns that entailed a much higher average level and a much lower variability than could readily be acquired on the market.

How about the bank in the *New York Times* story? Well, it effectively did the same thing. In not honestly marking its assets to market and, therefore, reporting losses as they accrued, the bank presumably kept the market value of its own shares above what would otherwise have been the case. Hence, it produced returns on its own stock that were, effectively, made up. Anyone who cashed out her shares of the bank stock during this period got away with (was effectively paid) a higher return than was warranted. This is no different from those Madoff clients who withdrew their holdings based on Madoff's fabricated return reports.

So is Wall Street running a Ponzi scheme? Yes. Insofar as any financial company does not fully disclose the current market value of its holdings, it's fundamentally playing the same game as Madoff. And most of Wall Street appears to be engaged in this practice and has been given license by the government and the accounting industry to continue making up returns. On April 2, 2009, the Financial Accounting Standards Board voted unanimously to let banks exercise more judgment in applying mark-to-market accounting of their assets and liabilities.[48]

William Poole, a very fine economist and former president of the St. Louis Fed, had this to say about the new ruling:

> I think it's a mistake. If it's too cold in the room, you don't fix the problem by holding a candle under the thermometer. . . . It may increase reported bank earnings by 20 percent, but it has nothing to do with the reality of bank earnings.

From Ponzi Schemes to Full Disclosure

The mortgage-backed securities crisis began in June 2007 with the failure of prominent hedge funds that were heavily invested in mortgage-backed securities. By February 2009, more than a dozen of the nation's largest financial institutions had hit the skids thanks to direct and indirect holdings of these instruments.

Like Bear and Lehman, the other companies saw their market valuations plunge based on rapid changes in beliefs that assets previously worth tens of billions of dollars were now worth next to nothing. And like Bear and Lehman, the other companies failed to disclose publicly, let alone fully and precisely, what they owned and owed.

Let me make clear what I have in mind by full disclosure. I'm talking here, for example, about a current or prospective Citigroup shareholder being able to determine on the web that Citigroup has $X invested in the top tranche of a CMO, which I'll call ABC, and then be able to link to a listing of all the mortgages whose performance will determine the payoff to ABC. For each mortgage, one would be able to determine the location and appraised value of the mortgaged property as well as the borrower's credit rating, earnings history, and any other pertinent information that would not identify the borrower and, thus, not violate the borrower's privacy.

One might think that in taking over or effectively taking over each of the above-listed companies, Uncle Sam would have required full disclosure. Nothing could be further from the truth. Take, for example, AIG, 80 percent of which we taxpayers have owned, as of this writing, for almost one year. There is currently no way to determine the precise nature of the over $1.6 trillion in credit default swaps upon which AIG says it now sits. Unless AIG were to default, which Uncle Sam has clearly decided not to permit, these insurance policies represent our contingent obligations. Yet we taxpayers have no ability or, it seems, right to learn precisely what it is we owe or when we may owe it.

The fact that the *New York Times,* which has been covering the housing/mortgage/financial crisis in very close detail, took more than a year and a half to actually focus in on the precise degree of pretense in the valuation of what may be trillions of dollars of financial assets and liabilities is testimony to the "don't ask 'cause we won't tell" culture of Wall Street and Uncle Sam. Indeed, the above-referenced *Times* article states, "Most banks provide only a very general description of their holdings, because they consider the information privileged."

We've also reached the point that voluntary disclosure of the details of the holdings of financial institutions would not be believed. According to the *Times,* "Many analysts do not trust what they are told about the quality of the securities and loans held by banks and other financial firms." Moreover, the assets and liabilities of modern financial companies are so complex that even honest revelation may leave appraisers with more questions than answers.

The run on Bear Stearns was in full force on Friday, March 14, 2008, when JPMorgan Chase was "invited" by the Treasury to purchase Bear Stearns by the end of the weekend.[49] At this point, JPMorgan had, apparently, no better idea than the man on the street what Bear was worth. JPMorgan rushed in a team of 200 bankers to sit down with their counterparts at Bear to try to decipher Bear's book of business. At the end of the 48 hours JPMorgan concluded that it still had very little understanding of Bear's 35 to 1 leveraged exposure, at which point JPMorgan agreed to buy the company essentially for free provided the Fed take over $29 billion worth of the most dangerous of Bear's liabilities.

As things now stand, no one can really tell what he or she is buying when it comes to purchasing a share of *any* our nation's "prestigious" financial institutions. In effect, Wall Street has asked us to value its firms based on their top brass, who are the only people with full access to the particulars of their company's positions. This may help explain why the Street pays its CEOs so much. Yes, our firm has tens of thousands of individual financial assets and liabilities, which only our CEO, and maybe a couple of his close advisors, is allowed to know about in their entirety. But our CEO is a pure genius and can handle this knowledge and make the right risk–reward tradeoffs. Otherwise, why would we be paying him $200 million a year?

In short, pricing a Lehman Brothers, Inc., comes down to pricing its Dick Fuld. Well, we now all know only too well what Dick Fuld is really worth. We also know that we're asking for trouble leaving our financial system in the hands of people like him.

Disclosure Is Essential

Suppose we could, right this minute, discern all the details of the financial assets and liabilities of the top-secret companies making up our financial sector. Would that help people make more informed judgments about how much to invest in these companies? Absolutely.

Take today's 800-pound gorilla that still menaces our financial system, namely the trillions upon trillions of credit default swaps out there in the market, whose exact ownership and nature is unknown. We do know that for every seller of a CDS, there was a buyer. Hence, every dollar of potential insurance payout by one party is a dollar that would be received by another. Hence, we know that the net, worldwide CDS exposure across all financial companies and individual CDS buyers and sellers is zero. But any given institution, in the United States or abroad, may be terribly exposed depending on how events play out. AIG, for example, is now suggesting that its books include $1.6 trillion in CDS holdings. But we don't know if this is a gross or net position, and even if the $1.6 trillion is a statement of AIG's net CDS exposure, we don't know its risk.

AIG could, for example, be on the hook for $5 billion in CDSs that insure the holders of these securities against the default of Ford Motor Company bonds, while at the same time AIG may be on the hook for $50 billion in CDSs that insure their holders against default of Toyota bonds. Now if Ford goes bankrupt, but not Toyota, AIG will be stuck paying out on its Ford CDS, but its exposure with respect to the Toyota CDS position could well improve. Toyota and Ford are, of course, competitors, so if Ford were to fail, Toyota can be expected to pick up a lot of business from Ford's former customers, substantially reducing the already small chances of Toyota going broke. AIG would have to shell out $5 billion for the Ford CDS, but could take back some of the collateral it previously posted on its Toyota position as the risk of a Toyota default declines. Another way of saying this is that Ford's declaring Chapter 11 would increase the market value of AIG's Ford CDS liability, but reduce the market value of AIG's Toyota CDS liability.

Thus even having companies report their net CDS exposure is not enough. One needs to know the exact details of each CDS and other financial contracts in order to really understand what risks and rewards the company is facing and whether the company is worth what it costs.

Disclosure Is Not Enough

Even if we could get banks, hedge funds, private equity funds, insurance companies, and so on to lay out all the fine details about each of their assets and liabilities, individual members of the public would be at a loss in trying to sort out what any given financial company was worth because they would have to come up with their own valuations. Processing all this information is something Joe Six Pack is neither prepared nor wants to do.

Joe Six Pack

Joe Six Pack wants to earn his wage, grab his beer, root for the Red Sox, and buy financial assets that are worth their price. He's not interested in being forced to hold complex financial instruments either directly or in his role as a taxpayer. And he realizes that fully disclosing a hyper-complex system that is beyond his or anyone else's comprehension is not particularly helpful. He's looking for a financial system that's simple, transparent, and safe—safe from greedy CEOs, CFOs, and all other fancy sounding Os, self-dealing directors, corrupt politicians, insider raters, and incompetent regulators.

Joe understands that economic life, in the best of circumstances, is not for sure. So a safe financial system does not, in his mind, mean one devoid of risk. Joe's willing to take some risk with his savings given the high average return investing in the economy can deliver. What he doesn't want is his investment risk to go beyond the economic to the human. He doesn't want to have his stock earn super-high returns one year because some politician delivered the goods and get slaughtered the next year because some rogue bankers ran a scam to "earn" a huge bonus.

Joe also knows that in fixing the financial system, the government could kill the goose that's laying the golden eggs. That's not what he's after. Joe doesn't want to stifle economic or financial innovation any more than he wants to stifle medical innovation. He wants the government involved, but not overly involved. By analogy, he wants a profit-driven private pharmaceutical industry to work on new medications, but he also knows that without the FDA (the Food and Drug Administration), he'd have no way of knowing what new drugs are reasonably safe and what new drugs will almost surely kill him.

(Continued)

(*Continued*)

When Joe looks at the FDA he sees the kind of disclosure system he seeks. It's one that keeps him and 300 million other Americans from duplicating the same effort to find out the same information. That is, it's one that gets the point that information is a public good—a good that can be used by Joe without diminishing its use by Sally. A steak sandwich, in contrast, is a private good; the more Joe eats, the less Sally has left to scavenge.

When Joe looks around, he sees all kinds of public goods being provided by the government for the simple reason that if their use doesn't limit someone else's use, they need, from the perspective of economic efficiency, to be provided for free, at the margin. But no private company can do so and make a profit.

National defense is an example. A single nuclear missile ballistic system can protect all Americans at once. We don't need each American to build his or her own system. And if the government didn't provide it, the system wouldn't get built since Joe would know that if Sally built it, he'd get to use it for free and Sally would know that if Joe built it, she'd get to use it for free. So Joe would let Sally build it, and Sally would let Joe build it, and it would never get built. This, in economics, is called *the free-rider problem*.

Product safety information, including financial product safety information, is a public good and needs to be provided by the government. Joe totally gets Elizabeth Warren, a Harvard Law School professor, now chairing the congressional panel overseeing financial bailouts. According to Warren, "Giant lenders compete for business by talking about nominal interest rates, free gifts and warm feelings, but the fine print hides the things that really rake in the cash. Today's business model is about making money through tricks and traps. . . . In the early-1980s, the average credit card contract was about a page long. Today, it is more than 30 pages. . . . I am a contract law professor, and I cannot make out some of the fine print. . . . Study after study shows that credit products are designed in ways that obscure the meaning and trick customers."[50]

Joe realizes that full disclosure of financial product safety information is no less important than is medical disclosure of a new drug's side effects and clinical test results. Joe also knows that leaving public safety trials and information in the hands of the drug companies wouldn't work. Too many extremely dangerous fly-by-night miracle cures would be invented, fully certified by high-paid "experts," leaving Joe with no idea which medicine was real and which was cyanide. Joe also knows that in recent years the FDA has gotten into trouble by letting the drug companies play far too large a role in the drug approval process.

Finally, Joe knows that our drug approval system works because it's not too strict. It doesn't keep us from buying herbal and other medications that haven't been clinically tested. Nor does it keep doctors from prescribing such medications. If a non-FDA drug appears to be really dangerous, it will likely be quickly investigated by the FDA and banned, but otherwise the FDA rates these medications by not rating them—by saying "Joe and Sally, these are untested drugs. Use them at your own risk. We can't test all medications, sorry. Doing so is too expensive. So what we know about this drug is that we know nothing, which means it could, from our perspective, just as well do harm as good."

If you think about it, rating by not rating is a way of providing a public good—the information that there is no information—at a very low cost. So not knowing is knowing and also represents a public good that needs to be publicly provided.

In the case of financial products, having the government indicate that these products over here, on the right, have been inspected, disclosed, verified, and separately rated by government-paid, nonconflicted, independent rating companies, and that these financial products over here, on the left, have not been inspected, disclosed, verified, or rated, provides the public with valuable information about products on both the right and the left.

Uncle Sam's Ponzi Scheme

We need a Federal Financial Authority (FFA) to protect us from predatory financial companies no less than we need a Food and Drug Administration to protect us from predatory drug companies. But when you look at the government's financial policy, you see the exact opposite of public financial product safety provision. Rather than compel full financial disclosure, Uncle Sam is hiding what he knows about the financial companies we now own.

Indeed, when it comes to nondisclosure, Uncle Sam is the father of all financial malfeasants. He's been systematically misrepresenting our nation's finances for decades and been giving the private sector an in-depth, ongoing tutorial on duplicitous, misleading, and deceptive accounting. In the process, he's run up an undisclosed fiscal bill that makes our current financial bailout look like chicken feed.

Unlike Madoff, the U.S. government hasn't been claiming to beat the market. But like Madoff, Uncle Sam hasn't provided an honest statement of what he's doing and how different citizens will fare over time with respect to what they'll contribute over their lifetimes and what they'll get back. In particular, Uncle Sam hasn't shown how its policy toward current adults will affect future generations. The reason is simple. Such generational accounting would show that future generations face tax rates over their lifetimes that are roughly twice as high as those facing current adults.

Generational accounting is a well-established methodology. It was developed in the late 1980s by myself, Alan Auerbach (now at UC Berkeley), and Jagadeesh Gokhale (now at the Cato Institute) and has been applied to roughly 35 countries around the world. It was included in the final budget of President George H. Bush and the first budget of President Clinton. But even though the analysis, which was produced by the Office of Management and Budget with the assistance of myself, Auerbach, and Gokhale, was tucked safely away in the appendix to the huge federal budget, it received enormous press attention. Indeed, it received so much attention that it began to threaten the status quo practice of fiscal policy, namely taking from the young and giving to the old. Hence, when it came to including generational accounting in President Clinton's second budget, it was censored two days before publication.

Fiscal Gap Accounting

A generational account for any given generation measures what the generation's remaining lifetime net tax bill—what the generation will pay net of what it will receive, all valued as of today—as a present value. If you add together all the generational accounts of all current and future generations, assuming no change in fiscal policy, you arrive at what all current and future citizens are going to pay, on net, in taxes to the government, measured as a present value. Call this amount A. This amount has to cover the amount B—the sum of the government's official debt plus the present value of all of the government's future purchases of goods and services (its so-called *discretionary spending*).

If you now take the difference between B (what the government intends to spend plus what it owes its bondholders)—and A (what it will be collecting in net taxes), you arrive at a measure called the *fiscal gap*.

Note that the fiscal gap and the generational accounting analyses incorporate all of the government's fiscal activities; that is, both are comprehensive analyses. This means that all of the government's fiscal obligations to pay for Medicare, Medicaid, Social Security, welfare, un-employment benefits, tanks, highway repairs, interest and principal on government debt—you name it—are being put on the same footing in assessing the overall sustainability of fiscal policy.

The U.S. fiscal gap is currently estimated by two distinguished economists—Jagadeesh Gokhale and Kent Smetters (at the University of Pennsylvania)—at $77 trillion dollars, which is more than five times current GDP and an absolutely enormous sum.[51] Indeed, were we to try to raise $77 trillion in present value by raising the FICA payroll tax, we'd have to more than double the employer plus employee tax rate, which is now 15.3 percent. And we'd have to do this immediately and permanently!

Gokhale and Smetters first formed an estimate of the fiscal gap in 2002 when Smetters was working for the U.S. Treasury and Gokhale was working for the Federal Reserve. Their meticulous fiscal gap mea-surement project took the better part of a year and received considerable assistance from several government agencies. The fiscal gap study was authorized by then Treasury Secretary Paul O'Neil with the goal of including the analysis in President George W. Bush's FY03 budget to be released in February of 2003. Gokhale and Smetters completed their study in early December 2002, but on December 7th of that year, Secretary O'Neil was summarily fired, leaving Washington the same day.[52] Two days later the Bush administration, which was keen on passing Medicare Part D (drug benefits for the elderly) and more tax cuts (and getting reelected), censored the study.

The reason for detailing these acts of censorship by both Democratic and Republican administrations is to clarify that if misleading the public about a financial enterprise defines a Ponzi scheme, then Uncle Sam's fiscal policy certainly fits the bill.

Why Is the U.S. Fiscal Gap So Large?

Can the true measure of our federal red ink really be $77 trillion? Indeed, it can. Just ask David Walker, former chief comptroller general of the United States and now president and CEO of the Peter G. Peterson Foundation (yes, the same Pete Peterson that Dick Fuld was out to beat). Pgpf.org reports that our liabilities to Medicare, Social Security, and the Federal debt alone now total $56.4 trillion.

To see why such figures can be so large, consider the fact that there are now roughly 33 million elderly in the U.S. When the 78 million baby boomers retire, we are going to have more than twice the number of oldsters, but only 18 percent more workers to help pay their Social Security, Medicare, and Medicaid benefits. These programs' benefit levels are already sky high. Indeed, if you calculate today's total spending on the elderly by just these three programs and divide by the number of elderly, you arrive at an average Social Security, Medicare, and Medicaid benefit payment per oldster of $30,250, which is 80 percent of per capita U.S. GDP. In 20 years when the baby boomers are fully retired, the average benefit per oldster will be $50,000, measured in today's dollars, and will represent roughly 110 percent of per capita GDP!

This $50,000 estimate is, by the way, based on very optimistic assumptions about growth in Medicare and Medicaid age-specific benefit levels. Between 1970 and 2002, the average level of real Medicare plus Medicaid age-specific benefits grew at a 4.6 percent annual rate. In contrast, real per capita GDP grew at only a 2.0 percent rate.[53] Since 2002, the growth rate in real age-specific Medicare and Medicaid benefits appears to have been even higher thanks primarily to the introduction of Medicare Part D. Nonetheless, the $50,000 estimate assumes that the Medicare plus Medicaid real average benefit will grow at only 3.6 percent per year.

If you take $50,000 per boomer and multiply by 78 million, you arrive at an annual sum that is close to $4 trillion; that is, we are, under highly optimistic assumptions, on our way to handing out some $4 trillion per year, measured in today's dollars, to retired baby boomers. Adding up all these $4 trillion or so annual amounts coming down the pike, and discounting for the fact that they are in the future, helps explain why the fiscal gap is $77 trillion valued in the present. By "present" I mean we are short the $77 trillion right now, not sometime down the road. Think of the $77 trillion as Uncle Sam's credit card balance. If he doesn't pay it, it will grow with interest.

In forming the values in the present of the fiscal gap, how one does the discounting (the marking to market) in forming the fiscal gap can matter quite a lot. There is reason to believe that the $77 trillion figure would be even larger were one to discount the government's future cash flow, taking into account that future benefit payment outlays appear to be more certain than do future tax receipts. The one example where such risk adjustment has been conducted is Social Security, although work is now underway to do such adjustment for all government spending and receipts.

Let me tell you briefly about the Social Security findings.

Social Security's Unfunded Liability

According to the Social Security Trustees Report, Social Security is, all by its lonesome self, 27 percent underfunded; that is, achieving long-term solvency requires an immediate and permanent increase by 27 percent in the 12.4 percent employer and employee payroll tax rate financing Social Security.[54] This calculation treats the Social Security trust fund as an asset of the system—a debatable assumption. And, like Gokhale's and Smetter's comprehensive fiscal gap accounting, the calculation of Social Security's fiscal gap fails to adjust for the riskiness of the system's cash flows. Instead, an arbitrarily selected 2.9 percent real discount rate is used in these analyses.

In a recent study, Steve Ross (an MIT economist), Alex Blocker (a statistics PhD student at Harvard), and I showed how one can use Steve's theory of Arbitrage Pricing to risk-adjust Social Security's fiscal gap—that is, to properly mark Social Security's future benefit payments and tax receipts to market.[55] Our analysis, while highly preliminary, suggests that Social Security's failure to risk-adjust its cash flow may be leading to an understatement of its long-term fiscal gap by more than one-fifth.[56]

If our findings hold up after further analysis, Social Security can be said to constitute a Ponzi scheme in that it is misrepresenting its long-term funding gap. But two things may be said in Social Security's defense. First, the valuation mistake is relatively small compared to the overall fiscal gap of $15.1 trillion fiscal gap that it reports.[57] Second, Social Security's trustees, in its infinite horizon liability calculations, do attempt to measure the system's fiscal gap. Indeed, Social Security's fiscal gap analysis is the only such analysis being done by any branch of the federal government for any of its programs.

Is the U.S. Bankrupt?

Bankruptcy is always in the eyes of the creditor. And there are clearly people and countries continuing to voluntarily lend the U.S. government money at what appear to be absurdly low rates. But I'm not one of them because my answer to this question is a firm yes. Given the magnitude of our fiscal gap, our country is absolutely and desperately broke. We were broke before the financial crisis hit, and we are now in much worse shape given the vast sums we've spent trying to save Main Street from Wall Street.

Uncle Sam brought us to this fiscal nadir by operating his own massive Ponzi scheme. And we, the people, are in for some very tough times when we finally wake up to what we're facing. Today's close to 80 million baby boomers aren't going away. They will all soon be enrolled in AARP (the American Association of Retired Persons) and be asserting their "rights" to annual Social Security, Medicare, and Medicaid payments, which, on average, exceed per capita GDP.

This is the very sobering reality from which we must consider financial reform. We didn't have the luxury of the letting the current financial catastrophe occur, and we certainly don't have the luxury of letting it happen again.

Think of our nation as the driver of a car whose gas pedal is stuck and whose breaks are busted. He's doing 60 mph and is about to head over a 100-foot cliff. What's he to do? Maintain the "safe" status quo and stay in the car? Or make the "radical" move of opening the door and jumping out? Obviously, he jumps out. He realizes that staying in the car—the conservative choice—is actually the radical option, whereas the radical choice, jumping out the door, is actually the safe or, at least, the safer move.

■ ■ ■

Two chapters from now, I'm going to ask you to jump out of the car with me with respect to radically restructuring our financial system. But please be aware that this jump is actually much safer than it seems. I'm going to slow the car to two miles an hour before asking you to make your leap, and I'm going to convince you that you'll be jumping into a very soft bed of grass that's been waiting for years to receive you. But before detailing the financial fix, let me indicate why our current course of policy is so dangerous.

Chapter 3

Uncle Sam's Dangerous Medicine

President Obama is an inspiring leader doing his utmost to make sure we end up with the Great Recession, not another Great Depression. But inspiration is one thing; developing effective financial policies are another. To date, the president's economic brain trust has neither proposed nor made any fundamental changes to our financial system that would reassure us that the interconnected problems plaguing the current system will be solved. In leaving the status quo in place, the president's economic team places the economy in ongoing and very serious jeopardy.

Yes, the Federal Reserve and FDIC are being given wider authority to regulate nonbank financial institutions.[1] And yes, the administration is seeking to set up four new oversight/regulatory authorities: the Financial Services Oversight Council, the National Bank Supervisor, the Consumer Financial Protection Agency, and an Office of National Insurance. And yes, the rating companies will be more closely supervised with respect to conflicts-of-interest restrictions. But these "reforms" add more cops to the beat, without necessarily locking the barn door.

This assessment is shared by the *New York Times*'s Joe Nocera, whose front-page commentary of the plan on the day it was announced included this summary: ". . . the Obama plan is little more than an attempt to stick some new regulatory fingers into a very leaky financial dam rather than rebuild the dam itself. Without question, the latter would be more difficult, more contentious, and more expensive. But it would also have more lasting value."[2]

Simon Johnson, former chief economist of the IMF and professor at MIT's Sloan School, fully endorses Nocera's views and points out that the administration's proposal was heavily influenced by Wall Street firms who were brought into the reform process at an early state.[3]

It's hard to believe we need more regulatory and oversight agencies. We already have over 115 that don't seem able to do their jobs. They include the Federal Reserve, the Federal Deposit Insurance Corporation, the Office of Thrift Supervision,[4] the Controller of the Currency, the Securities and Exchange Administration, the Office of Federal Housing Enterprise Oversight, the Federal Housing Financing Agency, the Commodities Futures Trading Commission, the General Accountability Office, the National Credit Union Administration, the Federal Trade Commission, the House Banking Committee, the Senate Banking Committee, the Financial Industry Regulatory Authority (industry-based), the Municipal Securities Rule Making Board, North American Securities Administrators Association (industry-based), the newly created Financial Stability Oversight Board, 50 state banking regulators, and 50 state insurance commissioners.

Apart from adding new regulators, the team-Obama financial medicine consists of continuing to administer two drugs previously prescribed by the Bush Administration as well as two new drugs not yet administered. The first is the extension of deposit insurance. The second is providing direct or indirect bailouts to financial and nonfinancial corporations deemed too big to fail, while continuing to let them trade on their "own" account; that is, gamble at the taxpayers expense.

The third drug is new, has yet to be implemented, but involves gradually strengthening capital requirements, but not by much. The fourth drug is also new and requires that the companies selling derivatives sell their products in an organized market (a clearinghouse) except when they don't want to do so.

Sam's Got Your Back

Consider the increase in deposit insurance, specifically the Bush Administration's decisions to: (a) raise the FDIC insurance limit from $100,000 to $250,000, and (b) have the Treasury insure that money market mutual funds never lose money.

The 1980s Savings and Loan (S&L) debacle showed what this can bring. Institutions that were essentially bankrupt paid high interest to attract deposits from people with nothing to fear because the government was insuring repayment. The S&Ls then threw very high-risk investment dice, praying to survive. But the dice were poor, and the S&Ls went under, leaving taxpayers with a huge bill.

Hopefully, the FDIC won't end up with an S&L-type crisis on top of its current debacle. With its new insurance obligations, it's now staring at $6.4 trillion in potential liabilities, yet it holds only $19 billion in reserves.[5] Talk about financial malfeasance! Madoff was short $65 for each dollar he ensured. The FDIC is short $337 for each dollar it's insured.

Were the public to digest this fact and withdraw its deposits en masse, Uncle Sam would likely have to print upwards of 24 trillion more dollars.[6] Public knowledge of this action would surely trigger hyperinflation and extract a major loss in purchasing power for anyone who failed to withdraw and spend his or her money immediately.[7]

So right here, right now, we have the basis for a national bank run. The run would not be to secure our money (dollar bills), but to secure our real spending power—the amount of goods and services our dollars can buy.

This concern is not new. We've had the basis for a national bank run ever since FDR introduced FDIC insurance in March 1933. Fortunately, Americans didn't call FDR's bluff by continuing their run on the banks (one-third had already failed). Had they done so, they would have demonstrated that, with respect to their real money balances, FDR was insuring the uninsurable.

Argentines learned this painful lesson during their 2002 financial crisis, when their government was rigidly pegging the peso to the dollar and promising, in effect, to insure the dollar value of peso bank accounts. After finance ministers began turning over on a weekly basis, people realized the gig was up and hit the banks running to get their dollars. But by the time they got there, the dollars were gone—given away to those who arrived first. And the pesos the banks handed out meant precious little thanks to that currency's very rapid 80 percent devaluation.[8]

The Argentine experience is instructive for another reason as well. The fact that, in the bank run, those who got to the bank first made out better than others could, in theory, have been offset by having the government tax the winners in the bank run to benefit the losers. But the government didn't keep track of those who ran first.

Furthermore, the bank run took down not just the country's leading banks, but large chunks of the private sector as well; the specter of financial failure led to public panic and a self-fulfilling belief that times were tough. Employers assumed households would spend less and employed fewer workers, and households assumed there would be layoffs and spent less. Sound familiar?

In short order, Argentine output plummeted, with unemployment reaching 25 percent.[9] Everyone got hurt, leaving the Argentine government with neither the revenue capacity nor the interest in fully compensating, with respect to purchasing power, those trusting Argentines who were the last to ask the banks for their money.

For the United States, the lesson from Argentina's and other nations' hyperinflations is clear. Fractional reserve banking—the facts that: (a) George Bailey doesn't keep his *demand* deposits safe, (b) George need keep only 10 cents in reserve against each $1 dollar of potential *immediate* withdrawal, and (c) Sam can insure the nominal (dollar amount), but not the real value (purchasing power) of deposits—builds economic fragility right into the heart of our financial system.

Maturity Transformation in Theory and Practice

Why on earth, then, would the government set up a financial system that permits banks to hold only a fraction of deposited money in reserve?

One answer (my answer) is pressure from bankers itching to make a profit by lending out idle money. But an economic justification was provided in 1983 by economists Douglas Diamond and Philip Dybvig.[10]

The Diamond-Dybvig model says three things. First, we value liquidity—immediate access to our money to pay for emergencies—shopping sprees, for example. Second, since not all of us will need all our money at once, banks can lend out most of it and use the high returns they will earn from investing for the long term to pay a good interest rate even to those withdrawing early. But the key thing is that not everyone asks for her money back in the short-term. If this happens, the banks fail because they have to liquidate their long-term investments at a loss in trying to meet the run. So the third thing the Diamond-Dybvig model says is that the government must do something very specific to prevent those of us who are patient (don't need our money immediately) from running on our banks if we hear rumors that others are doing the same.

That something is guaranteeing that even if there is a bank run, not just our deposits, but the *purchasing power* of our deposits will be protected. Thus, Uncle Sam needs to guarantee that if prices, for example, double, Uncle Sam will hand us two dollars for every dollar we have deposited in an insolvent bank so that our deposits will be able to purchase the same real goods and services as in the absence of a run.

Neither the U.S. government nor any other government that provides deposit insurance actually insures the purchasing power of deposits. Instead, they simply tell us we'll be able to get our money back. That's not much of a guarantee if the run eventuates in prices going through the roof.

Thus, the key condition needed in the Diamond-Dybvig model as well as in the real world to justify fractional reserve banking and prevent bank runs doesn't actually exist. Fortunately, this scary little secret hasn't dawned on the public, or on most economists, for that matter. But it should give us pause when we consider: (a) the FDIC's huge recent expansion of deposit insurance, and (b) the fact that our policymakers are retaining the old financial system pretty much as it was.

The FDIC's expansion of deposit insurance, by the way, totals $1.4 trillion and has raised the FDIC's liabilities from $4.8 trillion to the aforementioned $6.4 trillion. Yet the FDIC is only reporting the

$4.8 trillion on its balance sheet, claiming the $1.6 trillion is a "temporary liability" and, therefore, doesn't need to be disclosed.[11]

The FDIC increases its liabilities by one-third, but doesn't think it needs to tell us this fact? This is an example of the many horrendous lessons in deceitful nondisclosure that Uncle Sam has spent decades teaching the private sector.

Backing the Buck

To date, the government's single largest systemic risk insurance commitment is the Treasury's decision to either explicitly or implicitly guarantee that investors in the nation's 1900 money market mutual funds can redeem their shares at par value.[12] This means that $1 invested in a money market fund can never "break the buck"—never be worth less than $1 because Uncle Sam has pledged to make up the difference. Some $3 trillion in money market mutual funds were covered by this new insurance.

The decision to insure the market price of money market funds was taken on September 19, 2008, in the wake of the September 15 collapse of Lehman Brothers and the fire sale of Merrill Lynch to the Bank of America.[13] The steps were taken as panicked investors, including many retirees, realized for the first time that they could lose money in a money market fund and started selling their shares.

Money market funds are open-end mutual funds, meaning that if the shareholders sell their shares, the mutual fund has to settle up by the end of the day. In other words, it has to buy back (redeem) these shares at the net asset value (the market value) of the underlying assets in the fund that prevails at the close of trading on the day the shares are sold.

So if on September 15, 2008, millions of investors in the Reserve Primary Fund, the nation's oldest money market fund (which, apart from the word "reserve" has no connection to the Federal Reserve), sold their shares, the Reserve Primary Fund would need to sell off, for whatever price it could get, a large chunk of its underlying asset holdings in order to be able to redeem the shares being sold.

As of early September 2008, the Reserve Primary Fund held $64.8 billion in assets, but $785 million of this consisted of short-term paper issued by Lehman Brothers (that is, short-term loans made by the Reserve Primary Fund to Lehman Brothers). When Lehman went bust on the 15th, poof, the Reserve Primary Fund was out $785 million.[14] This made the ratio of the Reserve Primary Fund's assets, valued at market, less than the amounts its shareholders had invested; that is, the ratio was less than 1, which is the meaning of breaking the buck.

The Reserve Primary Fund announced on the 16th that it had broken the buck, which represented only the second time a money market mutual fund had publicly committed this sin.[15] During the rest of the week, money market funds in the country saw 14 percent of their assets head out the door. In trying to meet the demand for share redemptions, fund managers sought to maintain as much liquidity as possible, which meant not using funds on hand to make their standard short-term loans to banks and corporations. So this part of our capital market, the so-called *shadow banking system* (because it involved financial transactions among parties not directly regulated by the FDIC or Fed) froze up, driving up short-term corporate borrowing rates from 2 percent to 8 percent. This scared the daylights out of Treasury Secretary Hank Paulson, Federal Reserve Chairman Ben Bernanke, and, presumably, President Bush, if he wasn't off chopping wood.

Uncle Sam had two options. Option one was to say, "Gee folks, sorry your assets lost value, but no one, or at least no one down here in Washington, ever said there were perfectly safe. If you had wanted to invest on an insured basis, you should have deposited your money in an FDIC-insured checking or savings account." Option two was to say, "My gosh. You folks just lost several percent of your savings and you never, in your wildest dreams, expected this to happen. We, the government, will temporarily cover your losses by making sure that for the next few months you can get back at least what you put in."

The Treasury opted for option two and, voilà, our government was in the business of guaranteeing that the $3 trillion or so invested in money market funds as of September 19, 2008, never have a really bad day.

This provision of insurance is not quite as large in scope as the FDIC's, but it's very large. Creation of the FDIC was the most significant financial reform undertaken in the Great Depression. And it was announced with great fanfare. President Roosevelt shut the banks for a week and then made a special radio address to the nation on March 12,

1933, declaring the creation of what ultimately became the FDIC. In contrast, creation of the Treasury Guaranty Program for Money Market Funds was announced via a press release.[16]

Stop and think about this policy for a moment. If you bought say, $5,000 worth of Verizon stock, your investment could fall in value from one minute to the next and be worth far less than $5,000. You wouldn't expect Uncle Sam to guarantee that you could always sell your Verizon stock for at least $5,000. But if you invest $5,000 in a money market fund, Uncle Sam is saying, "Relax, don't worry. We'll guarantee you'll get your $5,000 back no matter what. It's just as safe as if you had deposited the money in an FDIC-insured checking account."

The government is charging money market mutual funds for this form of deposit insurance, so it's not giving this insurance away scot-free. But is Uncle Sam charging a price that's commensurate with the risk he's taking on or, to put it more accurately, the risk to which he's exposing us taxpayers? The deeper question, raised above, is whether the government can actually insure, in any real purchasing power sense, against systematic collapse.

Uncle Sam's clearly worried about ending up on the short end of his guarantee. He's now proceeding to issue regulations on how the money market funds, covered by his insurance, will invest their money. These regulations are on top of the primary regulations that govern money market mutual funds under the 1940 Investment Company Act. This act makes the Securities and Exchange Commission the primary regulator of money market funds and tells the funds to invest primarily in the highest-rated debt.

Funny thing, then, that the Reserve Primary Fund was holding Lehman paper on September 15 when Lehman declared bankruptcy. Inquiring minds should want to know why the Reserve Primary Fund had such a large holding of Lehman paper if the fund was supposed to focus on highly rated debt and why the fund apparently warned some, but not all, of its investors about the risks it foresaw in its Lehman holdings and why, if the rating companies were supposed to have properly rated Lehman debt and if the SEC was supposed to keep track of the fund's investments, the fund got into trouble. All these little questions popped up immediately when the Reserve Primary Fund broke the buck. And these and other questions are now being raised in lawsuits.

Thanks to the pending litigation, the Reserve Primary Fund is no longer the oldest money market fund. It's no longer in business. On September 30, 2008, the fund declared it was liquidating its holdings and closing its doors.

Opening Pandora's Box

A key but little-known feature of the Treasury's money market fund guarantee is that it applies only to money market shares held as of September 19, 2008. If you or I take $10,000 today and buy shares of a money market fund and the money market fund buys, say, AT&T short-term AAA-rated paper and it drops through the floor, leaving our $10,000 investment worth, say, $7,000, Uncle Sam is formally saying "tough luck." But were this to happen Uncle Sam would likely step back in and "back the buck" for fear of causing another run on money market funds in not so doing. It's hard for the government to treat one set of people one way and another set of people a different way when everyone is, for all intents and purposes, in the same boat. This is especially the case given that investors in money market funds that break the buck in the future will surely start screaming that they were under the impression their money market accounts were insured.

This is particularly true when you realize that foreign governments are some of the largest investors in U.S. money market funds. China purportedly had over $5 billion in the Reserve Primary Fund when Lehman collapsed. This may explain why the Treasury moved so quickly to back the buck in money market funds.

The Chinese, incidentally, hold north of $750 billion in U.S. Treasuries and roughly half of their $2 trillion reserves in dollar-denominated assets. Were they to dump these on the market, interest rates would soar, the dollar would implode, and the U.S. economy would suffer even greater damage. So keeping the Chinese happy seems to be a full-time occupation of our Treasury. Indeed, prior to the crisis, China was the world's largest purchaser of Fannie Mae and Freddie Mac bonds, and Fannie, Freddie, and Ginnie Mae mortgage-backed securities.[17] It held some $340 billion worth of the bonds of these GSE (government-sponsored enterprises) at the time Fannie and Freddie were "rescued"

in early September 2008.[18] This fact helps us understand why Uncle
Sam felt compelled to maintain the value of Fannie and Freddie bonds,
despite effectively wiping out the holdings of its shareholders.

Had the Chinese held $340 billion in GSE stock, the Treasuries
policy would no doubt have been quite different. It may also help us
understand why the Treasury and the Fed are so actively purchasing GSE
securities. Their official explanation is to help lower mortgage rates, but
another important reason is preventing the Chinese from experiencing
a capital loss on their holdings of these bonds.

This view connects to Perry Mehrling's reading of the core cause of
the financial crisis. Mehrling is an economist at Columbia University's
Barnard College and one of the world's preeminent students of current
and past financial markets. As Mehrling points out in his forthcoming
book, *The New Lombard Street,* in the prelude to our R or D, China and
the rest of the world developed a deep thirst for safe, dollar-denominated
securities. And as the prices of Treasuries were bid up, Wall Street and
Pennsylvania Avenue sought ways to meet that demand, namely by
manufacturing "safe" securities that were anything but.

As I write these words, I've just returned from a conference in China
attended by many of that nation's top economic thinkers and advisors. I
found myself astounded at the extent of anxiety being expressed about
U.S. policy and its potential for causing inflation, which would visit
huge capital losses on China's bond holdings. The economists were so
concerned that they proposed having the U.S. government explicitly
guarantee that Chinese investments in the United States not lose value.
Their anxiety also extends to the value of the dollar, which is why
senior members of their government are proposing the creation of a
new reserve currency to replace the dollar.

Economics Diary, September 14, 2009: Trade/Financial War with China?

The United States and China appear to be heading toward a trade war
or at least a trade skirmish. A week or so back, the United States placed
a 35 percent tariff on tires imported from China. This was met by a
formal protest by China, but then the Chinese public got into the act—
blogging en masse on that nation's web sites that the United States

was being "shameless" and that China should immediately dump all its holdings of U.S. Treasury bonds.[19] This public pressure has led/forced the Chinese government to place tariffs on U.S. automotive products and chicken meat.

This is not a good sign. World trade has already dropped by 9 percent, according to the World Trade Organization.[20] The last thing we need right now is returning to the policy of the 1930s in which countries placed high tariffs on each other's products in order to gin up more local demand for labor. The policy proved disastrous, and will prove so again.

Our Once and Future Horrible Mess

I've spent a decent amount of your time telling you about Uncle Sam's backing of the money market buck and protecting China for a reason. I want to focus your attention on the point that the horrible mess we've created is not just today's horrible mess. It has ramifications for tomorrow and beyond. Here and elsewhere, Uncle Sam has gone down a very slippery slope in setting precedents and expectations not only with respect to the investment returns of American citizens, but also with respect to the financial needs and aspirations of foreign governments.

We economists use the term *moral hazard* to reference our proclivity to take extra risk when someone is protecting our tush. This entire financial crisis has been a case study in moral hazard with self-declared financial gurus placing the bets, while bearing essentially none of the risk. Indeed, our remarkable collection of financial thieves transformed moral hazard into immoral certitude. And the more Uncle Sam guarantees people and institutions against financial loss, the more risk they will take and the more restrictions Uncle Sam will try to impose on their behavior.

The Germans have an expression, which was popular among young cynics in the sixties, for where this will all end up: *Est wird böse enden.*[21] The literal translation is: It will end angry. The official translation is: It will suck big time.

Big Brother, Can You Spare One Hundred Billion?

Uncle Sam's second policy, discussed above, is bailing out companies whose failure would have major ripple effects on the domestic and international economy. Apart from the cost, bailouts lead institutions that are too big to fail to undertake undue risks. This has happened in the current crisis. AIG alone issued $2.7 trillion in credit default swaps to counterparties like Goldman Sachs who knew full well that Uncle Sam would cover AIG's liability if AIG couldn't pay up.[22]

And Uncle Sam has been paying out the wazoo ($2.5 trillion to date, as mentioned above) to cover the losses of AIG, Fannie Mae, Freddie Mac, Bear Stearns, Bank of America, Citigroup, GM, Chrysler, and many others.[23] None of these "rescues" has, so far, actually rescued the economy, which still has massive unemployment. And all of the "rescues" have been inframarginal; that is, they didn't change incentives at the margin for institutions to act differently in the future from how they have in the past.

Meanwhile, as we've seen, the government is running astronomical deficits and printing money. All this is, of course, prelude to the extraordinarily large costs of paying the Social Security, Medicare, and Medicaid benefits to the Baby Boomers that will really kick in starting in about a decade.

Bailing out failed businesses, borrowing like mad, and printing money like crazy are policies one would expect of Third World countries, not the United States of America. And so far, none of it has done more than stopped the free fall. Indeed, there's reason to believe that in pushing so hard and so fast, the Treasury and Federal Reserve have caused much of the panic they have been paying so much to prevent. And the bailouts are teaching corporate America a very bad lesson about looking to the government in times of trouble.

One company, AIG, has learned this lesson better than any other. On March 6, 2009, AIG released a 21-page white paper, which is like none other in U.S. corporate history.[24] The paper, whose title is "AIG—Is the Risk Systemic?" represents an economic hostage note. It says in very clear and emphatic terms that if Uncle Sam stops bailing out AIG, AIG will fail and bring down the world economy.

Although AIG exaggerates its destructive power, its basic threat is credible. AIG claims to be able to take down the aircraft business (AIG, to repeat, is the world's largest aircraft leaser and Boeing's largest customer), the world shipping industry (AIG is the third-largest insurer of cargo shipments), the accident and health insurance industry, particularly in Japan, Korea, and China (where AIG is the top provider), the world's commercial insurance industry (AIG insures 70 percent of the world's largest banks, the Panama Canal, the UN, the U.S. military, reconstruction projects by international firms in Iraq and Afghanistan, a significant share of the world's oil rigs), and the operations of global corporate boards (AIG is the world's largest provider of directors' and officers' insurance).

These are the minor threats. They don't include the threatened loss of income by seven million Americans, many of whom are retired teachers, who have purchased annuities and other retirement products from AIG. Nor do they include the demise of corporate lending (AIG is the second-largest investor in U.S. corporate bonds). And they don't include AIG's thermonuclear economic device—"a run on the bank" in the $19 trillion global life insurance industry, which AIG says would create a "catastrophe."

The run to which AIG refers is on the cash surrender policies issued by the life insurance industry. These policies include whole and universal life policies, equity indexed annuities, variable annuities, and guaranteed investment contracts. In selling these policies, the life insurance industry, like the banking industry, has borrowed short and lent long. For example, whole life and universal life insurance policies entail making premium payments each year to buy not just insurance coverage for the current year, but also to build up an internal savings account, called the policy's cash surrender value.

For all intents and purposes, these cash surrender values (balances) are like checking and savings accounts. The term "surrender value" means that policyholders are free to demand these balances from the insurance company any time they'd like, including times when they think the insurance company is going under. But unlike standard checking and savings accounts, which are insured by the FDIC, cash surrender values aren't insured by any federal government agency for their nominal (face or dollar) value, let alone for their real purchasing power.

Life insurance companies hold reserves, and there are also state insurance guarantee funds, which are supposed to step in to cover insurance company failures and runs on their cash surrender values. But were AIG to fail and precipitate a cash-surrender-value run, the long-term investments held in insurance company general reserves would likely have to be sold in a fire sale—that is, for pennies on the dollar. And once these reserves were depleted, state insurance funds would be tapped. But the state guarantee funds specify very low limits on how much individual policyholders can recover.[25] Moreover, their reserves are tiny—less than $9 billion—and would be instantly depleted.

The party left holding the bag would, as always, be dear old Uncle Sam. From what one can learn from people in the industry, Uncle Sam would need to cover cash surrender claims for U.S. policy holders totaling roughly $3 trillion. This is far less than the $19 trillion figure AIG recklessly bandies about, but it's still a fantastically large number.

How would Uncle Sam come up with 3,000,000,000,000 dollars? He'd print it.

Bailing Out Corporate Pensions

As we've seen, Uncle Sam has made all manner of promises during this crisis in his quest to stabilize the economy. These new promises come on top of all the promises he's made to current and future retirees, either out of concern for the elderly or in response to a more malevolent force, namely the desire of each generation to expropriate the next. Think of the old economically eating the young, and you've got the picture.

In the scheme of things, Uncle Sam's Pension Benefit Guarantee Corporation (PBGC) is relatively small in the government's overall handout/assistance/redistribution/insurance/call-it-what-you-will policy, but it's a little gem for purposes of illustrating this book's central premise: Our root financial/fiscal problem is the leveraging of the public (particularly our children) on an involuntary basis, not the leverage voluntarily chosen by the public. Again, *it's the leveraging, not the leverage.*

The PBGC guarantees the defined benefit pensions of 44 million Americans participating in 29,000 pension plans. Such pensions are gradually going by the wayside, but they still are a major feature of our retirement system. Now, if a private employer's defined benefit pension plan is terminated because, for example, the employer goes bankrupt and the plan is underfunded, the PBGC steps in. When this happens, those workers and retirees promised very high benefits can get hurt. The PBGC pays out a maximum annual benefit, whose current value is $54,000.

But the taxpayers also stand to get very badly burnt because the PBGC, like the FDIC, doesn't have reserves to cover even the red ink we already know about—the pension benefits the PBGC owes to pension plans that it insured and that failed in the past.[26] The PBGC's assets are currently some $33 billion short of the present value of these pension benefit claims.[27]

The $33 billion is, if you can believe it, the good news. What we don't know is the claims the PBGC will face going forward. But we economists have started to ask the same question about the PBGC that we've started to ask about Social Security: namely, what's the size of this net liability valued on a marked-to-market basis? In other words, how much would we, today, have to pay a third party, say China, to take the PBGC off Uncle Sam's hands? In this case, China would agree to cover all the claims that the PBGC might have to pay out in the future and receive all the insurance premiums PBGC will collect. The answer appears to be well north of $100 billion.

Let me hasten to point out that in marking the PBGC or Social Security or the government's entire fiscal operation to market, we economists are doing the same kinds of calculations that the folks on Wall Street firms do every day in pricing the illiquid (rarely traded) assets and liabilities they either hold or are thinking of holding. And just like Wall Street's asset pricing, the pricing of government programs really represents best guessing; that is, we don't have an active market for buying and selling government insurance guarantees that can be used to find out exactly what the market is charging at the present time for taking on exposures of this kind. So this analysis is asking what would the market (China being a potential market player) charge if we did put the PBGC or Social Security up for sale (at a negative price!).

There are four reasons we're now stuck with what we think the market would say is not really a $33 billion problem—the number the PBGC is disclosing—but a $100 billion problem—the number it doesn't bother trying to measure and doesn't want to mention. First, the PBGC didn't charge companies large enough premiums for the insurance it was providing. Second, corporations were permitted to gamble with their pension fund assets knowing that if their gambles did poorly, the PBGC would back them up. The gambling took the form of investing a sizeable share of the pension fund's assets in stock and high yield bonds.

As things would have it, this gambling has gone pretty darn böse. According to Towers Perrin, a human resources consulting firm, the pension funds of the 300 very large U.S. companies that Towers surveys experienced a collective loss of almost $400 billion during the crash of 2008. This is a huge share—23 percent—of the liabilities these pension funds are supposed to cover! So now, rather than being $47 billion over-funded, these pension funds are underfunded to the tune of $339 billion and thinking a lot more carefully about how they might pass this big liability to Big Brother.

As Boston University finance professor Zvi Bodie has repeatedly stressed to deaf ears, the fact that the pension funds invested in risky assets represents a violation of their fiduciary duty, at least as economists understand this duty.[28] The appropriate policy for a corporation running a defined benefit pension plan is to fully fund its obligations and to match liabilities with assets to the maximum extent possible. Thus, if a pension fund owes a fixed payment each year to a set of retirees, it should fund those payments with Treasury bonds of equal maturity.[29] It should not invest pension fund assets in the stock or corporate bond market and hope to make a killing, which is precisely what has been happening.

The third reason underlying the emerging private pension debacle is that actuaries developed rules for valuing pension liabilities that had no basis in modern finance, but were designed to let their corporate bosses underfund their pension obligations.[30] Shakespeare is famous for his line "First kill the lawyers." When it comes to pension funding accounting, we economists would readily substitute the word "actuaries."

Just to be clear, some of my best friends are actuaries, and they are a surprisingly fun group, at least compared to my ilk. The standard definition of an economist, let's recall, is "someone who's good with numbers, but doesn't have the personality to be an actuary." So this isn't personal. And actuaries play a critical role in answering all manner of very tough questions they are extremely well trained to answer.

But actuaries aren't trained to value risky future income and expenditure streams. They aren't even trained to value safe future income and expenditure streams, which is as simple as it gets in the world of asset pricing. If, for example, you have to make a payment for sure in the future, you have to ask yourself the following question to price, in the present, this future obligation: How much would I have to spend today on a safe asset (in this case, U.S. Treasury bonds) to have enough money for sure to pay that obligation when it comes due? The answer amounts to forming a present value by mathematically discounting (making less of) the future payment, taking as the discount rate the prevailing yield on Treasury bonds of the same maturity. For example, if the payment is due 10 years from now, you use the prevailing 10-year Treasury bond yield to do the discounting. If the payment is due five years from now, you discount using the prevailing five-year Treasury bond yield.

Actuaries don't do this. Instead they say, "Well, if you are investing in stocks, not Treasury bonds, you should discount at the much higher average yield on stocks, not the relatively low yield on Treasury bonds." Were they to make this statement in an introductory finance exam, they'd get an F. Yes, stocks yield more on average, but what they yield is not for sure. And because of this, stock have to pay, on average, a higher return in order to compensate people who buy stocks for taking on the extra risk, including the risk that the value of their stocks may go to zero, in which case their realized yield is negative 100 percent.

In concocting rules for funding adequacy, the actuaries have played the same game as the rating companies did in rating toxic assets and the accounting companies did in rating Enron and similar companies. They committed financial malpractice/violated their fiduciary responsibility/took a bribe in order to appease their clients.

The final reason the PBGC is in such bad shape these days is the Bush administration's choice of Charles Millard, a former Lehman executive, to serve as its director. Charlie appears to be another "Brownie" appointment—a lawyer with no formal training in finance, but a loyal political apparatchik, who was sure he knew it all when it came to investment risk.

Charlie was gung-ho on Wall Street. He was convinced that stocks are safe long-term investments, despite very strong evidence to the contrary, and that the PBGC would make a killing by investing its meager assets with the right Wall Street firms. The *New York Times's* Floyd Norris described discussing this strategy with Charlie: "My interview with Mr. Millard was surreal. He insisted over and over again, that his policy was less risky than the old one."[31]

For Charlie, the right Wall Street firms included those with whom Charlie was shopping for his next job. Presumably, he viewed this as a confluence, rather than a conflict of interest. Members of Congress disagree. On May 20, 2009, the Senate Special Committee on Aging invited Charlie over to discuss how he came to award Goldman Sachs, Blackrock, and JPMorgan a contract to invest $2.5 billion of the PBGC's assets. The senators, you see, had read a report issued by the PBGC Inspector General stating that Millard and his staff had hundreds of phone calls and e-mail exchanges with the three firms after they had put in bids for the contract and prior to Charlie's choosing them—all while Charlie was seeking post-employment assistance. To give Charlie his due, he answered each and every one of the Senators' questions. But he did so with the same words: "I plead the Fifth."

The PBGC has a board of directors charged with overseeing its director's decisions. But its members appear to be off playing bridge with Jimmy Cayne. Between February 2008 and August 29, 2009 (the date of this writing), the PBGC's board met exactly zero times.[32] And in the prior 18 years, the board typically met only once a year.[33]

Zero is not a lot of meetings for fiduciaries of a very large insurance institution, which is at least $33 billion in the red, already has 1.2 million beneficiaries, and could soon have millions more. Prospective new claimants include one million past and present GM and Chrysler workers. Both of these companies have, as indicated, declared bankruptcy, and their pension plans could shortly terminate. If this happens, which seems highly likely, the PBGC's deficit will double to $66 billion.[34] To put this figure in perspective, it exceeds the value of all output produced by Hawaii, Delaware, Rhode Island, and ten other states in the course of a full year.

So how did Charlie's investment strategy turn out? Well, his intent was to invest 45 percent of the PBGC's assets in the stock market. He didn't keep his job long enough to achieve this result. But he did succeed in putting a chunk of the PBGC portfolio in the market and quickly lost $3 billion.

Recapitalizing the Banks

Bank capital is the difference between a bank's assets and liabilities as valued on the books by the company's accountants. It's the amount of skin shareholders have in the game. Given the current regulations, banks insured by the FDIC can lend 10 times their capital. But if their capital shrinks to zilch (Yiddish for bubkes) because the value of their assets drops to nothing, what can be lent out is bubkes (Yiddish for zilch).

Take Goldman Sachs. Let's suppose the company has close to $1 trillion in assets and $100 billion in capital. (The actual figures as of this writing are $890 billion and $63 billion, but I use these values because they are easier to deal with.) So of the $1 trillion that's been invested, only 10 percent is actually money owned by the stockholders (owners) of Goldman. The rest—$900 billion—Goldman has borrowed from other banks, from individuals, from pension funds, from municipalities and state governments, from foreign governments, and so on. These parties have lent Goldman $900 billion because they believe Goldman knows how to invest their money and will pay back the promised interest and principal on the bonds/paper/IOUs/credits they bought from Goldman. They also know that if Goldman's investments fail, Uncle Sam will bail them out because Goldman is too big to fail. So Goldman is able to borrow money at a lower interest rate and make more profits because of this implicit government guarantee.

This is 10-to-1 leverage, which is still very high if you think about it. If, from one day, one month, or one year to the next, Goldman loses 10 percent on its investments, it will still owe $900 billion, but only have assets worth $900 billion. So its owners will have a company worth nothing. If the company loses 20 percent on its investments, it will still owe $900 billion, but only have assets worth $800 billion to cover this obligation, leaving Uncle Sam to cover the missing $100 billion.

Once Goldman loses 10 percent or more, it is, theoretically at least, out of business. If Goldman's shareholders don't have any skin in the game, they can't play the game—they can't borrow any money from anyone and invest it for them. They can't play financial intermediary anymore or, going back to the gas station analogy, they can't pump any gas. They can try to sell $100 billion of new stock to new or existing shareholders, but having just wiped out the existing shareholders, this may be hard to do.

But Goldman's failure would trigger global financial panic and flip us into a bad equilibrium. So Uncle Sam can't apply the rules. It can't shut Goldman down and, in the hypothetical example in which Goldman loses 20 percent, it not only has to bail out Goldman to the tune of $100 billion to make sure its creditors don't lose any money (because they have their own power to force Goldman into bankruptcy if it misses any bond payments), but also to give Goldman's existing shareholders a free $100 billion to get them back into the game.

Yes, Uncle Sam could give existing shareholders, say, only $50 billion for free, but given the 10-to-1 capital requirement, $50 billion worth of shareholder's capital would support only $500 billion in asset holdings. Hence, Goldman would be forced to sell off $400 billion in assets and use the proceeds to repay $400 billion in borrowing. In the context of a panic, having Goldman sell $400 billion of assets quickly into the market is not something Uncle Sam would wish to see.

Now I've used Goldman as the example not because it received much of a bailout or necessarily even needed a bailout during the crisis. The company was, arguably, the most cautious big player on Wall Street throughout the financial crisis, realizing very early on that the subprime market was going to implode. I've used Goldman as an example because it came so close to going down even though it wasn't itself the cause of the financial mess or fundamentally in trouble.

When the crisis hit, the market value of Goldman's assets dropped through the floor, forcing the company, which prides itself on mark-to-market accounting, to book losses, which reduced the value of its capital to about $20 billion. As Goldman got close to failing, it realized it needed to cozy up to its potential savior, Uncle Sam. It did so by reorganizing itself as a commercial bank whose deposits would be insured by the FDIC. Most important, in becoming a conventional bank, Goldman obtained ongoing access to the Fed's discount window, which allowed Goldman, if need be, to discreetly borrow money at potentially very low rates.[35]

When a bank borrows from the Fed, the bank can be thought of going to the Fed's teller window and handing over an IOU promising to pay back monies in the future. The Fed looks at this promise and figures out what to make of it—how much to discount it (make less of it), given the chance the bank won't actually pay up. This is why this Fed lending facility is called the discount window.

Now if a Goldman, in tough times, bellies up to that teller's window and says, "Here's a promise to pay you back $10 billion in three months," the Fed, if it's trying to bail out Goldman's bondholders and shareholders (so they can keep pumping gas), can tell Goldman: "Okay, here's $10 billion. Just pay us back the $10 billion three months from now." This entails charging Goldman a zero percent interest rate, and now Goldman has $10 billion that it can lend out for three months and earn interest.

This lending by the Fed at below-market (or, if it chooses, even zero) interest rates is, then, one way Uncle Sam can recapitalize the banks, which in this case is a euphemism for giving them money for free. Another way is to have either the Treasury or the Fed simply buy up assets from a Goldman at a price above market. Say Goldman is holding a Fannie Mae bond that the market says is worth $10 billion and the Treasury or Fed says, "Hey, that Fannie bond you've got sure looks good to us. How about selling it to us for $30 billion?" "Well," says Goldman, "You twisted my arm. I'll do it. And if you need to buy some more of these, let me know. I'll help you out."

This appears to be the main path by which the Federal Reserve has been recapitalizing the banks and insurers that really got into trouble, which again, does not include Goldman. The last bit of the story is explaining how the Fed comes up with $30 billion. The answer is that it simply prints it.

For its part, the Treasury has been recapitalizing impaired banks by buying up their "troubled assets" at, one suspects, above-market prices and by buying up their shares and becoming a co-owner. To see how the share-buying mechanism works, take the above example in which Goldman's assets fall to $900 billion and it owes $900 billion. Now suppose the Treasury comes along and says, "Goldman shareholders, you have an asset here that's worth absolutely nothing. And we're not going to pay you anything for it. Instead, issue a large number of new shares that make the number of shares that you guys hold peanuts in comparison. We'll buy up all those new shares for $100 billion. This will give us essentially 100 percent ownership of your bank. And now we'll have a bank with $1 trillion in assets, $900 billion in liabilities, and $100 billion in shareholders' capital; that is, we'll have a bank that can continue to pump gas, albeit one that we have to completely run in all respects."

The Treasury can't print up $100 billion in fresh money to do this, but it can print up $100 billion in fresh Treasury bills and bonds and sell them to get the $100 billion to buy the shares. This is a financial wash if the Treasury didn't overpay for the bank it just bought.[36] But the Treasury is not in the banking business, so it may not be able to get $100 billion in value out of running this bank if it doesn't know how to run it or it starts making business decisions based on politics.

And politics has played a huge part in the financial crisis. Leading up to this crisis, politicians and political appointees have pushed regulatory agencies very hard to permit subprime lending to help poor people get into homes—homes they couldn't afford. How much of this reflected a sincere desire to help the poor and how much reflected a sincere desire to get reelected is hard to say. In any case, government-owned banks are likely to come under lots of pressure over time to make loans at favorable rates (buy mortgages at above market prices) to help certain constituencies at the behest of members of Congress and the administration.

Buying Up Toxic Assets

The public has had enough when it comes to the Fed and the Treasury directly buying toxic assets at what everyone suspects are highly inflated prices. The public's also had it with all the borrowing, in the case of the Treasury, and all the money creation, in the case of the Fed. Yet, despite all the spending, the banking system is still potentially $1.5 trillion short of the capital it needs to operate the pumps. The public is also infuriated by the fact that the financial handouts have been used to pay massive bonuses and come with no strings attached. The deal between Pennsylvania Avenue and Wall Street seems to be this: "We'll cover your losses, and you'll restore the economy."

But there is nothing to enforce the deal. In an economy like ours, bank shareholders may simply convey Uncle Sam's largesse directly to themselves in the form of dividends or stock repurchases. Alternatively, the bank managers, who seem to be in charge of the shareholders, may simply use the bailouts to set higher compensation levels for themselves, but via higher salary payments, rather than via bonuses, since uttering the word "bonus" is now taboo.

What to do? Well, the right thing to do is to stop wasting money (much of which is our kids' money) and focus on the basic problems of the financial system and fix them. But that will require, as we'll see, real changes in the system, which the administration's *political* economists aren't prepared to recommend.

GASP—The Geithner and Summers Plan

The wrong option, which is what Treasury Secretary Timothy Geithner and National Economic Council Chairman Lawrence Summers are pursuing, is to continue with the Bush Administration's "no strings attached" handout policy, but to do so surreptitiously. Their latest proposal is the $1 trillion Public-Private Investment Program (PPIP). It was purposely designed to be highly complex so the public wouldn't be able to see the massive freebie involved.[37]

Under PPIP, the FDIC provides preferential loans to large hedge funds (like the one Summers "worked" for) to buy up the banks' toxic assets at auction. Thanks to the very attractive loan terms, the hedge funds, in competing with each other, will bid up the prices received by the banks for their securities beyond their current, that is, true market values. And voilà, the banks will have more money to gamble with or give to their shareholders or use to "retain" their management.[38]

To get the essence of this scam, lets look at a Mardi Gras Beads example.

Mardi Gras Beads

Suppose Uncle Sam wants to hand his friend Ethel $1 million for free. Assume that Ethel has a large amount of something that's worth absolutely nothing—a truckload of Mardi Gras beads that she's been collecting for the last 50 years. Let's also assume that Sam sets up an auction for the beads in which he tells prospective bidders that he will match the winning bid two dollars for every dollar bid up to the point that his payment totals $1 million.

Even though Ethel's beads are worthless, the amount that will be bid and that she'll receive is $1 million. Why? Well, anyone bidding more than $1 million will end up with a worthless

(Continued)

(Continued)

pile of beads plus $1 million (the maximum subsidy) from Sam and, therefore, lose money. So no one is going to bid more than $1 million.

But anyone bidding less than $1 million will walk away with a profit for free, which will lead others to enter the bidding until there is no profit to be had. This occurs when the bidding hits $1 million. At a bid of $1 million, Sam's $1 million subsidy offsets the $1 million bid and the winning bidder ends up on balance with one thing and one thing only—a pile of crap.

To see why a bid of less than $1 million—say, $900,000—would turn a net profit, note that such a bid, if it won, would garner a $1 million subsidy, leaving a net profit of $100,000. A bid of $500,000, were it to win, would also garner a $1 million subsidy by Sam, and thus make a net profit of $500,000. A bid of $100,000, were it to win, would lead Sam to hand out $200,000 in a subsidy, and the bidder would net $100,000. If you check, any bid short of $1 million makes money for the bidder, so the bidders will try to outbid each other right up to bidding $1 million.

Had Sam just written Ethel a $1 million check, the result would be the same. Now, Summers and Geithner's PPIP doesn't include a direct subsidy. That would be too honest. Instead, it provides hedge fund bidders with a very inexpensive loan, which they get if they win the bid. The loan is very inexpensive because it comes with this neat feature—it doesn't have to be repaid if the toxic assets being purchased end up not doing well (e.g., the CDOs experience more defaults than expected). The PPIP plan does suggest the government will recoup some of its downside exposure by having the winning hedge fund give it warrants/options to collect extra money if the toxic assets perform really well. But the entire structure is sufficiently complex that no one will really be able to say for sure how large is the government's subsidy. This Rube Goldberg mechanism also has the interesting property that the very banks that created the toxic assets could arrange to pay the hedge funds to bid for their assets so as to enhance Sam's subsidy and their windfall.[39]

Moving toxic assets from private entity A to private entity B is not going to change the fact that these assets exist and that someone is going to end up holding them and pray they pay off. Playing musical chairs with toxic assets can't make any fundamental difference to the economy. So the real objective in ridding banks of toxic assets has nothing in fact to do with the toxic assets themselves or with the banks holding them. The true objective in "cleaning up" the toxic assets is very simple. It's giving the banks, which are still perhaps $1.5 trillion short of capital, close to that amount for free and doing so without the public's knowledge and inevitable outrage. This explains why when Secretary Geithner announced the plan in March 2009, bank stocks shot through the roof.

The real problem with the toxic assets is that: (a) they were produced in the first place, and (b) now that they exist, they are not being fully disclosed. What's needed is clear and reliable labeling of what these toxic assets really are so that anyone can identify and buy them if they so choose. What's also needed is a means to make sure that more toxic assets aren't added over time to the current supply, where I'm referring to toxic assets as assets that are labeled X, but that are actually Y. To me and to other economists, a tranched CMO, a subprime mortgage, a CDO squared, a CDS, or any other of a large and growing variety of products that have recently been developed by financial engineers is not, per se, a toxic asset. What makes these and many old-fashioned financial products, like whole life insurance, toxic is that they aren't being properly disclosed (which includes indecipherable disclosure), verified, and independently rated. As I write, there is nothing to prevent Countrywide Financial (now owned by B of A) from issuing more liar loans. After all, it has plenty of experience doing so. And if trillions more in such "securities" (note the irony) were issued, our economics brain trust could, presumably, end up over time extending PPIP to include new issuances of toxics.

If Geithner and Summers really wanted the existing toxic asset market to work they would just require full, minute, crystal-clear (as in intelligible to the typical layperson), and independently rated disclosure of the cyanide-laced securities and leave the market to figure out what they are worth. But this isn't their objective. Their objective is to give the troubled banks massive amounts of money for free so the banks can return to business as usual. When I say massive, I don't exaggerate. PPIP is designed to have hedge funds "purchase" $1 trillion in troubled assets.[40]

The PPIP policy does have one saving grace. So far no one seems to want to implement it. The FDIC appears to have no interest in carrying the water for the Treasury on this one.[41] The FDIC has already had plenty of extra liabilities dumped in its lap in the course of this crisis. And the banks aren't eager to surrender their option to decide for themselves what their toxics are worth even if the market says otherwise.

Putting More of Someone Else's Skin in the Game

Looking forward, the administration intends to raise capital requirements, meaning that a larger share of bank's investments would be owned by bank shareholders. The idea here is to: (a) limit how much the banks can hold in risky assets compared to their own skin in the game, and (b) get shareholders to be more careful with the bank's lending and other investments because more of it is their own money.[42]

But managers, not shareholders, are the ones making the investment decisions, particularly in the huge financial corporations with their highly dispersed shareholders. And the managers are pushing sales of the next Sure Thing because their bonuses are tied to sales. The more of the bank's assets they pour into the Sure Thing, the more they can convince others to buy it. Hence, the bank's capital is part of the managers' me-first compensation strategy, not a precious resource to be preserved. And changing capital requirements, even doubling them, won't matter much to managers on the make.

In addition to the Modigliani–Miller theorem, economics has a second line of argument that says using leverage can be either okay or a good thing. The argument, which interestingly enough shows up in some of Fed Chairman Bernanke's work, is that it's costly for investors to monitor what managers are doing with their money so that having some of a corporation's finance come from borrowing "keeps the managers feet to the fire." If the managers steal too much of the company's assets, they won't be able to repay the debt; the companies will go bankrupt and managers will lose their jobs. This makes good sense except for the issue of timing and dissimilation. Today's top managers are very skillful in pillaging their companies for years before missing any debt payments.

Enron's top management wrote the playbook on this. They cooked the books so well that they were always able to borrow from a new source or even the same source to pay back on time what they owed. *Fortune* magazine named Enron "America's most innovative company" for six straight years.[43] They got this right, except they left out "accounting" after "innovative."

Anyone who thinks you can hold managers' feet to the fire in any way, shape, or form given today's legal impediments, should talk with Carl Icahn, the famous corporate raider. Icahn has a web site devoted to explaining how corporate managers have been able to wrest control of corporations from shareholders. Below are the six major methods identified by Icahn that corporate managers use to retain control of their companies and expropriate their shareholders. The failure of corporate governance is of critical importance for understanding the financial plague we're now confronting.[44]

Carl Icahn's Six Ways to Steal From Shareholders

1. The "poison pill." This device, which is permitted in many states, allows a company to issue a plethora of new stock when a potentially hostile investor acquires a large stake, such as 15 percent. The provision has the effect of blocking any offer for a company, no matter how beneficial it may be for shareholders. According to the Corporate Library, nearly one-third of U.S. public companies have a poison pill in place, but others can simply institute them if they face a threat.

2. The staggered, or "classified," board. This device, also permitted in many states, allows a company to hold elections for only a minority of board members each year, effectively blocking stockholders from removing an entire board and instituting change.

3. "Advance notice" provisions. These corporate bylaws allow companies to demand an array of often arbitrary and irrelevant data from any investor wishing to propose a resolution for vote at a company's annual meeting, including board

(Continued)

(Continued)

candidates or resolutions on director pay, for example. These demands can be significant hurdles for any shareholder wishing to propose resolutions and often are simply pretexts for a company to deny a vote on a proposal.

4. The "right of domicile" provision. In many states, it is the sole right of management to determine where a company is incorporated, meaning they often domicile in management-friendly jurisdictions.

5. Division of CEO and chairman role. The CEO is the chief manager of a company, while the chairman is the main representative of stockholders. Unfortunately on many boards, this role is occupied by the same person, which often poses a conflict of interest.

6. Supermajority vote provisions for major transactions. These rules generally require that well over a majority of shareholders must approve major transactions like mergers or charter amendments, which is often an onerous impediment to change. A simple majority is sufficient for all such changes.

Corporate governance problems arise even when managers themselves own large parts of the company. In Lehman's case, management owned 30 percent of the shares.[45] But the only manager that really mattered was the CEO—Richard Fuld. As indicated, he and his henchmen had essentially sole knowledge of the company's risk exposure (not that they could necessarily process that knowledge), so what any individual manager did in terms of taking risk with respect to his own part of the business had, to that manager's knowledge, no clear relationship to the firm's overall risk, which means no clear impact on the probability of the manager losing money on his or her holdings of Lehman shares.

The other big problem here is that in good times, the government will be under strong pressure by the financial community to relax capital requirements. After all, if times are good, what's to worry? And in bad times, the government will be under even stronger pressure to relax the requirements. Not doing so will limit the amounts banks can lend and require more asset sales to meet capital requirements just at a time when there already is lots of selling going on in the market.

Finally, the amount of leverage a bank takes on is only partly determined by its capital requirement. It's also determined by the degree to which it buys leveraged assets. Banks can have the same amount of effective leverage regardless of the capital requirements simply by buying more leveraged and, thus, riskier assets.

Leverage upon Leverage

To see this, consider Goldman Sachs again with its $1 trillion invested in, I'll assume, risky assets, its $900 billion in borrowing, and its $100 billion in capital.[46] This portfolio position meets the current 10 to 1 capital requirement. To keep the story simple, suppose that the $1 trillion in risky assets are all invested in stock of companies with no debt. And to make the story concrete, assume that the risky assets in the companies consist of 1 trillion widgets that are going to produce a product that may or may not sell very well.

Now suppose the government raises the capital requirement from $1 of capital for every $10 of risky assets to $1 dollar of capital for every $5 of risky assets. Assuming it doesn't raise any more capital, Goldman will need to sell off $500 billion in stock and use the proceeds to pay off $500 billion in debt. This will leave it owning, effectively, 500 billion widgets and $400 billion in debt, leaving the company with $100 billion in capital. So doing this meets the new 5-to-1 capital requirement. But now suppose Goldman sells off its remaining $500 billion in stock holdings of the debt-free widget companies and uses the $500 billion to purchase the shares of companies that are themselves leveraged 2 to 1; that is, each of these companies has $1 trillion in widgets, but also $500 billion in debt. So they are worth $500 billion on the market.

In spending its $500 billion to purchase these leveraged companies, Goldman has gotten back to where it started, that is, it's gotten back to 10-to-1 leverage. Its $500 billion in assets now represent claims to 1 trillion widgets, but also obligations to cover $500 billion in debt. Add this obligation to Goldman's direct $400 billion of debt obligations and we're back to Goldman holding $900 billion in debt. And owners' capital is still $100 billion.

The basic point here is that capital requirements are meaningless without knowing the precise nature of the risky assets being held. Given this, for the regulators really to gain control of the risk of banks, they need to approve each risky asset purchased by the banks. But if this is the case, having private banks is worthless. If Uncle Sam has to approve all the decisions, better just to have him nationalize the entire banking system and make all the decisions directly.

This point is not simply theoretical. In Larry McDonald's insider account of the fall of Lehman, he repeatedly points out that Lehman was leveraging itself to purchase highly leveraged assets. So it was effectively much more leveraged than the 31-to-1 ratio indicated by its balance sheet. According to Richard Fuld, Lehman's leverage was 10 to 1 at the time it went kaput. But the Street must have figured, for two reasons, that the effective leverage was many times greater, since it decided Lehman wasn't worth peanuts. Reason one was that the assets Lehman held were much riskier than it was letting on, and reason two is that the assets Lehman held were worth a lot less than Lehman was saying they were worth, making its true ratio of risky assets to capital much higher than reported.

"Weapons of Mass Financial Destruction"

This is Warren Buffett's definition of derivatives. And there sure are lots of derivatives out there to worry about if Buffett's characterization is correct. Recall, the Bank for International Settlements reports a total gross volume of derivatives of $592.0 trillion.[47]

In the context of our current financial system, Buffett is 100 percent correct. But we need to be clear. These securities are not the culprit, and were they banned entirely, they would not cure the financial plague facing our country and, indeed, the world. Derivatives are new variants of a very large number of preexisting, old-fashioned securities, which are fully capable of precipitating financial and economic meltdown on their own.

The Great Depression wasn't kicked off by problems with collateralized debt obligations, interest rate swaps, or credit default swaps. These derivatives didn't exist at the time.[48] It was caused by the failure of 30 percent of the banks, which collectively were too big to fail and also too big to save (with no Jimmy Stewart to stop the serial bank runs). In other words, their collective failure kicked the economy into a very bad, long-term equilibrium, and the government could well have gone broke had it tried to prevent each one of their failures. "Broke" here means raising taxes through the roof, borrowing massive amounts, or printing huge quantities of money.

Thus, the problem is fundamentally not the nature of the securities being traded in the market. Nor is the problem the volume or complexities of the securities. The problem is that losses from these securities, whether they arise from the net exposures of a small number of extremely large financial companies or a large number of small and medium-sized financial companies, can bring down the financial system because it has no firewalls. Losses in one part of the system lead to losses in other parts, financial failures, and collateral damage in the form of collective panic, which flips the economy to a bad equilibrium.

Old and new financial securities are also armed and dangerous, with one explosion triggering a chain reaction. The potential for an explosion is particularly large in our modern world in which trades can be executed in milliseconds—far faster than a regulator can see, let alone stop. Even had the Office of Thrift Supervision assigned an army of regulators, rather than just a single person with real insurance expertise, to oversee AIG, the company could still have ended up with what it says is $1.6 trillion in CDS exposure.

And letting CEOs like Jimmy Cayne "manage" their financial company's massive financial risk is asking for trouble. Such "managers" can easily approve a trade or a series of trades occurring in a short space of time that leave their banks or insurance companies with a net exposure that totals in the hundreds of billions, if not trillions, of dollars. And if the Jimmys and Anthonys and Stans and Charles and Joes and Dicks and Franks and Roberts all helicopter each week to their favorite country club to play a round and then divulge over Lychees their latest brilliant market plays, we can see, as we've just seen, large numbers of major companies engage in copycat financial plays. In this case, the risk of collective meltdown has changed without their realizing it.

The point, then, is that these guys and gals—their decisions, their moves, their conversations, their personalities, their knowledge, their competitiveness, and their addictions to gambling, power, drugs, booze, interactive golf, or card games—are themselves a large source of systemic risk. And there is no purpose to this risk. It's not economic risk. It's man-made risk, which we neither need, nor can afford.

Proposed "Control of Derivatives"

The administration knows that derivatives-trading, particular CDS trading, is a Wild West activity these days, with many of the trades being very poorly documented. So the powers that be are proposing that CDS trading take place via a clearinghouse. But such clearinghouse trading, as proposed, would be voluntary. So any given seller of any given CDS or other derivative that could be construed to be a CDS could simply opt to sell the CDS over the counter, meaning in a private deal without the knowledge of those overseeing such trades.

Furthermore, even if all derivatives were traded in a clearinghouse, this hardly limits net open positions by financial firms that, to the extent they are leveraged and are "too big to fail" (at any time or at special times when their failure would be contagious), are implicitly laying off the risk of their bets to the taxpayer.

Selling insurance in the open light of day is better than selling it in the dark. But if you are insuring something you can't really insure, you are committing fraud. This is what AIG did, and this is what so many other Wall Street firms did in selling CDSs. They were insuring against defaults of securities in all situations (what we economists call *states of nature*), and they were in no position to do so even if they had been safely reserving every dollar they collected in premiums (in CDS sales receipts).

The Dangers of Putting Wall Street on a Leash

Having the federal government intervene in our economy's financial sector in the short term is one thing. Having it run, and therefore micro-manage, the financial sector over time is another, and very dangerous, thing. But that's the direction we're headed as part and parcel of resurrecting a failed financial system that, in the end, the public won't really trust. And because it's been burnt so badly, the public is going to put lots of pressure on public officials to do whatever it takes to keep this from happening again. In the context of our financial structure, this means having Uncle Sam micro-manage essentially everything any financial company does.

This prognosis is supported by the facts. Uncle Sam is already starting to set executive compensation based, in large part, on politics.[49] He's also deciding who should get mortgage relief and on what terms. He's gearing up to regulate appointment of directors to corporate boards. And he's also going to help decide bank dividend-, share repurchase-, and preferred stock-conversion policy.[50]

The bankers, of course, have only themselves to blame for this state of affairs. The public is outraged over Wall Street compensation in particular, and executive pay in general—at its fantastic magnitude, at the disconnect between pay and performance, and at the rising cost to taxpayers.

The latest uproar was generated by a July 30 report issued by New York State Attorney General Andrew Cuomo. The report shows that over 5,000 bankers from nine banks received bonuses in excess of $1 million in 2009. A total of 836 bankers received bonuses exceeding $3 million.[51] The nine banks were singled out for a reason. They were all huge and all on the government dole. Each received tens of billions of dollars from Uncle Sam under TARP—the Troubled Asset Relief Program (TARP). Take Citigroup and Merrill Lynch. Together they lost $54 billion in 2008, received $55 billion in TARP money, and then proceeded to reward their managers' incompetence by handing out $9 billion in bonuses. Bank of America's net income in 2008 dropped by 71 percent, yet it paid its management no less in 2008 than in 2007.[52]

Andrew Cuomo's no economist, but he can put two and two together. He made these and other comparisons between the banks' profits and their bonuses and concluded, "There is no clear rhyme or reason to the way banks compensate and reward their employees. In many ways, the past three years have provided a virtual laboratory in which to test the hypothesis that compensation in the financial industry was performance-based. But even a cursory examination of the data suggests that in these challenging economic times, compensation for bank employees has become unmoored from the banks' financial performance."[53]

The problem of executive pay goes far beyond the U.S. financial sector. Today, the typical CEO of a large U.S. corporation earns over 250 times what the average worker brings home! Two decades ago that CEO would have averaged "only" 80 times the pay of the average worker. Either CEO productivity relative to that of average workers has risen by a factor of three since the early 1990s, or CEOs are being paid miles more than they're worth.

The public has opted for the latter interpretation and is increasingly coming to understand that top management and boards of directors pay each other to pay each other, which translates into stealing from shareholders. And since the average Joe is a shareholder, via his 401(k) plan, in corporate America, the average Joe is feeling ripped off. And rightly so. Corporate management appoints the directors of their boards, and the directors decide how much to pay the managers not just for the fancy title they've been given, but also for the opportunity to set their own pay for serving as directors. Talk about crony capitalism![54]

■ ■ ■

On July 31, the day after Cuomo issued his report, the House of Representatives said enough is enough. The House voted 237 to 185 to restrict executive pay via a number of channels.[55] The legislation, which may or may not see the light of day, given its need for the Senate's and president's approval, calls for nonbinding shareholder approval of executive pay and independence of the directors and outside consultants who are determining executive compensation. It also requires banks and other financial companies to disclose their bonus plans, and, most important, it lets government regulators decide if the incentive schemes are "aligned with sound risk management."[56]

Regardless of what one thinks of the House bill, and I think some features (particularly independence of those on compensation committees) have real merit, what we are really seeing is public realization that the banks and insurance companies need a baby-sitter on an ongoing basis. But the public also knows that there were plenty of baby-sitters in place before the financial system collapsed and none was closely monitoring their baby.

Chapter 4

"This Sucker Could Go Down"

Former president Bush uttered these encouraging words on September 25, 2008, in a meeting with members of Congress in which he pleaded for passage of the $700 billion TARP (Troubled Asset Relief Program) bank-bailout bill.[1] The former president wasn't hyperventilating or whatever he might call it. He was scared stiff. Over the prior two weeks, Fannie Mae, Freddie Mac, Lehman Brothers, and AIG had either failed or been taken over by the Feds.

Treasury Secretary Hank Paulson was equally panicked. Paulson was so worried about the potential for further financial meltdown that he literally got down on his knees and begged Speaker of the House Nancy Pelosi to help pass the bill.

Not exactly what you'd expect from a tough-talking Texan and the former head of Goldman Sachs. But everyone was sure financial Armageddon was about to occur. And if they weren't sure, they wanted to make sure they were on record as raising the possibility in case it did happen; that is, they wanted to protect their derrières.

Presidential candidate Senator McCain suspended his campaign, announcing: "We are running out of time. . . . [The nation] faces an historic crisis in our financial system." McCain next issued a joint statement with then Senator Obama that "the effort to protect the American economy must not fail," whereupon he rushed to Washington to muster support for the TARP bill among his fellow Republicans.[2] McCain even canceled a presidential debate, suggesting he would be too busy fixing the world's economy to devote to that incidental pursuit. Later, when it became clear that the economy could actually survive for a couple of hours without McCain's help, the senator rescheduled the debate.

The hysterics or histrionics were all duly reported by the press and worked wonders with Congress. On October 3, Congress approved the bill, and the president signed it. But the sight of our leaders in full panic mode did a real number on the market. Starting on Monday, October 6, the stock market began to vaporize, dropping sharply day after day. By the end of the week, the market was down 20 percent—the worst weekly decline ever.[3] And by the end of December, the market stood at half its peak value recorded in October 2007.

This was a stock market muddle—the opposite of a stock market bubble. Pessimism fed on itself, and our leaders did their best to encourage it by making clear that the D word was front and center in their minds and finally spiting the word out. They held lots of press conferences and uttered some reassuring sounds, but their grim faces and body language said it all. They spoke of "saving the economy."[4] They said, "We are in the most serious financial crisis in generations."[5] They warned, "We have inherited an economic crisis as deep and dire as any since the Great Depression."[6]

Taking Stock

There are many critical lessons from what happened in the fall of 2008 and over the following year. First and foremost, we saw the amazing fragility of the current financial system and the fact that our politicians are fully prepared to publicly advertise its fragility in order to score political points. Second, we've seen that the federal government is, to a large extent, a wholly-owned subsidiary of the financial sector. Professor Simon Johnson, who is hardly a card-carrying leftist, puts it this way:

> I think the banks have control of the state. . . . They got the bailout, they got the money they needed to stay in business, they got a vast line of credit from the taxpayer. . . . they got everything they wanted. . . . If the economy turns around, even if we get a recovery that's not completely convincing but we sort of feel like we're not falling, and we're not having the massive unemployment of the '20s and '30s, the pressure will come off the banks. They know this. This is why they think they won. They faced down the dangers and they've gone through this difficult phase, and they came through it stronger than ever.[7]

Third, we've seen that the federal government is willing to explicitly and implicitly guarantee gargantuan bailouts that it is in absolutely no position to guarantee. This is particularly the case given that the country is already clearly bankrupt; its certain fiscal commitments far exceed its capacity to pay. Fourth, we've seen that Uncle Sam, having done Wall Street's bidding, is now facing tremendous public anger and is responding by extracting his own pound of flesh from Wall Street, namely explicitly or implicitly transforming the private financial sector, including those parts with no direct government ownership, into a wholly-owned subsidiary of the state.

Fifth, we've seen that despite $2.5 trillion in direct expenditures and another roughly $10 trillion in contingent commitments, the economy remains in deep trouble. Unemployment is still rising. And Uncle Sam can't employ 130 million plus workers on his own. He needs the private sector to do the hiring, and for that to happen he needs the private sector to trust that he knows what he's doing.

All presidents see their approval ratings fall after the first few months in office. But President Obama's rating, while still very high, has dropped more rapidly than that of prior presidents. This is not to pile on our new leader. In general, I believe the president is doing a tremendous job. But his job approval rating is a sign of unease with the general economic policy approach, which he inherited, but which his economic generals have maintained.

This policy entails trying to control/influence animal spirits by spending like there is no tomorrow. But the animals Uncle Sam is trying to psyche up are we, the people, and we, the people, aren't stupid. We realize that it's our own and our kids' money that Uncle Sam is ultimately spending or committing to spend if things get worse.

And yes, we realize that much of this actual and contingent spending could end up paying for itself if it really delivers the goods—a restoration of full employment in short order. But after almost two years into this D or R thing, we, the people, not to mention China and many other foreign countries, are increasingly worried that that the Bush-Obama economic rescue effort is violating the Hippocratic Oath—*First Do No Harm*. The rescue effort has been meant to convince us that the slow response to financial collapse that occurred in the early 1930s would not be repeated and that the economy and financial markets would quickly return to normal. That hasn't happened, notwithstanding the current hopeful economic signs. And we, the people, are now very worried that this "rescue" won't, in fact, work, but instead will spell massive tax hikes, hyperinflation, and sky-high interest rates.

We Are Not All Keynesians Now

Sixth, we've learned that decades of research on multiple equilibria and coordination failures by economists has been entirely ignored in favor of 1960s-style Keynesian economics in which government spending, rather than calm economic assurance coupled with actually fixing the microeconomic financial-market problems that need fixing, is the appropriate policy tool.[8]

President Nixon, in the midst of the economic fiasco of the early 1970s that he helped to create, famously stated, "We are all Keynesians now." But as he was announcing his conversion, the economics profession was in the process of largely rejecting the Keynesian school of thought, which is predicated to a large extent on assumptions about price and wage rigidity and public myopia/stupidity that were always hard to swallow and have certainly not characterized the current economic decline. Instead, we've seen the public quickly comprehend that the economy was in trouble. We've seen workers volunteer to take pay cuts to save their own jobs. We've even seen workers take pay cuts to save their coworkers' jobs! But what we've really seen is employers deciding almost overnight to cut jobs because they've been told that times are now bad and that everyone else is going to lay off workers so no one will be able to buy what they have to sell. In effect, employers have been told that the only thing to fear is fear itself and that they damn well better fear it or get terribly burnt.

Although it's not widely known, Keynes did not consider himself a Keynesian. He was not particularly enamored of the mechanical IS-LM economic model of price or wage rigidity that his disciples developed in the 1940s in their attempt to decipher his often quite imprecise, if not downright cryptic, magnus opus, *The General Theory*. Unfortunately, Keynes's concerns were ignored, and this new IS-LM testament prevailed, becoming standard fare in undergraduate macroeconomics pedagogy. And it is precisely this IS-LM model that is being applied to the current economic crisis.

The IS-LM model says two things—you fight major economic downturns both by spending and by printing money like mad. We've done both, but rather than admit the strategy's not working or not working very well, many Keynesian economists are claiming we need to spend and print even more money.

Paul Krugman, a Princeton economist and economics columnist for the *New York Times*, is the chief proponent of more federal spending. He's also a card-carrying Keynesian and proud of it. In his September 6, 2009, *New York Times Magazine* article, "How Did Economists Get It So Wrong?" Krugman paints a picture of the economics profession as divided into two camps—saltwater macroeconomists from Princeton (Krugman's department), Harvard, and MIT who live relatively close to the ocean, and freshwater macroeconomists from Chicago and Minnesota who live close to lakes. According to Krugman, the saltwater economists are the Keynesians and have gotten things right because they believe markets don't work, whereas the freshwater economists have gotten things wrong because they believe markets not only work, but work perfectly. Krugman portrays the freshwater economists as overly enamored with mathematical models of rational economic agents, whereas the Keynesians know that lots of people are "idiots" (the blunt term he uses in his article, but correctly attributes to Larry Summers) and subject to behavioral problems (that is, act irrationally) when it comes to handling their finances.

Krugman is a Nobel Prize–winning economist. In his day he used plenty of sophisticated math with rational agents to make the advances in the theory of international trade for which he is rightfully famous. So the math and nonmath distinction he draws is fatuous; economists in every major economics department throughout the world use math because it is the language in which we communicate and pinpoint our ideas. And the suggestion that everyone in Chicago and Minnesota has one point of view and everyone at Princeton, Harvard, and MIT has another, and that these five schools constitute the known, relevant world of macroeconomics is equally ridiculous.

Krugman's suggestion of a bifurcated economics profession, one that's living in a perfect-markets fantasy land and one (his) that's grounded in a real world of imperfect markets populated by idiots, makes for a lively column, but badly disserves his readers. Yes there are economists with extreme views close to those Krugman portrays. Indeed, at this point, Krugman comes as close to his stereotype of an old-time Keynesian economist as anyone in the profession.

But what's needed is not pointing fingers at particular schools of thought, but putting one's finger on what's really going on. Here Krugman is missing the essence of the macroeconomic problem, namely the inherent fragility of the economy's performance because, as Keynes was the first to make clear, beliefs about the economy's underperformance can be self-fulfilling. It's not that prices and wages don't adjust to clear markets. It's that they can adjust to clear markets at different levels of economic activity—ones in which there is full employment and ones in which there is massive unemployment. Today's multiple equilibria mathematical models show that confident economies can have functioning markets and scared economies can have also have functioning, albeit poorly-performing markets and that there is nothing that ensures we end up with a confident economy, particularly when we have politicians screaming that the sky is falling in.

Think back about Alex and David trying to coordinate their market in fish and hotdogs. If they can't figure out when to meet and neither swims to the middle of the lake, they'll both end up in a very unpleasant economy—an economy with perfect market clearing and price setting, but no real joy. It's an economy in which Alex sells his fish to himself at a price at which he's willing to buy and eat it all (and then get sick).[9] And David sells himself his hotdogs at a price that clears his own unpleasant but absolutely perfect market. If the two can coordinate meeting in the middle of the lake, they can make a completely different market characterized by a completely different set of market-clearing prices, but a market that's delivers much better outcomes. So setting market prices is not the problem. *The problem is settling on the right market.*

The economic problem here is really one of public finance. A market is, itself, a public good. Each party can use a market without diminishing its use by other parties. But as with other public goods, like defense, private parties are inclined to free ride on each other when it comes to providing a service whose value they will not fully capture. Alex wants David to swim to the middle of the lake to scream out when they should meet each week, and David wants Alex to do so. And each waits for the other to take the plunge.

Krugman's also missing the essence of the microeconomic problems that kicked off this macroeconomic debacle, namely that we've constructed a financial system with a host of interconnected structural (that is, microeconomic) problems, which are almost guaranteed to periodically crash our financial system, scare us to death, and take down our economy.

You can't blame the public for not knowing what Jimmy Cayne and Dick Fuld were doing when people in their own companies and our top regulatory agencies had no idea. You can't say wages don't adjust when workers are fired without being asked if they'll take pay cuts. You can't say prices don't adjust when sellers are running huge sales and gas prices fall by 60 percent in five months.[10] You can't say investors have "behavioral" problems because they bought DDD securities, which they were told were AAA. And you can't say that securities markets are inherently subject to bubbles when those driving up the prices were using stolen money—money borrowed on fraudulent terms.

At this point, Krugman is a full-time newspaper columnist, and his trying to revive 30-year-old academic disputes and calling the public names may work for his employer. But he's not helping us see the real problems we face or how to fix them.

Reviewing the Case for Radical Surgery

Carpenters are guided by a wise principal—*measure twice and cut once*. So before prescribing Limited Purpose Banking's radical financial surgery, let me restate briefly the case for fixing things from the ground up.

Our country needs a well-functioning financial system. The principal goal of a financial system is to bring together suppliers and demanders of funds. It's not to run a gambling operation that takes a fundamentally risky economy and makes it much riskier by leaving massive gambling debts for John Q Public to cover. The problem is not the risk taking or the leverage used to expand risk taking. People should be allowed to take on risk, particularly given the fact that reducing risk A may require taking on risk B. The problem is the leveraging of the taxpayer by people with no formal training in finance or economics, no personal downside, an assortment of Napoleonic complexes, the money to buy ratings in New York and policy in Washington, and the ability to run circles around regulators.

■   ■   ■

Without truly radical surgery on our financial system, there is a small but significant chance of total financial meltdown that would make what we've seen to date penny ante. Uncle Sam can insure our checking accounts, our savings accounts, our CDs, our money market accounts, our cash surrender values, the debts of our major financial and nonfinancial corporations, and the dollar-denominated reserves of China and Lord knows what other countries, but he can't insure anybody's purchasing power. He can make dollars. He can't make goods and services. And it's the goods and services that people and governments are being promised or think they are being promised.

The meltdown, if it comes, can be triggered by runaway inflation, runs on the banks, runs on insurance companies, the crash of the U.S. Treasury market, a run on the dollar, or another huge run on U.S. stocks. And in this environment, in which our remaining firewalls are barely standing, any one of these events could, and likely would, trigger all the others.

Chapter 5

Limited Purpose Banking

There is a better way to restore trust in our financial system and get our economy rolling than by having Uncle Sam pledge always to clean up the mess, which he can't actually do. The better way is not to let the mess happen to begin with. As indicated above, this alternative reform is called *limited purpose banking* (LPB). It's a simple and very low-cost change to our financial system, which limits banks to their legitimate purpose, namely connecting (intermediating between) borrowers and lenders and savers and investors. The costs of limited purpose banking are negligible for a good reason. The reform builds off the existing mutual fund industry, which has been functioning very smoothly for more than half a century. It also dramatically rationalizes and simplifies financial regulation.

Under limited purpose banking, all *banks*—all financial and insurance companies with limited liability (e.g., C-corps, S-corps, LLPs) that are engaged in financial intermediation—would operate as *pass-through* mutual fund companies, which sell mutual funds—safe as well as risky collections of securities. That is, the banks would simply function as middlemen. They would never themselves own financial assets or borrow to invest in anything except those specific assets, such as computers, office furniture, and buildings, needed to run their mutual funds' operations. Hence, banks would never be in a position to fail because of ill-advised financial bets.

No-risk banking? Yes, no-risk banking. Intermediation requires no risk taking whatsoever. And we've just had an object lesson in what happens when you let intermediaries gamble—they can go broke, and in the process drive the country broke. With limited purpose banking, financial intermediation never breaks down. Moreover, we the people are never leveraged, and consequently never subjected to "economic blackmail," as FDIC Chairman Sheila Bair puts it.[1]

Full Disclosure—No Plan Is Perfect

In considering limited purpose banking (LPB), please bear in mind that no proposal is perfect. We live in an uncertain world with a goodly number of devious people. We have to do the best we can with our scarce resources and protect ourselves to the maximum extent possible without throwing the baby (economic growth) out with the bathwater (financial malfeasance).

Limited purpose banking is, I'm convinced, the best and simplest solution to our horrendous and, unfortunately, ongoing financial plague. But there are, no doubt, elements in this plan that you are going to like less than others.

Fortunately, the plan is so simple—has so few elements—that you'll be able to see immediately what you like and don't like. But I hope you'll agree that each of the elements is critical for the plan to work. So the real question is not whether you like every detail of LPB. It's whether you like LPB better than maintaining the current system, with its extremely dangerous risks. I also hope you'll agree that LPB offers a way to reform our financial system with the least possible intrusion by the federal government in what are ultimately private financial matters and decisions.

In considering LPB, please also bear in mind that the proposal is not coming completely out of left field. If you look carefully at some of the reform ideas emanating from Congress these days, you'll see a number of LPB-type features. But you'll also see that they come attached with a very heavy and unnecessary dose of government regulation and financial micro-management, not to mention political kickbacks masquerading as reform.

This is no surprise. If we let the Street's Jimmy Caynes continue to call the shots, we have two options. Either we have federal regulators sit at their elbows while at work and shadow them when they leave the office. Or we make their every significant financial move subject to federal government approval. This amounts to effective nationalization of the banking system and the end of free financial enterprise.

In my view, we're likely to flip from dramatically underregulating to dramatically overregulating the financial sector while still leaving the system at risk. Recall that prior to September 11, we had plenty of airline security, with all of us forced to spend lots of our travel time passing through metal detectors and having our carry-ons X-rayed. Yet no one in charge of air travel security figured out that the most effective way to stop airline hijackers was simply to give the pilots a loo and some sandwiches, lock the cockpit doors, and adopt the rule of never opening them under any circumstances. So we spent years thinking airline hijackers would follow our script, rather than devise their own plans, which they did again this Christmas. Unless we have a foolproof financial system, homegrown financial terrorists will once again find the hole in our financial security system and drive a truck through it!

But I may be wrong. It may be that Congress does essentially nothing to clamp down on Wall Street, leaving us fully exposed to ongoing financial fiasco. As I write, it's less than 15 months since Lehman's collapse, but the *Wall Street Journal* is claiming on its front page that financial reform is essentially a dead letter and that major Wall Street firms are taking on more risk than ever. Indeed, the top five U.S. banks now stand to lose $1 billion in a single day were their trades to turn sour, compared to $600 billion in 2007.[2] The *Journal* also reports that banks "are selling exotic financial products similar to those that felled markets and the world economy last fall."

The *Journal* article appeared one day after a *New York Times* column by Andrew Ross Sorkin stating, "As we approach the anniversary of some of the most cataclysmic failures in our economic history, we appear to be in perhaps no better position to manage the failure of an investment bank, a hedge fund, or an insurance company than we were before. Absent any legislation that would prevent another 9/15

(Lehman) . . . from happening, our only options are to throw money at problem companies or arrange shotgun marriages to keep them from failing. That hardly seems like a long-term solution."[3]

Two days later, the *Times* ran a front-page story with this headline: "A Year after a Cataclysm, Little Change on Wall St." plus this text: "Wall Street lives on. One year after the collapse of Lehman Brothers, the surprise is not how much has changed in the financial industry, but how little. Backstopped by huge federal guarantees, the biggest banks have restructured only around the edges. . . . The Obama administration has proposed regulatory changes, but even their backers say they face a difficult road in Congress. For now, banks still sell and trade unregulated derivatives, despite their role in last fall's chaos."

Banks = Mutual Funds

Under limited purpose banking (LPB), banks would let us gamble, but they would not themselves gamble. That is, banks would be free to sell all manner of mutual funds, including the 10,000 or so now on the market. These mutual funds include traded equity funds, private equity funds, real estate investment trusts, commercial paper funds, private mortgage funds, credit card debt funds, junk bond funds, funds that invest in put options on U.S. Treasuries, inflation-indexed bond funds, currency funds—you name it. Limited purpose banking is completely open to financial innovation with respect to the type of mutual funds offered. But at a minimum it would include two additional types of mutual funds—cash mutual funds and insurance mutual funds, which I'll describe momentarily.

The Federal Financial Authority

Beyond the prohibition against financial companies borrowing short and lending long and the introduction of two new types of mutual funds, there is only one other critical feature of LPB, namely replacing the roughly 115 federal and state financial regulatory bodies with a single financial regulator—the Federal Financial Authority (FFA) referenced above. The FFA can be thought of as an FDA (Food and Drug Administration) for financial products. The FFA would verify, supervise custody, fully disclose, and oversee the rating and trades of all securities purchased, held, and sold by the LPB mutual funds.

Here's an example of how the FFA would operate.

The FFA as the Financial Regulator

Consider Robby, who seeks to borrow money to buy Frank's house in Cleveland "using" a bank; call it WLM Bank (which stands for *We Love Money Bank*). WLM would initiate the mortgage, by which I mean it would help Robby fill out a mortgage application. Next WLM would send the paperwork to the FFA for processing. The FFA would verify Robby's income statement using federal income tax records; it would certify his credit rating; it would verify, using independent local appraisers, the value of the home he intends to purchase; it would verify the property taxes and insurance costs on the home; and it would specify all other pertinent information that would help a mutual fund understand the value of buying Robby's mortgage.

Most important, the FFA would hire private rating companies to provide independent ratings of the risk of Robby's mortgage. The rating companies would be free of any financial conflicts of interest; that is, they would not be permitted to work for companies or individuals whose securities they are rating.

The FFA would disclose everything it has learned about Robby's mortgage on a public web site, without disclosing Robby's identity or the precise location (inside, say, a mile) of the house in question. And once the FFA has done its work, it would return the now fully disclosed mortgage to WLM, which would put the mortgage up for public auction and purchase either by its own mutual fund that invests in home mortgages or by the mutual funds of other banks investing in home mortgages.

Robby's mortgage would fund when purchased and not a second before, with the acquiring mutual fund wiring the funds to Frank's account. Hence, WLM would never hold the mortgage and never be exposed to the risk of Robby's defaulting. It would simply intermediate the transaction, for which it would charge Robby a fee.

Ending Insider Rating

The FFA would eliminate insider rating, a key cause of our financial debacle. Standard & Poor's, Moody's, Fitch, A. M. Best, and other rating companies could still operate, but the public would have an independent assessment of financial products. Indeed, the current rating companies would likely receive considerable business from the FFA, provided they didn't cross the conflict-of-interest line. Alternatively, Robby would be free to hire them privately if he felt their assessment of his risk of defaulting would help sell his mortgage at a higher price, and thus ensure him a lower interest rate. Such private rating information would also be included in the public, online disclosure of Robby's mortgage prior to its sale at auction. Again, this would be done without identifying Robby by name.

Bye-Bye, Bernie, Bye-Bye, Allen

The FFA would oversee third-party custodial arrangements of all mutual funds. This would ensure that no Bernard Madoff or Allen Sanford could ever again self-custody his clients' assets and spend their money illegally.

Initiation, Not Securitization, Is the Problem

Given the packaging together for easy sale of literally tons of bundles of thousands of fraudulent subprime mortgages, it's easy to blame securitization for our financial troubles. After all, if the subprimes hadn't been securitized either in whole or in tranched parts, banks could not easily have sold them, and would instead have had to hold them, and would therefore have made sure they weren't fraudulent—or so it is said.

I disagree. Bundling together a bunch of risky assets and selling them is a way of helping the public limit the risk of investing in that asset class. A stock market index fund does this diversification for stocks, and a pool of mortgages does this diversification for loans to homeowners. So pooling subprime mortgages, or prime mortgages, for that matter, to let people easily and inexpensively diversify this type of investment can't be a problem. And once such pools are created, selling them can't be wrong; what's wrong with selling a legitimate product?

The real problem with the bundling and sale of the subprimes was that the products being sold weren't legitimate. Sellers of these mortgage bundles, whether sliced and diced into CDO/CMO tranches or not, were lying about what they were selling. They were misstating income, appraisals, credit ratings, and other critical details about the loans. This was no different from selling cyanide as a painkiller. And when you learn this fact, the immediate response is not to blame the bottling and sales process, but to blame the labeling process—the disclosure process—the fact that the bottle had a product name and not the name of the dangerous chemical.

The problem with the subprimes then was not their securitization and sale, but rather their initiation, by which I mean their false and misleading disclosure. Had the subprimes that we now call toxic been sold as such, there would have been no problem. They would have sold for what they were and are worth, which is very little. But when they were sold as being honestly documented loans or derivatives on loans, the sellers were committing fraud, pure and simple. And those who did this should be placed in jail.

Clearly, we can't rely on Wall Street to police itself in these matters. Nor can we trust the private rating process. This and the fact that the information about Robby's mortgage constitutes a public good is why the FFA needs to fully oversee the initiation process, not just for new mortgages, but for all securities being purchased by LPB mutual funds.

We must also realize that forcing banks to hold the mortgages they initiate to change their behavior is an experiment that was tried and failed. In this crisis, the Wall Street firms that got into trouble did so because they were holding vast amounts of these securitized toxic assets on their books. Presumably they did so because they drank their own Kool-Aid and believed their own sales pitches about the safety and high returns available from these securities. Alternatively, those managers within the firms manufacturing these securitized assets realized that their bonus wasn't connected to who, including their own company, bought the product, but how much was bought. In many ways selling in-house may be easier than selling out-of-house. And if you know you are selling financial sludge to your employer, but can safely sock away large bonuses for several years before it's discovered and you're fired, you are still ahead.

Securitizing Death

Securitization, which again is not the problem, is perfectly compatible with LPB. Mutual funds can purchase individual assets or securitized bundles of assets as they wish. But unlike the current system, with the FFA's oversight, they'll know what they are buying, which will make all the difference in the world.

Again, securitization itself is an increasing and useful feature of modern finance, even if some of the securities being packaged together can seem pretty darn smarmy. Wall Street's most recent foray into securitization is called "Life Settlement Funds."[4] It entails selling bundles of life insurance policies on people it claims will drop dead fast. The specific traders selling these securities say they have located a bunch of particularly sick oldsters with life insurance policies and that these policies will pay off soon provided the sick oldsters cooperate by dying in a timely manner.

What's in this for the oldsters with good death prospects? Well, they don't have to wait to die to collect on their policies. They can sell their policies right now to Wall Street traders for ready cash, albeit for a lot less than the face values of their policies.

Should we let Wall Street trade bundles of death assets? The answer is yes provided there is an FFA to prevent the two types of fraud that will otherwise arise. The first is that oldsters will be persuaded to hand over their policies for a lot less than they are really worth because these oldsters are conned into believing that they are a lot healthier than is actually the case. The second is that Wall Street will advertise the death assets as having excellent payoff prospects, when, in fact, the oldsters named on the policies held in the *death* settlement funds aren't all that ripe and ready to go.

The FFA's precise role here would be to spot check the potential decedents whose policies are included in the death settlement funds and make sure they are, indeed, as sick as advertised. If they are and they need some extra money so they can party until they drop, why shouldn't they be allowed to make that deal? The problem again is not buying or selling financial products. It's buying or selling fraudulent financial products, and only the government can be trusted to help us understand what financial products are and are not snake oil.

Cash Mutual Funds

Now that the FFA's role has been established, I want to explain why we can do away with the other 115 or so financial regulators, including the FDIC (whose employees can, by the way, be put to work for the FFA). To do so, I need to describe the two new mutual funds that will arise under LPB. The first is cash mutual funds.

A cash mutual fund is just what it says it is, namely a mutual fund that holds only cash. This is a general property of LPB mutual funds. Each mutual fund would hold what it says it holds and nothing else. For example, a six-month T-Bill mutual fund would hold six-month Treasury Bills, and that's it. A U.S. pharmaceutical stock fund would hold only stocks of U.S. drug companies in the proportions established by the mutual fund's charter. A Los Angeles commercial real estate equity trust mutual fund would hold only commercial real estate (with no mortgages on those properties since such mortgages would entail the REIT borrowing) in Los Angeles.

All mutual fund assets will be held by third-party custodians (to be supervised by the FFA), so if Sophie buys, say, $1,237 of shares in a cash mutual fund, she will know there are literally 1,237 dollar bills (or the electronic equivalent) sitting in an account, under the control of the third-party custodian, with Sophie's name on it.

All mutual funds would be marked to market. Cash funds would obviously be valued at $1 per share and could, therefore, never break or exceed the buck. All other funds, including today's money market funds, could and would break or exceed the buck based on fluctuations in market valuations.

Owners of cash mutual funds would be free to write checks against their holdings, use debit cards to access their cash from ATM machines, and use debit cards to pay for purchases online or in stores. These cash mutual funds would thus represent the demand deposits (checking accounts) under limited purpose banking.

Obviating FDIC Insurance
and Capital Requirements

In requiring that cash mutual funds hold just cash, LPB effectively provides for 100 percent reserve requirements on checking accounts. This eliminates any need for FDIC insurance and any possibility of traditional bank runs, where people with checking and savings accounts worry about losing access to their money.

Moreover, since no bank holds any risky assets apart from the value of its furniture, buildings, and land, and holds no debts, apart from the mortgages on its property and any loans used to finance its mutual fund operations, there is no need for capital requirements. The associated loss of work will give many a bank regulator apoplexy but, again, I think they'll find good and meaningful jobs with the FFA.

In pointing out that we can eliminate essentially the entire financial regulatory system and do just fine with a single regulator, the Federal Financial Authority, I don't mean to sound as though I'm bashing financial regulators. In the current financial environment, their job is critical, and even though they performed it miserably of late, primarily due to political interference, they have, as a group, served the nation extremely well over the years.

Cash Mutual Funds and Narrow Banking

One hundred percent reserve requirements on checking and other accounts subject to immediate demand was, by the way, advocated under the heading *Narrow Banking* by Irving Fisher, Henry Simons, and Frank Knight in the 1930s and endorsed by Nobel Laureate Milton Friedman, Robert Litan, and other economists in the postwar era.[5] Simons and seven of his colleagues at the University of Chicago developed a specific narrow banking plan, called the Chicago Plan, which they presented to Congress for its consideration. Yale's Irving Fisher was sufficiently intent on narrow banking that he wrote a book on the subject entitled *100% Money*.[6]

Fisher and Keynes were the worlds' leading economists of their day. The world listened to Keynes, but ignored Fisher, who had famously assured the world on the eve of the 1929 crash that the stock market was still looking good.[7] I think it's fair to say that in recent years, narrow banking has been viewed by the economics profession as something of a crackpot proposal. It seems to undermine the ability of the banking system to provide liquidity insurance via maturity transformation à la the Diamond-Dybvig model discussed above. And its ability, discussed below, to provide the government more control of the money supply is viewed suspiciously by Keynesian economists, like Paul Krugman, who advocate using fiscal rather than monetary policy to influence the economy's performance. These economists likely view narrow banking as a policy that would permit monetarist economists (of whom Milton Friedman was the most prominent) to focus attention on the wrong set of macroeconomic tools.

Finally, narrow banking, like limited purpose banking, places limits on banking behavior, and any interference in free markets goes against the grain of economists who spend years studying the ability of un-fettered competition to improve economic well-being and learning to measure what's called *excess burden*—the economic costs arising from the government's interference in the market, whether via regulation, taxation, or subsidization.

I'm neither a Keynesian nor a Monetarist economist. I think both schools of thought are outdated and miss the fundamental source of macroeconomic instability, namely multiple equilibria associated with coordination failures. But I also think that there is no single right model of the economy, and that both old-timer Keynesians, including Krugman, and Monetarists have something to teach us about today's economy. Finally, I think we economists become enraptured all too quickly by particular mathematical models of the economy, because of their elegance, and, as a consequence, end up waging silly doctrinal fights.

All this said, I want to be clear that I'm not an advocate of narrow banking in of itself. Narrow banking is a small feature of limited purpose banking and would hardly suffice to deal with today's multifaceted financial problems. The problem is not that banks are borrowing just from those with FDIC-insured deposits and then gambling, at our po-tential expense, with simply those borrowed funds. The problem is that banks are *also* borrowing from many other lenders (including sovereign nations) whose loans are implicitly guaranteed by our government because the banks individually or as a group are too big to fail.

The "too big to fail" problem references another elegant strand in economic theory and modeling, namely the economics of moral hazard and the optimal design of private and social insurance contracts.[8] I view limited purpose banking from these headlights. It's not a proposal to restrain free financial trade with all the excess burden such a policy would entail. It's the opposite. It's a proposal to resolve market failure, and moral hazard is a form of market failure arising from incomplete information, in this case our inability to easily monitor people like Joseph Cassano.

One doesn't need to denigrate the deep insights in the Diamond-Dybvig's model to also realize that: (a) it is a model of insurance that critically relies on a re-insurer, namely the government, doing something it can't do and, in point of fact, doesn't claim to do, namely provide real as opposed to nominal deposit insurance; (b) it ignores the moral hazard problem arising from the government re-insurance of liquidity risk; and (c) it suggests there are no other effective means of providing liquidity to lenders than telling them they can get their money back on the spot and to the penny at any time and under any circumstance.

Regaining Control of the Money Supply

A by-product of 100 percent-reserved checking accounts is that the government would gain full control of the M1 money supply. M1 is the sum of currency held by the public (money tucked in our pant pockets or, these days, hidden under our pillows) and our checking account balances. Under LPB, M1 would equal the sum of currency plus our cash mutual fund balances (i.e., our LPB checking accounts).

Since the government prints every dollar of currency in the economy and since each of those dollars would either reside, at any point in time, in our own physical possession or in a third-party custodian's physical possession (as custodied securities of the cash mutual funds), the sum of the currency printed would equal the sum of our own physical holdings plus the value of our cash mutual fund shares, which exactly equals the custodians' holdings.

Under LPB, since M1 is currency plus the value of the holdings of the never-break-or-exceed-a-buck cash mutual funds, M1 corresponds to precisely what the government has printed. Thus, under LPB, the government has direct control of M1.

This is far from true under the current system. Currently, the government has only indirect control of the money supply because the extent to which checking account balances are created depend in large part on the *money multiplier*, which is ultimately determined by the banking system. When the banking system contracts its lending, the amount of checking account balances in the financial system declines as borrowers deposit less money into their checking accounts for the simple reason that they've chosen to borrow less or have been able to borrow less and just don't have as much to deposit.

So when the banks stop lending, M1 shrinks, as does the ratio of M1 to the amount of money originally printed by Uncle Sam, which is what we call the money multiplier. During our current financial crisis, the M1 multiplier declined from 1.6 to 0.9, although it now appears to be heading back up.

Milton Friedman and Anna Schwartz argued strongly that the cause of the Great Depression was the collapse of M1 as opposed to, for example, the economy's flipping from a good to a bad equilibrium. In their view, there is a tight connection between M1 and the price level, and the contraction of M1 put downward pressure on prices, which caused the substantial deflation that arose in the early years of the Great Depression. Wages fell as well, but not as fast as prices, so the real cost of hiring labor—the real wage—rose, leading firms to lay off workers.[9]

One can question the Friedman-Schwartz view of the Great Depression, which I and many other economists strongly do, but my goal here is not to debate the origins of the Great Depression. My point is that under limited purpose banking, M1 would be fully determined by the government, so that the Friedman-Schwartz concern about the government losing control of the money supply and, thus, the economy's price level and performance, *to the extent that it's valid*, would not arise.

Incidentally, Schwartz's reading of the cause of the current Great Recession—that it was due, in large part to non-disclosure, is, in my view, spot on.[10] Here is a snippet of her July 25, 2009 *New York Times* column on the reappointment of Ben Bernanke to a second term as Fed chairman.

> Last year, when the credit market became dysfunctional and normal channels for borrowing broke down, the Fed misread the situation. It persisted in believing that the market needed more liquidity, even though this was not a solution to the market disturbances. The real problem was that because of the mysterious new instruments that investors had acquired, no one knew which firms were solvent or what assets were worth. At the same time, these new instruments were being repriced in the market. The firms that owned them then needed to restore their depleted capital. When big firms experienced enormous losses, the Fed did not respond in a way that calmed markets. Most of all, Mr. Bernanke ultimately failed to convince the market that the Fed had a plan, and was not performing ad hoc.

I think Schwartz is a bit tough on Bernanke and by implication, Paulson, who were in the economic fights of their lives. But this crisis wasn't caused by people deciding overnight and for no reason that they no longer wanted to lend. It was caused by large financial companies collapsing because their lenders realized they were being cheated and decided that enough was enough. Had the Fed and Treasury required immediate and minute disclosure of all companies' financial assets and liabilities and organized their independent rating, verification, and custody, the same people who realized they were being cheated would have realized it was once again safe to lend (purchase paper) because they could see what they were buying.

Insurance Mutual Funds

What's the role of insurance companies under limited purpose banking? This is a good question because the difference between financial securities and insurance policies is simply a matter of words. Today we can purchase financial securities that insure us against the stock market crashing, the dollar falling, the price of oil rising, and company X's bond defaulting (via the CDSs mentioned above).

Given that today's insurance companies are fundamentally engaging in the same business as today's banks, insurance companies would be considered banks under limited purpose banking. And like all banks under limited purpose banking, they would be free to market mutual funds of their choosing. But the mutual funds that insurers would issue would be somewhat different from conventional mutual funds. The first reason is that their purchasers would collect payment contingent on personal outcomes and decisions as well as economy-wide conditions. The second reason is the insurance mutual funds would be closed-end mutual funds, with no new issues (claims to the fund) to be sold once the fund had launched.

Illustrating a Life Insurance Mutual Fund

Take, for example, a three-month closed-end life insurance mutual fund marketed by a financial company called Die with Us First Bank to males age 50 to 55. Let's assume the fund closes on January 1, 2011, meaning males in this age bracket can buy shares up to that date. Like all other limited purpose banking mutual funds, FBH would be required to custody its securities. In this case, FBH would simply hold every dollar contributed to the fund (spent on shares) in three-month Treasury bills.

At the end of three months, the pot (the principal plus interest on the Treasuries less the fee paid to fund managers) would be paid out to all those who died in proportion to the number of shares they purchased. Shareholders who don't die collect nothing. Now clearly, the dead can't literally receive payments, but their heirs can, so when I say the decedents collect, I really mean their estates.

There are two important points to convey right off the bat. If Arthur and Edward both die, but Arthur bought twice the number of shares as Edward, Arthur collects twice as much as Edward. So the way to buy more insurance under LPB is simply to buy more insurance mutual funds shares.

Second, once the fund closes the size of the pot is given, so other things equal, the more shareholders who kick the bucket, the less any decedent will collect. Thus, insurance mutual funds have a natural firewall, given by the size of the pot, when it comes to what they have to pay out. The firewall is the pot. What's in the pot is everything that's available to distribute, and not a penny more. All investors in the mutual fund will realize that no one is going to add to the pot after the fact, particularly not taxpayers.

As I'll discuss momentarily, LPB insurance mutual funds can help society allocate aggregate risk, but limited purpose banking doesn't pretend to be able to eliminate aggregate risk. In other words, unlike our current system, it doesn't pretend to be able to insure the uninsurable, which represents a standing invitation for another financial disaster.

Insuring the Uninsurable—A Life Insurance Example

Today, when you purchase a life insurance policy for, say, $2 million, you're told that you'll be paid the $2 million if you die regardless of how many other people die. If you push life insurance executives on this point, they'll point to the state guarantee funds backing their promises. When you tell them these funds are peanuts, the execs will tell you that the industry manages aggregate mortality risk (the risk more people die than expected) by selling both life insurance and annuity policies. Annuities pay off based on how long people live, whereas life insurance pays off based on how quickly people die. So if the death rate rises, what the insurance companies lose on their life insurance policies, they'll make up on their annuity policies, which is why they pool together the premiums from both insurances businesses into what they call their general reserve.

This "logic" breaks down once you consider the fact that the people who buy life insurance are younger than those who buy annuities, and that we can simultaneously experience a disease, like AIDs, that kills the young, and find a cure for cancer that preserves the old.

This inability to perfectly hedge is, by the way, anything but unique to insurance companies. Well over 1,000 hedge funds have closed during the current crisis because their hedges were far from perfect. Back in 1998, the mother of all hedge fund failures Long-Term Capital Management (LTCM), showed us how much could be lost overnight, in this case \$4.6 billion—when a bank borrows huge sums to arbitrage market "mistakes" only to find that things that aren't supposed to happen just happen to happen.[11]

In this case, Russia was not supposed to default on its debt and trigger concern that the nation's largest hedge fund, LTCM, might fail, not because LTCM was invested in Russian bonds, but because if Russia's default caused people to think LTCM would fail, LTCM would fail. LCTM, you see, was short 30-year Treasury bonds and long $29^3/_4$-year Treasury bonds. LTCM took this position because it thought the price differentials between the two bonds would narrow and the fund would make a killing.

But the "on-the-run" 30-year Treasury bonds are more liquid that the "off-the-run" $29^3/_4$-year bonds for reasons that defy economic logic. And when there is a panic, the prices of on-the-run bonds rise relative to the prices of off-the-run bonds. This is what happened. Russia's default triggered a panic, but not about Russia. It was a panic that LTCM would collapse and bring down the financial markets. This panic led to an increase in the liquidity premium, which led to huge LTCM losses, which led to LTCM's collapse.

This is the ultimate financial irony. LTCM was looking at all the financial risks in the marketplace except its exposure to itself. And in the end, we had LTCM effectively causing its own collapse. The episode is a lovely example of multiple equilibria. Russia's default, per se, was immaterial. It was simply a sunspot that triggered a panic that was rational because it was based on a self-fulfilling financial prophecy.

LTCM's failure is minor by today's standards, but it rocked the socks off of Wall Street at the time—requiring the New York Fed to effectively order the Street to clean up LTCM's mess or face a major financial collapse. Interestingly, John Meriwether and a number of other LTCM partners moved on to start up a new hedge fund, which recently closed after losing 44 percent of its investors' money in the current crisis.[12]

Is there a deadly disease on the horizon today that might outfox life insurance company hedging strategies by differentially killing off the young? Well, yes. There is our current outbreak of swine flu, which the World Health Organization (WHO) declared, in early July 2009, to be a level 6 world pandemic after it had stricken some 29,000 people worldwide. This was WHO's first such declaration in 41 years, with level

6 being WHO's highest alert. And the disease does have a much higher mortality rate for those below age 65.[13]

The Financial Risk of Swine Flu

To date, the death rate from the swine flu has been moderate, and a new vaccine has been developed, so there is good reason to hope that we'll survive this disease relatively intact. But I want to assume the opposite for purposes of illustrating how the current financial system would deal with a really terrible outbreak of swine flu versus how limited purpose banking would respond. My point is that such an outbreak would not only kill large numbers of us. It would also kill our financial system given the way it's now structured.

The swine flu virus, depending on its strain, can be a pretty nasty bug. The 1918 swine flu pandemic killed at least 20 million, likely killed 50 million, and possibly killed 100 million people worldwide.[14] It killed more people than the bubonic plague (the Black Death) claimed when it struck between 1347 and 1351.[15] Worldwide, the mortality rate from the 1918 influenza appears to have been at least 2.5 percent. In comparison, the current U.S. mortality rate is 0.8 percent. So if you add 2.5 to 0.8, you see that swine flu could quadruple our death rate.

If swine flu deaths were concentrated among the very young and very old, both populations of which hold little or no life insurance, there would be little or no impact on the life insurance industry. But let's assume that the deaths were concentrated among those ages 35 to 70, who hold the bulk of life insurance policies. With enough swine flu killing large numbers of this population, we could find that the U.S. life insurance industry is short trillions of dollars in reserves.

Currently, there is $19.5 trillion of life insurance in force in the United States; in other words, were every American who is insured either via an individual or group (employer-provided) policy to drop dead, say in the course of a couple of weeks, American life insurance companies would need to immediately come up with $19.5 trillion.[16] But the life insurance industry only holds $1.1 trillion in reserves.[17]

Now even the worst-case swine flu scenario wouldn't wipe out all Americans with life insurance policies, but this thought experiment helps concentrate the mind and sensitize us to the industry's insuring of the uninsurable. In fact, the industry's reserves would be wiped out were only 5.6 percent of its insureds to die within a short period of time.[18] But it also would surely be wiped out by an even smaller death rate for two reasons.

First, much of the $1.1 trillion in reserves are reserves not to cover life insurance, but to cover the cash surrender values of whole life and similar policies.[19] The folks owning these whole life policies aren't going to be very keen on having what amounts to their savings accounts being used to cover someone else's death benefits. Second, life insurance reserves are generally invested in liquid assets, with the largest single holding being corporate bonds. But were the life insurance industry to need to cash out its holdings quickly, the sale of its securities into the market would depress corporate bond and other asset prices, meaning the industry would net less than $1.1 trillion in actual cash available to pay dead claimants.

The life insurance industry says their models incorporate the possibility of a bad outbreak of swine flu and that they could withstand such an occurrence with no or little sweat.[20] But if you probe, you find out the industry is counting on kids and oldsters to succumb to the disease, not their middle-aged clients. You'll also hear the industry say that if the middle-age death rate is high enough to bring down the life insurance industry, we'll have other things to worry about than insurance company failures. That's true, but it's precisely in such a dire situation that we wouldn't want to have to deal with a financial crisis that runs like the following scenario.

The public gets wind that the life insurance companies can't cover their obligations. There is a run on the $3 trillion cash surrender value of the industry. As "insurer of last resort," Uncle Sam steps in and prints trillions to cover not just the withdrawals, but the policy claims themselves. The public starts to worry about inflation and the safety of the banks. Dollars become hot potatoes. Inflation starts to skyrocket. The public begins to withdraw its checking and savings account balances in cash as sellers stop taking checks, which take days to clear—days during which prices can soar. Alternatively, the public starts using its debit cards to buy physical things, which will retain their values. The sellers of such items do the same the instant the receipt from the sale hits their banking accounts. But if it takes several days to get access to the proceeds of one's sales,[21] sellers will refuse to let customers use debit cards and simply request cash on the barrel, or, put more accurately, barrels of cash.

As the public starts taking its deposits out of the banks, the FDIC finds itself short some $6 trillion to cover its own guarantees. Uncle Sam prints an extra $6 trillion to meet its insurance commitments. This sparks even more inflation. The dollar plunges, and the Chinese, disgusted by their capital losses, start dumping their U.S. assets, which drives interest rates through the roof and U.S. stock prices down the tubes, which reduces asset values of U.S. banks and other companies, triggering massive additional money creation to cover what, in the summer of 2009 the FDIC calculated as $13.9 trillion in total new Treasury guarantee commitments, and . . . well, you get the picture.[22] It's Argentina, here we come!

This would never happen under LPS.

And, to be clear, it may never happen under the current system because the requisite triggering events may never occur. But as the fiduciary of our economy, the government needs to worry about such "black swan" events, the rare, not-to-be-believed, the absolutely-will-never-happen, the not-to-worry, the don't-be-silly, the you're-being-incredibly-naïve events like the one we are—guess what—experiencing right now.[23]

LPB Life Insurance Mutual Funds and Tontines

If *Die with Us First Bank*'s life insurance mutual fund has a familiar ring to it, you have probably heard of the tontine, which was invented by Lorenzo de Tonti. Born in Naples, de Tonti moved to France, where he started the first tontine in 1653.[24] Tontines were used to pool longevity risk. Participants would put money into the tontine, which would be invested on their behalf. Over time, those participants who continued to live would receive income and/or principal payments based on the tontine's investments, while those who died would receive nothing.

Although the French and British government initially used the sale of tontines to raise funds, tontines were not subject to any disclosure or third-party custodial supervision, so many were used to scam the public. This is not a statement about the tontine structure, which is simply a straightforward means of pooling longevity risks among people. It's a statement about the regulatory system, specifically a failure of government to provide a critical public good—the public disclosure, verification, custody assurance, rating, and, no doubt, rule of law that's needed to let securities markets operate.

But the key lessons here are that tontines are insurance mutual funds, and that such funds have been around for well over three centuries. In fact, when the New York Stock Exchange was established under a buttonwood tree in 1792, the Tontine Coffee House, located on the corner of Wall and Water Streets was chosen as the Exchange's first physical exchange.[25] A life insurance mutual fund is simply running a reverse tontine—paying the pot to those contributors who die, rather than to those who live. Under LPB banks would market not just life insurance mutual funds, but also longevity mutual funds (actual tontines), as well as a host of other tontine-type insurance funds.

Illustrating Other Types of Insurance Mutual Funds

Let me provide four more examples of LPB insurance mutual funds to give you the full flavor of the new financial products that can be safely developed and provided to the public via limited purpose banking. Indeed, limited purpose banking seems the perfect means for implementing the financial innovation advocated by Yale economist Robert Shiller in his book *The New Financial Order*.

The first example is using insurance mutual funds to construct a tranched CDO. The second is using insurance mutual funds to buy or sell credit default swaps. The third is using insurance mutual funds to share aggregate mortality risk. And the fourth is using insurance mutual funds to organize homeowners insurance.

The first example is one you've already seen. As noted in Chapter 2, a tranched CDO is effectively a mutual fund in which investors make agreements to differentially share the risks of their collective investments. This example illustrates a critical point about LPB, namely that it allows different people to take on different amounts of risk not only by purchasing different types of LPB funds, but by also taking (buying) different positions within a given LPB fund.

As we saw with the Robinson Crusoe example, leverage is one way to raise your risk exposure. It's not the only way. You can also just invest in more risky things, like using your own (unborrowed) coconuts to lure sea crocodiles onto your island and then fighting it out to see who eats whom. But the tranched CDO mutual fund example is, in fact, an example of those holding the lower tranches taking riskier positions by leveraging themselves via-à-vis those holding higher tranches.

LPB Lets Us Leverage Us, But Not Our Countrymen

To see the leveraging that's possible with an LPB mutual fund in an even simpler setting, consider a one-year, closed-end mutual fund where the asset purchased by the fund yields a zero return half the time and a 100 percent return the other half. Suppose that 30 people invest $1,000 in the fund on the basis of receiving $1,033.33 no matter what, while one person, Sandy, invests $1,000 understanding she'll receive zero when the return is zero and $31,000 ($62,000 less $31,000) if the return is 100 percent. Sandy is leveraged 30 to 1. Sandy has, in effect, borrowed $30,000 from the other fund members and promised to pay a 3.333 percent interest rate on the $30,000 she's borrowed. With the $30,000 that's been borrowed and her own $1,000 invested in this risky security, she can end up at the end of the period with either $31,000, on which she has to pay out $31,000, or $62,000, on which she has to pay out $31,000.

The key point is that what happens in Vegas stays in Vegas. Sandy and her co-investors put all their money out on the table (i.e., in the fund), jointly decide how to invest it, and also decide how to spread the winnings or losses. There are no third parties involved, so the mutual fund owes no money to any external party. This provides a natural financial firewall. The fund can lose all its assets, but nothing more. Its failure hurts its members, but doesn't infect others, financially speaking. To make this work effectively, there must be very simple and transparent rules that make it crystal clear how the fund's investment proceeds, both principal and return, are to be distributed under all circumstances. The tranched CDO has very clear and simple sharing rules. (Again, what wasn't clear, but what the FFA would make clear, was what mortgages the CDOs were actually buying.) Any mutual fund with complex sharing rules would have that fact publicly disclosed by the FFA, which would say, "This fund's rules for sharing investment proceeds among its shareholders are complex, making its purchase potentially highly risky." Every LPB mutual fund prospectus would be limited to one page. If Joe Six Pack isn't able to understand it, the FFA's disclosure would make that very clear. And the independent rating companies would presumably downgrade funds with complicated sharing rules. If there is one thing we have learned over the years, it's that financial complexity and financial fraud go hand-in-hand. The hallmark of LPB would be simplicity and transparency. If that means fewer financial products arise in the marketplace, so be it. It's imperative that Joe Six Pack knows what he's buying when he goes to the financial store. Part-and-parcel of transparency is limiting the discretion of mutual fund managers in investing fund assets. Funds that seek wide latitude with respect to the range of their investments and their ability to flip/time their investments would have to make that clear in their one-page prospectus. And the FFA would make it clear that "this fund is potentially highly risky, not only because of the nature of its investments, but also because of the latitude it gives fund management in switching investments."

One final point about mutual funds and their ability to permit shareholders to take on different degrees of leverage: This is not just a hypothetical possibility. Mutual funds have been around since 1924 and were formally regulated starting in 1940 with the passage of the Investment Company Act of 1940.[26] There are, as repeatedly stressed, a plethora of different types of mutual funds selling many different types of investments. Some of the funds on the market today issue preferred as well as common stock, and the preferred shareholders can be viewed as lending to the common shareholders in exchange for a more secure return on the fund's investments. As a formal matter, then, mutual funds in which their shareholders leverage vis-à-vis each other already exist.

Using Insurance Mutual Funds to Buy and Sell CDSs

Credit default swaps (CDSs) have gotten lots of bad press during the course of the financial crisis, but they themselves are not the problem.

They represent a means of people sharing risks by placing bets about economic outcomes, like IBM going bust and defaulting on its debt.

Norma, a marketing manager working for IBM, may well want to purchase insurance against that happening because Norma realizes that if IBM gets into trouble and defaults on its bonds, she'll likely be out of a job. Buying a CDS that insures Norma against the default on IBM bonds thus provides her with a hedge against the risk of lower future labor earnings. The reason is that as IBM gets into hotter water, the market value of Norma's CDS rises.

People who work for other companies in completely different industries, say an Exxon-Mobile engineer, Dan, may be willing to sell insurance against IBM's defaulting because Dan realizes that he stands to make money if IBM doesn't default and if it does, well, he'll lose money but not his job.

Insurance mutual funds handle CDS purchases and sales in a very straightforward manner with an airtight firewall. Take a credit default swap sold by Go for It Now Bank via its IBM-Defaults-in-2012 mutual fund. Purchasers would specify in advance if they want to get paid off if IBM defaults or the opposite. So Norma would put in her money in the fund on the basis of IBM defaulting on any of its debt in 2012. Dan would buy shares in the fund on the basis of IBM not defaulting over the course of the year. All money put into the fund by, say, January 1, 2011, would be invested in one-year T-bills and, at the end of the year, the pot will be paid out to the winners in proportion to their share holdings.

Note that there is no counterparty risk here. Dan's money is on the table. Norma's money is on the table. The money's held by a third-party custodian in the Treasuries. If IBM goes under, Norma gets paid off by Dan, no questions asked. If IBM stays afloat, the opposite is true. In contrast, under the current system, if IBM goes under and Dan stands for an AIG, well, the money's not on the table. It's been invested in some risky venture or paid out to AIG executives, and Norma is forced to turn to Uncle Sam to cover her claim.

Sharing Aggregate Risk

In describing the life insurance mutual fund, I indicated that the more fund shareholders who die over the duration of the fund, the less that's

paid out to any decedent. So if we have, for example, a terrible outbreak
of swine flu, there will be this aggregate risk, which the economy
must bear and which is not hedged by the life insurance mutual fund I
described.

Note that with LPB, life insurance and similar insurance mutual
funds that depend on individual outcomes would likely evolve to be
very large in size (have lots of shareholders) to improve diversification and
ensure that any risks that are not hedged out are, in fact, aggregate risks.

But the fact that the simple life insurance mutual fund I described doesn't cover aggregate mortality risk doesn't mean mutual funds
wouldn't arise that move this risk from people who are less able to bear
it to people who are more willing to bear it. In other words, we can't
eliminate aggregate risk—we can't insure the uninsurable—but we can
make sure that aggregate risk is borne by those who are best suited to
do so.

Under LPB, allocating aggregate mortality risk, or any aggregate risk
for that matter, is simple. You just set up a closed-end insurance mutual
fund where the shareholders place bets on the aggregate risk in question.
Thus, Mortality Is Our Middle Name Bank could set up, say, a one-year
aggregate mortality insurance fund that closes on a fixed date, pays out
a year later, and lets shareholders invest based on whether the economy-
wide mortality rate exceeds or is below the government's forecasted level.
Younger households would likely want to bet on mortality exceeding
this level, because if it does and they die, their life insurance mutual funds
will likely pay off less than they'd hoped. Older households would likely
want to bet on mortality ending up below the forecast rate because in
that outcome, their longevity insurance mutual fund holdings will do
worse than they'd hoped.

Note that there is nothing special about mortality. It's just one
economy-wide outcome. LPB insurance funds could help people allocate risks associated with GDP growth, changes in the nation's unemployment rate, changes in interest rates, changes in inflation, changes
in the stock market, changes in national or regional house prices—you
name it. There are many existing mutual funds that help us with these
aggregate risk allocation issues. But one of the beauties of LPB is that
it keeps things simple. Everyone should be able to quickly grasp what it
means to bet on the unemployment rate rising above 12 percent between
now and the end of the year if it's currently 10 percent.

Parimutuel Betting and Insurance Mutual Funds

If the IBM defaults fund and aggregate mortality rate fund sound to you like parimutuel betting at the racetrack, you're right. Parimutuel horse race betting dates to 1867, when it was devised by the Catalan Joseph Oller, while living in France.[27] An avid cockfighter and a professional bookmaker, Oller introduced his method of betting at the French race-tracks. In 1874 he spent 15 days in the slammer for illegal gambling. But in 1891, the French government accepted his method of racetrack betting, and his system soon spread around the world.

If you call IBM defaults (or mortality is lower than expected) horse A and IBM doesn't default (mortality is higher than expected) horse B, what we have is a horse race in which money is paid at the gate and at the end of the race, those who bet on the winning horse collect the pot.

Clearly, horse racing is a form of gambling and my drawing the connection between LPB insurance funds and horse racing runs the risk of readers thinking I'm advocating gambling. I'm not. The difference between gambling and insurance is that the former entails placing bets that leave one more exposed to risk, while the later is placing bets that hedge other gambles and thus leave one more exposed to a particular risk, but less exposed to risk in general. When Norma works for IBM, she's taking a gamble on IBM's longevity with respect to her own future labor earnings. By buying shares of the IBM defaults insurance mutual fund, Norma hedges that risk. She uses one bet to mitigate the adverse effects of another.

I'd also define gambling as taking on risks at unfavorable odds because the commissions being charged for running the betting are so high. This is why spending a weekend at Las Vegas is viewed by economists as eco-nomically insane. It's one thing to invest money in, say, the stock market via a mutual fund that invests in a stock index fund at very low costs. It's another thing to invest in the roulette wheel at the Hooters Casino Hotel on the Vegas Strip when your expected return from playing the game is negative, notwithstanding the potentially exciting distractions.

Betting on More than One Horse/Mortality Rate

There are many different ways to bet at the races. The types of bets include Win, Place, Show, Quinella, Exacta, Trifecta, Superfecta, and

Boxing Bets. I know this in theory—from reading up on racetrack betting. In practice, I have yet to go to the races. But now that I've written this book, I'm ready to give it a shot.

The Quinella bet is the only one I want to put in your brain. It entails betting on one of two horses, say Queen of Sheba and King of Hearts,[28] coming in first or second, regardless of which order that occurs. Now suppose you want to be protected against the aggregate mortality rate exceeding 2 percent, but you want to be even more protected if it exceeds 5 percent. And let's treat Queen of Sheba as a mortality rate arising that ranges from 2 to 5 percent and King of Hearts as a mortality rate that comes in above 5 percent. Then if you bet Quinella on these two horses in the aggregate mortality horse race mutual fund and also place a separate bet on King of Hearts, you'll win some money if the rate is between 2 and 5 percent and even more money if the rate is above 5 percent.

And the point is?

The point is that you may want to buy some aggregate mortality risk protection for small outbreaks of the swine flu, but more protection for large outbreaks. And insurance mutual funds would arise that permit you to do so by investing on both a Quinella and straight-bet basis, as well as in many other forms.

Illustrating a Homeowner's Insurance Mutual Fund

My final example of an insurance mutual fund is a six-month homeowner's insurance policy sold by the First and Last Bank of Homes. Purchasers of this fund would buy their shares by January 1, 2011, but collect on May 30, 2011, only if they experience a fire, flood, robbery, or some other loss to their homes. This mutual fund's payoff is a bit more complicated because it depends not just on how much each shareholder contributes to the fund and whether or not he or she experiences a loss, but also on the size of that loss.

Specifically, each dollar of loss would be multiplied (weighted) by the number of shares of the shareholder experiencing the loss. This would establish the number of loss shares for the shareholder. The sum of all loss shares would be divided into the total pot available to be paid out on May 30, 2011. This would establish a payment per loss share for those experiencing losses. The payoff to anyone experiencing a loss would simply equal this amount times her number of loss shares.

Note that this payoff formula means that if two people, Joe and Sally, buy the same number of shares, but Joe's loss is twice Sally's, Joe's recovery will be twice as large as Sally's. In addition, if two people, Fred and Mark, have the same loss, but Fred purchases twice the number of shares that Mark buys, Fred's recovery will be twice as large. Hence, limited purpose banking permits people to buy as much insurance coverage as they'd like.

Helping Solve the Corporate Governance Problem

One of the major problems with today's financial system is that there is no clear way for shareholders of banks to measure any given banker's performance. Under limited purpose banking, the returns on the mutual funds provide clear evidence of how the bankers are performing. With LPB, bankers will move from "managing risk" to managing mutual funds. And whether their funds are open-end or closed-end funds, they will be marked to market by the market so that shareholders can measure how well their fund performed and compare that performance with other funds' performances. Fund managers that consistently outperform the competition will derive a reputation over time for doing so and be able to charge higher fees to shareholders.

The Federal Financial Authority would play a role in ensuring that fund statements provided clear and uniform disclosure of all fees so that investors would be able to understand immediately what they are being charged for the services being delivered. In my view, there are far too many fees charged by mutual funds today, and they are far too hard to follow.

Relationship of Limited Purpose Banking
to Glass-Steagall

The Glass-Steagall Act of 1933 established good-guy commercial banks, to be regulated and overseen by the FDIC, and bad-guy investment banks, who were free to do more or less whatever they wanted, but had no recourse to rescue by Uncle Sam. When Glass-Steagall was effectively repealed in 1999 by the Gramm-Leach-Bliley Act, it told good-guy banks they could do what bad-guy banks were doing, and they did. They started setting up structured investment vehicles, trading in fraudulent CDOs, and increasing their effective levels of leverage.

Some students of the financial crisis, including former Federal Reserve Chairman Paul Volcker, think we should just reenact Glass-Steagall and let the shadow-banking-bad-boy-system do its risky thing and let it fail if it fails.[29] But having seen the interconnected nature of counterparty relationships between commercial and investment banks, let alone the insurance industry, this is clearly a nonstarter. Lehman Brothers was Henry Paulson's attempt to see if a Glass-Steagall-type, tough-love policy would work. It didn't; it blew up in his face. Within a couple of days he was literally begging politicians to give him a huge war chest to rescue our financial house of cards.

If we reenact Glass-Steagall, the nonbank/shadow bank/investment bank industry will have a competitive advantage because they would implicitly be getting lender-of-last-resort protection by Uncle Sam without having to pay for it. This would lead the regular banking system to yell foul and push and pay for deregulation, leading us right back to where we are today.

The reality is that with today's financial instruments, there is no way to tell one financial enterprise from another. We need a common set of modern and very simple rules to govern all financial companies, which is precisely what LPB and the FFA would provide.[30]

Isn't LPB Simply Imposing 100 Percent Capital Requirements?

The answer is yes and no. Under limited purpose banking the banks are themselves simply financial intermediaries, while their mutual funds represent mini-banks, if you like, all of which are subject to 100 percent capital requirements. Mutual funds permit different shareholders to take more or less risky positions and, in that sense, leverage and deleverage one another. But the mutual funds themselves cannot borrow. Hence, every dollar the mutual funds own corresponds to a dollar of mutual fund shareholder's equity, hence the implied 100 percent capital requirement.

But if this is the case, why not just place 100 percent capital requirements on the banks and call it quits? Why force them to become mutual funds? Well, there is a lot more to LPB than simply 100 percent capital requirements. To see this, let's consider the various steps we'd need to take to transform Citigroup into a financial institution with the same characteristics as a large set of mutual funds under LPB.

To begin, we'd want to separate out and sell off Citigroup's investment banking business, by which I mean the group that helps take companies public; helps companies acquire new assets, including new companies; helps arrange mergers; and helps companies float debt. This investment banking business would have to stick to intermediating. Because it's not a mutual fund, it would not be allowed to either hold assets or borrow to buy assets. It would be a consulting company pure and simple. Hence, investment managers would no longer be allowed to invest, not their own money, but their shareholders' capital in these securities, and then turn to the market and claim, "See how good these securities are? We're holding large chunks of them ourselves."

Next we'd separate out and sell off Citigroup's trading business and require that it run without ever operating with open positions. Under LPB, trading would occur only via electronic exchanges that do not entail any exposure by the brokerage firm at any time. The brokerage arm of Citigroup is first and foremost a financial intermediary, and under LPB it would need to stick to its knitting. It would not be permitted to acquire assets or liabilities on its own account. It would simply connect buyers and sellers of securities and organize the secure and simultaneous transfer of money for the security in question. The FFA would need to supervise these arrangements to ensure that trades clear with absolutely no exposure to the brokerage firms.

Step three is dealing with the remaining Citigroup's business, namely asset management. Here we'd need to swap all of Citigroup debt for equity and prevent it from ever borrowing again to fund risky investments. We can now think of Citigroup as either one huge mutual fund with lots of different assets, one big commercial bank with a 100 percent capital requirement, or one LPB bank with a large number of different mutual funds corresponding to the different Citigroup asset classes.

We'd next need to set up the FFA to disclose, verify, and independently rate each of Citigroup's asset holdings so shareholders can tell what they are actually buying in purchasing Citigroup stock. Step five is marking Citigroup's assets to market so investors can compare the overall company's valuation with the value of its parts. We don't want Citigroup shareholders to wake up from one day to the next and realize they have no idea what assets the company is holding and come to believe these assets are worthless. We don't want investors to panic and dump Citigroup shares in a mad rush for the exit. This wouldn't lead to a Citigroup default because Citigroup would have no debt. But it could lead to an uninformed meltdown

To determine a true value for Citigroup, we will need to break up and sell off the different parts of Citigroup's holding so we'll have market-determined prices of the components. Otherwise, we'll be forced to take Citigroup's word for what its particular assets would sell for on the market. And we know how good Citigroup's word is.

This last step left us with a large number of small companies holding specific assets. They sound like, and indeed are, the individual mutual funds that arise under limited purpose banking. Finally, we'd need to make sure that no assets purchased by these Citigroup minis or arrangements to divide the proceeds of these assets to the shareholders of the Citigroup minis creates any claims that ever collectively exceed the value of the assets held by the minis. So the Citigroup minis could not, for example, buy an asset that entailed the receipt of a stream of payments under normal circumstances, but requires making a very large payment under special circumstances, which could exceed the value of the minis' assets.

In other words, the Citigroup minis could not hire a Joseph Cassano to sell CDSs, which have just this property—a stream of premium receipts in normal times, but a large settlement payment when a bond defaults or some other event is triggered whose value is not conditioned on the value of the mini's assets as of the triggering date. Recall that limited purpose banking lets people go broke. But it doesn't let banks or mutual funds run by banks go broke. So it wouldn't let the Citigroup minis go broke.

The requirement that LPB funds, such as the Citigroup minis, are never leveraged can be described differently. It amounts to saying that the funds or the minis or whatever you'd like to call them can never be leveraged regardless of the time or circumstances in which they find themselves. We economists would say that the LPB funds/Citigroup minis face not just an immediate 100 percent capital requirement, but also a *state-contingent* 100 percent capital requirement.

Chapter 6

Getting from
Here to There

L imited purpose banking is radically different from leverage-based banking. Much of our financial system, namely the almost century-old mutual fund industry, is already engaged in limited purpose banking. Indeed, if one interprets the word "banking" to reference "saving and investing," limited purpose banking is one of the major components of our modern banking sector. Prior to the crash of 2008, we Americans held about $14 trillion in retirement assets, which were almost exclusively invested in mutual funds.[1] This represented over one-third of total U.S. household financial assets.[2]

For the vast majority of us who are lower or middle class, mutual fund holdings represent virtually all of our financial wealth. We place almost all of our mutual fund assets in the place we do essentially all our saving, namely in our 401(k), IRA, and other retirement accounts. The fact that we save mostly in retirement accounts is not surprising given the tax breaks they afford. But the fact that our mutual fund assets are secured by third-party custodians is very reassuring and, I believe, a major factor in the popularity of retirement account saving. Congress mandated such custodial arrangements for a good reason—saving for retirement is tough and risky enough without having to worry whether our financial middleman is going broke and using our money to pay his bills.

Robert Maxwell did precisely this in 1991. Maxwell was a British tycoon who made and lost a fortune in the newspaper and publishing industries. In the process he stole more than £400 million from his workers' pension plan. But before this fact became public, Maxwell took a cruise on his 180-foot super yacht, the *Lady Ghislaine*, and either jumped, fell, or was pushed overboard. Regardless of how he died, the bottom line is that he drowned having just sunk the retirement dreams of 32,000 of his employees.[3] Thanks to this and other pension scandals, the British have enacted much tighter regulations on employer-provided retirement plans.

The other strong statement that can be read from the financial facts is that we've been moving toward limited purpose banking over time, but clearly not fast enough. Thirty years ago mutual fund holdings represented only 14 percent of total financial assets; today's figure is 34 percent.[4] So the glass is already quite full when it comes to implementing LPB.

Of course, fully implementing limited purpose banking requires going beyond just growing the mutual fund industry. It requires shutting down leveraged-based banking and insurance operations, establishing cash and insurance mutual funds, and replacing our existing hodgepodge of financial regulators with a single regulator—the Federal Financial Authority.

Implementing Limited Purpose Banking

Implementing limited purpose banking is straightforward. All financial corporations, if not already registered as mutual fund companies, would register with the Securities and Exchange Commission and begin marketing cash and other mutual funds subject to the third-party custody and other regulatory provisions of the Investment Company Act of 1940.

Depository institutions would immediately transfer all their checking accounts into cash mutual funds and use their reserves to provide the cash to back these shares.

As of early September 2009, demand deposits totaled $425 billion.[5] The banking system was holding over $829 billion in reserves.[6] So the banks have plenty of reserves today to fully back their cash mutual funds. This was not the case in the past. In September 2007, reserves totaled only $43 billion.[7]

Today's situation is highly unusual. In normal circumstances the banks would be holding only about $42 billion in reserves against their demand deposits since the reserve requirement imposed by the Federal Reserve is only 10 percent.[8] Hence, the extra reserves—the so-called *excess reserves*—of the banking system are now huge: $766 billion to be precise, when normally they'd be close to zero.

There are two reasons the banks are holding so much in excess reserves. First, the Federal Reserve is paying them to do so. Specifically, the Fed is paying interest to the banks on their reserves as a way of secretly slipping them more money. And they surely need whatever money they can get their hands on because, as previously indicated, they appear to be collectively insolvent. The second reason is that the banks are still skittish about lending to businesses, the public, state and local governments, and each other.

Zombies and Gazelles

Since they would no longer be allowed to buy financial assets or borrow to invest in securities, banks, as broadly defined, would, over time, need to shut down their old operations by either: (a) immediately selling off their assets, paying off their liabilities, and handing the net proceeds to their shareholders, or (b) retaining their assets and liabilities and simply paying out, over time, the associated net cash flow to their shareholders.

Thus, the transition to LPB can be very gradual with respect to unwinding existing bank assets and debts, but immediate with respect to issuing and marketing new mutual funds. Banks become zombies with respect to their old, illegitimate practice—gambling at our expense—

but gazelles in exercising their new and sole legitimate purpose—intermediation.

The banks would make distributions to their shareholders by paying them dividends or by buying up (repurchasing) their shares.[9] The banks' shareholders would, in turn, use these funds to purchase mutual funds issued by the banks. That is, money would flow out of the banks to households and from households back to the mutual funds operated by the banks. There would be no net drainage of funds from the banking system and thus no shrinkage in the size of the financial sector.

Deleveraging Investment Banking and Trading

The major bank holding companies would also need to spin off their investment banking and trading operations and restructure them on a no-risk, no-leverage basis. Thus, a Goldman's investment banking branch would be confined to providing consulting and intermediation services. It would not be permitted to co-invest, let alone borrow to co-invest, in the companies or securities it is helping market to the public.

And a Goldman's trading desk would be transformed into an electronic clearing system, not one that can go belly up by borrowing to take open positions that may turn sour. Today, such leveraged trading operations can take the form of Goldman traders borrowing a particular security from some third party and promising to return it with interest at a future date. In the meantime, Goldman sells the security to some other third party for ready cash. When the time comes to hand back the borrowed security, Goldman no longer has it, so it needs to buy it on the open market. If the market price for the security rises a lot, Goldman makes a loss. Indeed, the loss is, in principle, unbounded because the price of a security can, in principle, rise to any value.

This is called "short selling." But it's just one of many ways that traders can leverage and get their banks, which ultimately means us, into trouble. Another way is to simply borrow money and lend it to clients for use by the clients in purchasing securities. These securities can plunge in value, leaving the client unable to cover his or her debt and the broker dealer/trading operation with a loss. The loss can be huge if the loan was huge.

Broker dealers/traders limit their exposure by holding onto the securities purchased by the clients until the clients repay what they borrowed. They also ask their clients to put up additional collateral, in the form of cold hard cash or highly liquid assets, like Treasury bills, to help guard against getting egg on their face. And as the securities in question start to fall in value, the broker dealers/traders require their clients to put up more collateral in what's called a *margin call*.[10]

But prices of securities can change precipitously from one millisecond to another, so there is nothing to prevent things from going south very quickly and the egg hitting with a devastating impact. Just ask Barings Bank, if you can find someone who used to work there.

An End to Rogue Trading

One by-product of restricting traders to simply matching buyers with sellers of securities and never letting them take any risk whatsoever as part of that process is that these restrictions will do away with rogue trading, which has caused eight financial tsunamis in recent years.[11] Jérôme Kerviel appears to hold the world record for such shenanigans. He single-handedly lost $7.2 billion for the 145-year-old Société Générale, which is one of France's three largest banks.

Jérôme was a junior trader earning a paltry salary by Wall Street standards. But he used techniques to exceed his trading limits that the best and the brightest at the SEC would have a hard time detecting.[12] Apparently, Jérôme wasn't primarily out to make money for himself. He just wanted to help his company and was sure he knew how best to do so.

If we maintain our current banking system, we'll surely want to post a very large financial detective squad at Société Générale as well as at every other major foreign bank around the world because, they too, have become actual or potential wards of the U.S. taxpayer. France's would-be-hero, Jérôme, lost the $7.2 billion at a rather unpropitious moment, namely in 2008. And, thanks to this loss, Société Générale was in no position to lose a lot more money, including a $11 billion insurance claim owed to it by—drumroll—good old AIG.[13]

Consequently, when Inspector Clouseau, namely the Office of Thrift Supervision, let that financial genius Joseph Cassano sell CDSs cheap and with no reserves to Société Générale, little did Clouseau know he was putting the U.S. taxpayer into bed with a French bank that had just been clobbered by one of its least assuming junior traders, Monsieur Kerviel, and was not only too big to fail, but also ready to fail if AIG went under. When Lehman went down and our Treasury saw the nuclear fallout it had thus produced, it realized it had to take over AIG and that part of doing so required having AIG immediately wire $11 billion to AIG's largest claimant, Société Générale.

If you live in say, Lawrence, Kansas, and want to follow the money, it left your pants pocket and was sent to the Treasury in the form of tax payments or purchases of new Treasury bills or bonds. Then it was sent to AIG in exchange for worthless shares. Finally, it was sent by AIG to Société Générale under the direction of your government.

Pauvre Jérôme. Had he worked for Joey Cassano, he could have run a legal immoral scam and be sitting on a beach sipping Margaritas with tens of millions of dollars in his Swiss bank account. Instead, he ran a well-meaning but illegal immoral scam, and is likely facing an extended stay in jail.

There is, however, light for Jérôme at the end of his tunnel. Once he's out, he can compare notes with Nick Leeson, who killed Barings Bank barehanded by losing $1.3 billion. Barings was founded in 1762—a long, long time ago. But all it took Nick was just one day—January 17, 1995—to fully detonate that venerable company. Nick's explosive device was a short straddle that entailed taking a huge bet that the Tokyo stock market would not drop in value from the close of the market on January 16 to its opening on January 17.

But Nick missed a black swan—the Kobe earthquake that struck Japan at 5:46 A.M., well before the Tokyo market opened sharply lower and well before Nick could sell out his position anywhere near its former price.

Nick fled Singapore, where he was based, was arrested, spent six and a half years in jail, and is now doing extremely well writing books, including: *Rogue Trader: How I Brought Down Barings Bank and Shook the Financial World*. He's also writing books on coping with stress and has recently been appointed CEO of Galway United Football Club.

Financial crime pays as long as you steal along reasonably conventional lines. And big financial crime pays big time.

The Politics of Limited Purpose Banking

At a grassroots level, LPB should garner plenty of support. The public is dying to have the financial system fixed for good. People seek a transparent, safe system, which puts a definitive end to financial crises and public bailouts. And they are increasingly frustrated by politicians who seem to be doing nothing of real substance to achieve that end.

Banks and bankers, on the other hand, will likely fight this reform tooth and nail. They'll claim LPB is naïve, radical, a nonstarter, that it relies too much on the government, and that it's going to limit credit, leverage, and financial sector returns. But what they will really worry about is their bonuses, and for good reason.

Limited purpose banking will deliver on President Obama's September 14, 2009, pledge: "We will not go back to the days of reckless behavior and unchecked excess that was at the heart of this crisis. . . . Those on Wall Street cannot resume taking risks without regard for consequences."

The trouble is that the president's own financial reform agenda cannot deliver on this pledge without having the government oversee Wall Street's every move on a literally millisecond-by-millisecond basis. That's one heck of a lot of oversight and would leave us with the worst of all worlds—a financial regime that's so tightly regulated that Wall Street can't sneeze without getting approval from Pennsylvania Avenue.

We need Wall Street to be Wall Street in the best sense of that expression. We need modern finance and financial innovation. And we can get both safely and without the heavy hand of government by implementing limited purpose banking.

Hence, the best hope for LPB may, paradoxically enough, lie with Wall Street. If Wall Street realizes that its game is up and that LPB will let bankers earn a good and honest living that exceeds what Washington is otherwise serving up, Wall Street could become LPB's biggest proponent. That's my hope—that Wall Street will consider this proposal and after ranting and raving and calling it nuts, it will reconsider and get behind it.

■   ■   ■

But my sales job, I realize, has just started, so before bringing this first pitch to an end (followed by an afterword that addresses a couple of other "minor" problems our nation faces), let me respond in the next chapter to several reactions to LPB that I've received in the course of authoring and co-authoring columns about the proposal in the months leading up to my writing this book.

As I indicated in Note 2 in the Preface, these articles have appeared in the *New Republic,* Bloomberg.com, Forbes.com, FT.com, the *Dallas Morning News,* the *Boston Globe,* the *American Interest,* and the *Financial Times.* The financial editors of each of these publications stuck their necks out and published a radical proposal without blinking an eye. To me, this was very encouraging. I've also received encouragement from some of the top financial experts and policymakers in the world and co-authored several of the columns with some of the world's leading economists. This too tells me that the plan deserves serious consideration. Finally, the interest in the proposal has been bipartisan. For example, the column in the *New Republic,* a fairly liberal publication, was co-authored with John Goodman, president of the National Center for Policy Analysis, a fairly libertarian organization. And if you examine this book's endorsements you'll see big-time liberals and conservatives literally on the same page.

Chapter 7

What About?

Today talking has a bigger payoff than listening, and for good reason. It takes the same amount of time to read or listen to a sentence as it did one hundred years ago, but it's become incredibly cheap, in terms of time, to talk—to transmit a sentence to hoards of people. E-mail, txts, tweets, blogs, web sites, Facebook, and so on—they've created a veritable Tower of Babel. As in the biblical story, we're all physically linked, but we can't understand one another. It's not that we speak different tongues. We're just too busy talking to listen.

A good example of this is the Economists' Forum on the *Financial Times* web site run by economist Martin Wolf, who is himself a major contributor.[1] The forum is, in theory, a great place for economists to exchange their views about economic policy. And in the early days of our economic fiasco, other economists and I jumped on its opportunity to share our wisdom and educate the masses—masses of other economists who we thought were listening.

At the beginning, there were only a few speakers and lots of listeners. But as more and more economists learned about the forum, more started to contribute. Suddenly there were so many entries that one needed the entire day to read them, let alone comment on them intelligently. The entries grew so rapidly that Martin could only display them for a day or two before taking them down and replacing them with new ones. So the trick became to write even more often and repeat yourself if necessary so your point of view was always on display.[2] Another strategy was to skim the latest posting and enter a comment that reworked the contributor's point into your own.

In economists' tongue, talking crowded out listening. And to further economize on the time we listened, we skimmed what others were saying because reading their minds was faster than reading their words.

Given that you're on this page, you're a great listener, for which I sincerely thank you. But in presenting limited purpose banking in other forums, even in short shrift, I've learned that listening problems are widespread.

Let me provide an example. One "reader" of my LPB article with Christophe Chamley, which appeared in the May–June 2009 issue of the *American Interest,* wrote the magazine, commenting:

> The financial system is flawed, but it certainly does not support a rebuttal of the market system. . . . It is difficult to understand how replacing the market system with a bureaucracy can improve the efficiency of the financial markets. . . . Slapping a "lack of trust" label on banking is another false generalization. Have customers been closing their accounts and fleeing banks? Is there a greater demand for currency? . . . It is a fantasy to think that we can dispense with all risk.

What I find most interesting about these comments is that I agree with them. The goal of LPB is not to rebut the market system, but to save it. But let's be clear, our financial system is not a "market system." It's replete with market failure. And, hello—it's been nationalized. Uncle Sam is writing nine out of ten mortgages; he's operating the world's largest insurance company; he owns the largest stake of several of the country's biggest banks; he's about to set pay on Wall Street; and he's gearing up to micro-manage all remaining "private" banks before they too put him over the barrel.

LPB is designed to fix the market defects so we can have highly competitive trading in financial products—products that we actually understand and trust. Trusting a financial product doesn't mean the product will yield a sure return. It means knowing what risks the product actually entails.

And yes, it is a fantasy that we can dispel all risk. But it's not my fantasy. Instead, it's the fantasy our current system is perpetuating and our government (i.e., you, me, and the "reader") is underwriting. Uncle Sam is pretending he can guarantee, *in real terms*, all manner of irresponsible private financial commitments, when he can do nothing of the kind. And had he not gone to unprecedented lengths to make the pledges he's made—by extending deposit insurance, insuring money market accounts, nationalizing Fannie, Freddie, and AIG, guaranteeing loans of Citibank and B of A, and so on—we would have seen runs on the banks and insurance companies as sure as day follows night. Those runs are still waiting to happen because the government cannot, in fact, deliver on its implicit real promises.

Finally, I agree that replacing the financial system with a bureaucracy would be a terrible mistake. LPB does the opposite. It eliminates over 115 bureaucratic regulatory agencies and replaces them with one—the Federal Financial Authority (FFA), which will have a limited set of tasks. The FFA would not rate our credit or loans. It would verify the accuracy of our credit scores and hire private, independent companies to rate our loans. And because of this, parties other than Uncle Sam will again be willing to lend to us.

Can We Just Agree to Agree?

President Obama is after us, these days, to disagree agreeably. That's a fine goal. But I think the real challenge is getting us to agree agreeably. We seem to have to argue with each other even when we're on the same page. If we could just listen to what we're each saying, without immediately putting the talker into a red or blue, left or right, liberal or conservative box, we'd find a much greater commonality of views than we think.

This applies to LPB. Those who think it's too radical should check if they aren't themselves proposing a very close cousin of this reform, but just using different words and structures to achieve the same end.

This said, let me turn to some real questions and disagreements about LPB.

Will LPB Reduce Liquidity?

No, it should enhance liquidity. All LPB mutual funds, whether closed-end or open-end, will trade on the market, and since the public will know precisely what each fund is holding, it will be much easier to buy and sell financial instruments in times of economic uncertainty. Uncertainty is the real villain when it comes to liquidity. When people don't know where the economy is headed, they become unsure of the value of their assets and very reluctant to transact out of fear that they'll do so at what will prove to be the wrong price. By securing our financial system, LPB will greatly reduce the chances of financial panic and thereby make our economy more certain and liquid.

Will LPB Reduce Credit?

No. Under the current system, lenders put money in banks, which give it to borrowers.[3] Under LPB, lenders put money in mutual funds, which give it to borrowers. The difference is that the mutual funds, having issued equity, not debt, to the lenders won't guarantee full *and real* repayment to lenders based on a pledge extorted from Uncle Sam, which Sam cannot, in fact, actually fulfill.

Having said this, I want to repeat that for people who seek safety with respect to their nominal dollar returns, LPB offers cash mutual funds as well as existing and new mutual funds that invest in U.S. Treasuries bills and bonds of specific maturities or in combinations (e.g., indexes) of different maturities. For those seeking safety with respect to their real dollar returns, there are and will be plenty more mutual funds that invest in inflation-indexed bonds (Treasury Inflation Protected Securities, or TIPS) of different maturities.

Also, there is nothing in LPB that precludes households from purchasing individual securities. These days, one can buy TIPS and other

Treasury securities directly from the Treasury at www.treasurydirect.gov. Hence, anyone concerned about securing either nominal dollars (actual dollar amounts) or real dollars (real purchasing power) for specific years in the future and can't find a mutual fund holding the right maturity, can purchase his or her preferred maturity from the Treasury directly or in the secondary market.[4]

The other key difference with respect to credit extension is that under LPB, lenders will have full and truthful information about the people to whom they are lending. This should make it easier for most people to borrow; most people are honest, and under the current system, there is no way for a lender to know if the borrower's representations are true. Indeed, given what lenders have just experienced, they have every reason to believe that borrowers, with Wall Street's help, are lying about both their ability to repay and the value of their collateral.

Who Will Lend to Business?

Both small and large companies will borrow from mutual funds. That is, they will go to a bank and apply for a loan. The bank will have the loan processed by the FFA and then auction it off to mutual funds specializing in small business loans if the company is small, and large business loans if the company is large.

By the way, requiring banks to auction off, on the web, the loans they initiate, be they commercial or private (as in mortgages), will guarantee that borrowers get the lowest available interest rates. This is an important form of borrower protection that doesn't exist within the current system.

Will LPB Reduce Leverage?

Yes and no. LPB will keep banks from leveraging the public without its knowledge or approval. But it won't impose limits on leverage undertaken between consenting adults. As discussed, mutual funds can be, and in some cases already are, structured to allow shareholders to leverage themselves up or down relative to one another using common and preferred shares and other techniques. Indeed, as we've seen, tranched CMOs and CDOs are mutual funds that offer various degrees of leverage to investors via their selection of the tranche they wish to hold.

Will LPB Shrink the Financial Sector?

This is hard to say. There is no single right size for the financial sector. It will find its natural size when there is no explicit or implicit government subsidization of financial malfeasance. The real measure of the financial sector's contribution to output is the value of its intermediation services. Since the FFA will ensure that these services are meaningful, rather than elaborate scams, the economy may decide to make more use of financial intermediation. But if the sector does shrink, the capital and labor used in the sector won't be lost. It will go to work in the nonfinancial sector, although the adjustment will take some time.

Doesn't LPB Force Us to Become Our Own Bankers?

We are our own financial keepers. We've been so in the past and will continue to be so in the future. We're each ultimately responsible for how much we save, what insurance we buy, and how we invest our savings.

Under LPB, there will be plenty of financial advisors as well as mutual fund managers seeking to give us advice. But thanks to the FFA, there will be a way of verifying that one's assets are being invested as agreed. Also, LPB will be a much simpler and more transparent system than our current financial structure, with much more homogeneous financial products.

Isn't LPB Reducing the Amount of Safe Assets?

There are no perfectly safe assets available in our country or, for that matter, anywhere in the world. Even TIPS bear risk insofar as the federal government can default on their payment at any time. The market certainly thought there was a good chance of such default in the six months following Lehman's collapse. In December 2007, it cost only $600 to insure yourself for one year against default on $10 million of U.S. Treasury bonds.[5] But in early March 2009, the price exceeded $100,000![6] Campbell Soup's credit default swaps during this period were selling at a lower price, so the market thought Campbell's Soup was more trustworthy than Uncle Sam.[7] Although it's much cheaper these days to buy insurance against defaults on U.S. Treasuries, the market clearly believes there is still a major risk of this occurring.

That said, some assets are safer than others, and many observers think the government's guarantees are responsible for providing more safe assets in total in society. I disagree. In trying to make things safe, I believe the government has achieved the opposite. It's created a very unsafe financial and economic environment, in which financial companies take on much more risk because they keep the gains and hand the public the losses. The current episode has made this crystal clear.

And though the real values (the purchasing power) of our money markets, savings accounts, checking accounts, life insurance cash surrender values, and CDs have been preserved, at least so far, we've all taken a hit. Many of us have seen our other assets plummet or our jobs disappear. And we or our progeny will, over time, pay for the bailouts.

So no one should be under any illusion that our government can keep us economically safe. The best our government can do is try to keep the economy in a good place and, if it still heads south, redistribute within and across generations to spread the pain as fairly as possible. Giving financial firms what amounts to huge incentives to destabilize the economy, albeit on a random basis, is precisely the wrong way to run the show. Not only does the economy collapse, but the government ends up with a colossal bill that it has to pay to third parties, including, in this case, the Chinese government and the shareholders of Société Générale. These obligations clearly limit the amount of ex-post risk pooling the government can do.

Finally, I see little evidence that Uncle Sam is sharing the risks of the financial crisis fairly across generations. From what I can tell, most of the costs of this unfortunate episode are going to be foisted on our children and grandchildren. That's not intergenerational risk sharing. That's intergenerational risk making.

Does LPB Require Homemade Insurance Policies?

"Today, I can buy a life insurance policy that pays off no matter what happens. And you're going to force me to buy one mutual fund that insures my life, but leaves me exposed to aggregate mortality risk, and then I have to place complex bets within a second mutual fund that will let me hedge the aggregate mortality risk? You are forcing me to make two financial transactions when now I need to make only one."

The premise of the first sentence is false. Were, for example, swine flu to really break out, our life insurance policies would not fully pay off because our life insurance companies would either go bust or be bailed out. It they go bust, our heirs won't get paid as much as was promised, and if they are bailed out, our heirs, along with others, will face higher explicit or implicit taxes to cover the bailout.[8] Worst of all, the process of watching either the life insurance companies fall apart or be bailed out could push us off our precarious economic precipice. As we've seen, it's a long way down.

But the concern being voiced about having to buy too many financial products to achieve a given end is a valid one. Isn't there a way to make our financial lives under LPB simpler?

There is. It's called the market. Life insurance mutual funds will naturally compete to make it as easy as possible for households to purchase what amounts to a basic policy plus varying degrees of aggregate mortality insurance. For example, just as we can now bet on horses via online betting, we'll surely buy life and other insurance mutual funds on line, and the LPB mutual funds will do for this business what Gohorsebetting.com, Bodog.com, Youbet.com, and the very many other competing online racetrack betting services do for horse racing. They provide clear, simple instructions for taking on and laying off particular mutual fund risks.

For example, when younger households buy shares of life insurance mutual funds specific to their age, sex, and health status,[9] they can be asked (on line, on the phone, or in person), if they also wish to purchase aggregate mortality protection that will pay X, Y, and Z if this year's mortality rate falls in ranges A, B, and C.

Insuring Against Changes in Insurability

In today's financial system, one "can" buy renewable term life insurance, which effectively wraps together insurance against your dying with insurance against your living, but also experiencing an adverse health shock that limits your ability to purchase term insurance in the future at preferential rates.

Since younger households will want to buy life insurance through time and will also seek protection against changes in their health status, the life insurance mutual funds would also likely ask such households if they wish to protect themselves against a change in their health status that affects their future insurability by buying shares of health status insurance mutual funds.

These health status insurance mutual funds would probably run on a one-year rather than three-month basis, because the change in healthcare status would need to be assessed by independent healthcare professionals, again under the aegis of the FFA.

The need for this type of insurance mutual fund would depend on future government regulation. For example, Uncle Sam could simply decree that no life insurance mutual fund can take preexisting medical conditions into account in selling shares of its life insurance mutual funds. In this case, the Drop-Dead-If-You-Must, 30-to-35-Year-Old-Females fund could limit its shareholders to 30- to 35-year-old females, but couldn't require them to be in good health as specified by a medical review of the type you typically get these days when you apply for life insurance.

Ruling out insurers' use of preexisting medical conditions in setting insurance rates is, by the way, a key feature of the new Health Insurance Exchange that Congress and the administration are designing. The Health Insurance Exchange is meant to provide health insurance coverage to today's almost 50 million Americans with no current coverage. If policymakers think it unfair to charge the sick higher health insurance premiums, they're also likely to think it unfair to charge the sick higher life insurance premiums.[10]

With LPB You Don't Know the Odds
Until It's Too Late

When you bet at the racetrack, the odds aren't set until the betting window is shut at post time (when the race begins). At this point, the parimutuel fund is closed, and no more bets can be placed. People that wait until the last minute bear the risk of being unable to bet, while those who bet early do so with a less precise estimate of the final odds. So there is an advantage as well as a cost to betting late.

In my vision of LPB, I would expect there to be many large, highly competitive insurance mutual funds selling us protection against each particular type of risk. I would not expect the payoff odds (the ratio of what you'd get if you won to what you originally invested) to vary much across funds, and, absent a large aggregate shock, their variation across time should be gradual.

Actuarially speaking, it doesn't take large numbers of insurance mutual fund shareholders to achieve virtually all the potential risk sharing available via diversification. Indeed, having 100 women invest in the Drop-Dead-If-You-Must-30-to-35-Year—Old-Females fund would achieve virtually all the risk-sharing possible, and I'd expect the number of shareholders in such a fund to number in the thousands. So I think the issue of not knowing precisely how many other people are investing in your insurance mutual fund and how much they've contributed will not be of much concern once the LPB insurance funds are up and running and attracting large numbers of investors.

Why Not Simply Correctly Price
the Government's Guarantees?

Perry Mehrling believes that rather than radically reform our financial system along the lines of LPB, we should have the government charge a price for systemic risk insurance that is appropriate to market conditions and the amount of insurance being provided. At the early stages of the crisis, Perry persuaded me that this was the right financial fix. We penned several FT Economists' Forum columns, including one with Alistair Milne of City University London. Alistair is one of Britain's top financial economists and had independently reached Perry's conclusion.[11]

In Perry and Alistair's view, the government is not just the lender of last resort but also the insurer of last resort, and should intervene by selling credit default insurance if the price of such insurance goes nuts. Furthermore, the price of the insurance should be set high enough to deter excessive risk taking.

An example here would be insurance against the top (safest) tranche of a CMO defaulting. This insurance would pay off only under extreme circumstances, when the system has collapsed. If the government can, at a price, keep this from happening, it can safely intervene in this insurance market and effectively set a ceiling on the premium.

In my mind, this "if" is very big. There is nothing in the economic theory of coordination failures/multiple equilibrium that suggests that the government can actually choose the economy's equilibrium. Recall that, in such models, if everyone thinks everyone else is thinking that G (as in good equilibrium) will happen, it's in the interest of everyone to think G will happen and G will, in fact, happen. By the same logic, if everyone thinks that everyone else is thinking B (as in bad) will happen, we'll end up with B happening.

Now if everyone thinks that everyone else thinks B will happen and the government starts screaming, "It's G, you idiots! Everyone is thinking G!" well, there's no reason for anyone to believe the government, because it should scream this no matter what people are believing because it wants the economy to end up at G.

If tomorrow everyone came to believe that everyone else was going to run on their checking and savings accounts, their money market accounts, their cash surrender values, and so on and that the government was going to have to print money out the wazoo to service these runs as well as mitigate the economic fallout and that this money creation would cause hyperinflation, then everyone would run, because that would be the individually, economically rational thing to do. This would be true regardless of Uncle Sam's standing with arms outstretched in front of the banks, screaming, *"Don't run, you bloody fools!"* People would not only run. They'd run right over Uncle Sam.

And please don't take my word for this. Take the words of former Treasury Secretary Hank Paulson, current Treasury Secretary Tim Geithner, and former SEC Chairman Christopher Cox, all of whom apparently warned the nation's top bankers on the eve of Lehman's collapse that if Lehman collapsed, all of their banks could go down.[12]

Now some will say, "Yes, but Lehman collapsed and the government moved in and saved the day, so it does have the power to insure the system." My response is, "Hardly." We now have 14 states with unemployment rates above 10 percent. Michigan's unemployment rate is now north of 15 percent. The government has failed to save the economy from what will surely be its worst showing in 70 years, and *things could easily go south from here.*

So if the government can't really insure against system risk, how can it sell systemic risk insurance? It can't. It can sell, but it can't deliver. Just ask AIG.

How Will Monetary Policy Operate?

It will operate just as it does today. If the Fed wants to increase the money supply, it will print money and use it to buy assets from the private sector, typically the private sector's holdings of Treasuries. In this crisis, we've seen the Fed print money to buy other assets as well, indeed, even toxic assets. At the moment, the Fed's balance sheet appears to be about 50 percent invested in assets other than Treasuries, the majority of which appear to be of highly questionable market value.

Under LPB, the Fed, if it wanted, could purchase and sell shares of the various mutual funds. Thus, if the Fed wished to quickly lower mortgage interest rates, it could do so by buying shares of mutual funds investing in mortgages. Or if it wanted to intervene in the credit default insurance (CDS) market, as Perry and Alistair advocate, it could do so by buying or selling shares of corporate bond CDS insurance mutual funds.

For example, if it wanted to lower the cost of default insurance on IBM, it could buy shares of the IBM Defaults This Year or Not fund, taking the position that IBM won't default. In other words, the

Fed would put its money in the fund and be paid back its share of the pot only if IBM doesn't default. Those trying to insure themselves against IBM's defaulting now see a cheaper price of doing so. The Fed's intervention has made the pot larger, so for the same collective investment, they'll get a larger payoff if IBM defaults. Alternatively, they can make a smaller investment in the fund and get the same payoff they'd otherwise have received were IBM to default. Hence, Perry and Alistair's proposed policy of having the government intervene in default insurance markets can be safely conducted within LPB.

Note that in buying or selling shares in funds that entail bets on aggregate outcomes, the Fed or Treasury, for that matter, would not be insuring the uninsurable. It would be putting its money on the table (in the pot), like everyone else. And the pot is clearly paying off in nominal, not real dollars. So there is no implicit attempt to insure anything real.

What about Foreign Assets?

LPB would include mutual funds that hold foreign stocks, bonds, and real estate. The current mutual fund industry sells plenty of funds already that invest in foreign securities. The FFA would be responsible for disclosing what it knows or can discern at reasonable cost about these securities. Again, rating by not rating is a form of rating.

Won't Americans Just Bank Abroad?

If the United States adopts limited purpose banking, other countries around the world will likely follow suit. But if they don't and Americans want to bank in London, Paris, and so on, they should be free to do so with all the risks that a non-LPB-based banking system entails.

Lots of Brits and other Europeans learned a healthy lesson during this crisis about banking abroad. They opened up checking accounts in Iceland's three largest banks, assuming the Icelandic government would insure their deposits, at least in nominal terms. Collectively, these banks ended up taking in deposits and other short- or medium-term loans that appear to have exceeded four times Iceland's GDP![13] They then turned around and invested these huge (at least for Iceland) sums in U.S. mortgaged-backed securities and other "safe" assets.

When financial matters took a turn for the worse, all three of these banks collapsed and were nationalized. At this point, the Icelandic government had to make good on its deposit insurance. But it realized that printing vast hoards of krónur to cover the deposits of foreign nationals would lead to hyperinflation. So the Icelandic central bank told foreign nationals to take a hike. In anticipation of this treatment, the British and other governments seized the remaining assets of the Icelandic banks that were situated in their jurisdictions. The dispute over what was and wasn't insured, and whether the Icelandic bank assets could legally be seized, will go on for years and make lots of lawyers rich.

But even if non-Icelandic deposits get paid their krónur, they won't be worth much since the krónur has already devalued dramatically relative to the euro and the dollar and would really depreciate were the Icelandic central bank forced to print several times GDP to meet its insurance commitments.

Doesn't LPB Dramatically Shrink the Money Supply?

The precise definition of the money supply is largely in the eyes of the beholder. Even the Federal Reserve doesn't know what money supply measure to consider. The St. Louis Federal Reserve Bank keeps track of four different measures: M1, M2, M3, and L. As you move from M1 to L, each measure adds some additional components, which are viewed as less liquid, as in less easy to use in purchasing goods and services.[14]

Unfortunately, over the short run, where the short run can involve a goodly number of years, the different money measures aren't particularly well correlated with one another let alone the price level. This is an embarrassing situation; we economists have very precise mathematical models connecting M to P, which reference the money supply and the "price" level, but we really don't know how precisely to measure M or P, for that matter.

One thing we do know, though, is that dramatically increasing the monetary base—how much money the government prints to buy things—will over time lead all four money measures plus any reasonable measure of the price level to skyrocket. We can't say precisely how to measure money, but we know it when we see it, particularly when we see lots of it.[15]

As mentioned, under LPB cash mutual funds will be the most liquid of assets. They will never break the buck and can be accessed via ATM accounts or debit cards. And since the government will directly control M1 (the sum of cash in our possession and cash in our cash mutual funds), it can make M1 anything it wants just by printing more or less money, which must be held in one of those two places. Given this ability to print money, there is then no reason to think that the M1 money supply will be smaller under LPB.

What about M2 and broader measures of money? Well, M2 equals M1 plus money market accounts, savings accounts, and small denomination certificates of deposit (CDs). And the broader measures build on M2. So one way the government can make M2 or some broader measure of money larger, if it wants it to be larger, is simply to increase M1.

Now it's true that under LPB, savings accounts and CDs will no longer be issued by the banks, which, let's not forget, often entail a fee upon early liquidation. Nor will there be money market mutual funds whose market values are explicitly or implicitly insured by the federal government. So these elements of M2 and broader measures of money will be eliminated. But households who formerly held their savings in full or in part in these vehicles will be investing those same funds in LPB mutual funds that are highly liquid insofar as they can be sold at any time at prevailing market prices.

What's the Role of the FFA in Investment Banking?

Under limited purpose banking, a new mortgage, commercial loan, credit card, issuance of stock, new real estate trust, and so on would be initiated by a bank, sent to the FFA and private parties, as desired, for independent and multiple rating, income verification, and disclosure, and then auctioned by the bank to mutual funds, including mutual funds that the bank itself markets to the public. The new securities would fund upon sale to the mutual fund, so that the bank would never hold them;

that is, never have an open position. Once funded, the new securities would be held by the owners of the mutual fund—the people. This ensures that people, not institutions, hold risk.

Would individuals be free to buy and sell individual securities outside of mutual funds? Absolutely. And banks would be free to brokerage those purchases and sales. But banks would not hold inventories of securities of any amount or kind. To facilitate their brokerage services, the FFA would establish an escrow service, effecting the transfer of money to sellers and securities to buyers once it had confirmed receipt of both the money from the buyers and the securities from the sellers. That is, the FFA rather than broker-dealers could clear securities markets. Banks would thus assist people in buying and selling securities, but would never incur exposure in the process of this brokerage business.

What about Venture Capital, Private Equity Firms, and Hedge Funds?

Venture capital firms would simply be LPB banks that sell mutual funds specializing in buying the equity and bonds of new startups. Their principals would be free to purchase, as private individuals, the issues they helped initiate. And private equity firms? Such banks would simply sell mutual funds that invest in private equity.

Hedge funds could buy options and puts within mutual funds, but they couldn't short securities that leave their mutual funds in particular situations with obligations that exceed the value of the mutual fund's assets. Hence, many hedge funds would likely want to operate as non-LPB banks, in which case they would operate with unlimited liability—that is, with liability extending fully to those running the fund. Had LTCM been forced to operate in this manner, its owners, would no doubt, have taken on much less leverage in trying to capitalize on spreads that seemed sure to close, but failed to cooperate.

Is GE a Bank under LPB?

Is General Electric a bank under limited purpose banking, given that it has a major subsidiary, GE Capital, which engages in financial intermediation? GE itself would not be a bank. But GE Capital most certainly would be and would be precluded from doing anything other than initiating mortgages, getting them rated, selling them in the market, and operating its own mutual funds.

Can't Nonfinancial Corporations Play Conventional Bank?

Under LPB, what prevents a corporation like Papa Gino's from borrowing to invest in risky securities; that is, to act like a current-day bank? The answer is that corporations can borrow to expand their operations and to acquire other companies in their lines of business. But Papa Gino's could not buy stock in Dow Chemical, which would, presumably, violate Papa Gino's corporate charter, which instructs company officers to make pizza, not napalm. If Papa Gino's wanted to expand its charter to include financial services, nothing would prevent it from establishing the First Bank of Thin-Crust Pizza that operates, like all other banks, as a mutual fund company.

Why Let Proprietorships Run Traditional Banks?

Is it fair to let proprietorships and partnerships, *which do not have limited liability,* to operate as conventional banks, which can borrow short and lend long? The answer is yes, since the owners of these banks would be personally liable for all their losses, including the loss of deposits, which the government would not insure.

Will LPB Prevent Financial Panics?

To the enduring consternation of economists, people are human. There is nothing to stop them collectively getting overly excited about particular assets, be they stocks, bonds, or real estate, and then deciding from one minute to the next that they've made a huge mistake and all try to dump their assets at the same time. Such irrational exuberance and pessimism can't be stopped. The best we can do is discourage it by making sure our financial system is structured on sound principals, so that when the market crashes, the financial system doesn't crash as well.

Again, the gas station analogy is useful. It's bad enough that gas prices will occasionally shoot up to tremendous levels for no apparent reason. It would be many times worse if all of the nation's gas stations go broke at the same time that prices go nuts.

And the potential for the financial system to fail can, itself, trigger financial panic and runs on the market. If rumors spread that the gas stations are going down, this will drive up the price of gas and take the leveraged gas stations down. So having a financial system that's safe should mean much less financial market volatility.

LPB also builds in extra protection against asset fire sales because many, if not most, of its mutual funds would be closed-end funds. When the owners of closed-end funds panic, they can sell their shares to other owners or to third parties, but they can't force redemptions (sales) of the underlying assets held by the closed-end fund. Closed-end funds specify when and how the assets they buy will be liquidated. For example, a closed-end fund investing in 1,000 risky 15-year mortgages issued on a given date might specify that it will hold the mortgages for the full 15 years, paying out the net cash flow to the fund holders along the way. If people start panicking about the ability of homeowners to repay their mortgages, they may try to dump their mutual fund shares, but the 1,000 mortgages, themselves, won't be sold/dumped on the market.

Such runs could make it tough for lots of higher risk homeowners and businesses to borrow via mutual funds at reasonable interest rates, which is what we're seeing today. So I'm not suggesting that financial life will be perfectly smooth. I'm saying it will be much smoother under LPB than under the current system because LPB will remove, to a very great extent, the risk of fraud and systemic collapse.

LPB Will Destroy Valuable Relationships and Information Banks Have About Their Borrowers

This is a view straight from *It's A Wonderful Life*. Jimmy Stewart knows everyone in town. He trusts them; they trust him. Jimmy knows Sally's behind on her payments, but that she's good for them. And Jimmy knows why his golf buddy Frank is short on his loan. Frank broke three toes in an errant swing on the 14th and hasn't been able to pitch the *Three-in-One*—a marvelous cigarette holder that gives you three smokes at once.

This is a lovely story about a world that no longer exists if it ever did. Today's Jimmy is working for a huge conglomerate run by top managers and directors who care primarily about their compensation, not shareholder value. The quicker this "leadership" team can "manufacture" a profit, the sooner they can justify huge bonuses for themselves and take early retirement. There's another reason these thieves have to work fast. There's always the chance that a hostile takeover (by even more efficient thieves) will close down their scam. This means initiating Sally and Frank's loans, paying raters to lie about their quality (because there's no FFA to check), and selling them off for up-front money.

And, as previously indicated, forcing Jimmy to hold all the loans he issues doesn't work either because his bank will then face all the risk and have to charge Sally and Frank higher rates than a diversified, securitized market can deliver. In addition, Jimmy is not risking the loss of his own capital; if he's a manager of a major financial conglomerate, he's risking the loss of his shareholders' capital.

But there is a real concern here. Private information and the effort going into collecting that information has real value. If Jimmy is enduring Frank's awful golf game in order to learn more about Frank's business, he should be able to earn a return on that effort, not to mention physical risk. But under LPB, Jimmy can do this. He can manage a mutual fund that invests in startup firms and spend time and effort deciding which startups are most likely to succeed and buy relatively more of their paper. And, if his funds do well, he can charge larger fees. He just can't force the general public to co-invest with him.

Economics Diary, November 11, 2009: Whither the Economy?

The stock market continues to head north, but the economy remains in the tank. Mortgage delinquencies are at a record high with 10 percent of all households with mortgages at least one month late in their payments. Fourteen percent of these households are either delinquent or facing foreclosure.[16] Consumer confidence remains very low and unemployment has hit 10.2 percent. A total of 263,000 of our landsmen lost their jobs in September, including close to 16,000 teachers.[17] Another 571,000 workers dropped out of the work force. The national unemployment rate is now 9.8 percent. And the duration of unemployment is reaching levels last seen in the 1930s.[18] The ranks of the unemployed include almost 7 million seniors, aged 65 and older, most of whom lost both their jobs and large chucks of their savings over the past two years.[19]

Add up the officially unemployed (those who looked for work in the past week), the unofficially unemployed (those who've looked for work over the past year, but not the past month), and those who are working part-time but would like to work full-time, and you reach 17.5 percent of the nation's workforce.[20] This broader measure of unemployment appears to be higher than at any time since the Great Depression.

Today, CNN identified 10 states in severe financial peril, with budget shortfalls ranging from 12 percent, in the case of Michigan, to 49 percent in the case of California. New Jersey, Nevada, Arizona, and Illinois have budget gaps of 30 percent, 38 percent, 41 percent, and 47 percent, respectively. Florida, with a budget gap of 23 percent, is shrinking. More people are moving out than are moving in for the first time since World War II. My guess is that the young and middle-aged workers in Florida are the ones who are bailing and leaving the elderly, with their high Medicaid price tag, to fend for themselves.[21]

Meanwhile, Morgan Stanley, JPMorgan Chase, and Goldman Sachs are back to "God's work," preparing to hand out $30 billion in bonuses.[22] This is obscene and is outraging the entire nation. I suspect these companies are digging their own graves.

And if all this weren't depressing enough, the FDIC reported last week the 115th bank failure of the year. The bank failure rate is accelerating, with 1,000 more failures expected in the near term.[23] And the Treasury just announced its 2009 fiscal year deficit was $1.4 trillion—the largest deficit since World War II when measured as a share of GDP.

Oh, and by the way, the FDIC is now completely broke and needs to borrow to cover its obligations to insured depositors.[24] The FDIC doesn't want to borrow from the Treasury. Apparently, the two heads of these agencies—Sheila Bair and Timothy Geithner—don't play nicely in the sandbox. So the FDIC is borrowing from private banks; that is, private banks are bailing out the FDIC, which is supposed to bail out private banks. But this is also part subterfuge to keep the Treasury out of the headlines. Recall that the private banks are being given or lent money by the Treasury and Fed for free or on what appear to be highly favorable terms. So what we really have here is the government bailing out the government, but letting the private banking system pick up a nice fee along the way. The Federal Housing Administration is also starting to run in the red and will shortly need massive infusions from the Treasury or the Fed.[25]

The Fed's massive money creation is starting to take its toll on the dollar. In the past nine months, the dollar's value relative to the euro has fallen by 13 percent. It now takes almost $1.50 to buy one euro. Part of the reason for the dollar's decline is that foreign governments are buying fewer dollar-denominated assets in which to hold their reserves.[26] This could reflect more faith in foreign economies or more fear of U.S. inflation.

The M1 money multiplier remains very low and, to date, the monetary base hasn't risen by as much as I feared when I first began writing. But the Fed is still printing money like crazy; indeed, it's still committing to buying up hundreds of billions more of private as well as government securities. And if and when the money multiplier returns to normal, there will be an awful lot of money chasing a relatively small number of goods. This is dawning on Wall Street. Morgan Stanley just issued a warning about high future inflation and long rates are rising.

Credit markets remain extremely tight. Several weeks back, the *New York Times* ran a lead story on the moribund nature of private credit markets.[27] Notwithstanding $1 trillion in federal injections, the mortgage, commercial real estate loans, commercial paper, student loan, auto loans, and other debt securitization markets, which account for 60 percent of new credit creation, remain on life support.

Yale's Robert Shiller can call a spade a spade: "The securitization markets are dead." In the case of mortgage-backed securities, private lending is running for the year at $8 billion, compared with three-quarters of a trillion dollars back in 2005. Were it not for new mortgages issued by Uncle Sam through Fannie, Freddie, and FHA, we'd have almost no housing market, period. But now the Fed is threatening to pull the plug on continued support of residential and commercial real estate lending. This is raising lots of concerns, particularly among investors in commercial real estate. Some $50 billion of their securitized borrowings are coming up for refinance in a few months.

The reason the private credit markets remain frozen except for those with top credit ratings and lots of collateral is simple. No one trusts that the securities being bundled together are as advertised. Or to quote the *New York Times*, "Many investors have lost trust in securitization after losing huge sums on packages of subprime mortgages that had high default rates."

Trust in insurance companies is also terribly weak. Today, a purchaser of an AIG annuity who lives in California sued the State of California to make sure AIG doesn't transfer any assets out of state; she's worried (for good reason) that (a) Uncle Sam will eventually stop bailing out AIG, (b) AIG will go belly up, and (c) she'll lose her annuity. If the California courts approve approves her suit, she'll in effect force California to run on AIG's reserves. This would likely trigger a run by all the other states on "their" claims to AIG's assets, which could trigger a run on AIG's cash surrender values by its multitudinous policyholders.[28]

In short, nobody trusts anybody these days when it comes to their money. In negotiating with the former Soviet Union, President Reagan used to quote a Russian saying, "Trust, but verify." A better saying in this context is "Verify, then trust." But over two years into this financial abyss, we have no mechanism in place for independent verification, rating, custody, and disclosure and no firewalls against insuring the uninsurable. Nor do we have any plans for such a mechanism. Until we do, via Limited Purpose Banking and its federal financial authority, our financial system and economy will remain dead in the water and in ongoing peril.

Just ask Neil Barofsky, who was appointed Inspector General of the Troubled Asset Relief Program, and indicated in July in a 256-page report that "the total federal support (of the financial sector) could reach up to $23.7 trillion."[29]

As Barofsky told CNN,

These banks that were too big to fail are now bigger. . . . Government has sponsored and supported several mergers that made them larger and that guarantee, that implicit guarantee of moral hazard, the idea that the government is not going to let these banks fail, which was implicit a year ago, is now explicit, we've said it. So if anything, not only have there not been any meaningful regulatory reform to make it less likely, in a lot of ways, the government has made such problems more likely. . . . Potentially we could be in more danger now than we were a year ago.[30]

Barofsky is not only concerned about the "too big to fail" problem. He's also highly skeptical that we are going to do the independent verification, disclosure, and rating needed to restore confidence in the financial system.

Speaking of ratings, Gretchen Morgenstern, the *New York Times* ace financial reporter, reported today on wea culpa Congressional testimony by Scott McCleskey, head of compliance at Moody's from 2006 through 2008. McCleskey focused on Moody's ratings of municipal bonds issued by some 29,000 local governments, school districts, water authorities, etc. He disclosed that Moody's fails to rerate these bonds on a timely basis, while conveying the impression that it does. In fact, McCleskey indicated that "the vast majority" of the thousands of outstanding Moody's-rated municipal bonds hadn't been re-rated for years and some hadn't been re-rated for up to two decades! When McCleskey raised a red flag with his superiors, he was told "not to mention the issue in any e-mails or any other written form."[31]

For his part, Uncle Sam has been busy sharpening his knives when it comes to Wall Street pay. He's just announced 90 percent cuts in the compensation of top execs at AIG, Citigroup, and Bank of America.[32] And he's poised to start micro-managing pay levels at all the major banks in the country via the Federal Reserve.[33] Just ask Kenneth Lewis. Ken was forced to work the entire year for B of A for nothing—not a single penny, which presumably is why he resigned.

But let's not worry about Ken. He'll be able to find work. Maurice (Hank) Greenberg is hiring. Hank's been working overtime to build AIG II under the name C. V. Staar and Company.[34] Greenberg, recall, built AIG into a financial colossus, with many solid insurance businesses, before hiring one Joseph Cassano to sell credit default policies that the company couldn't possibly cover.

Hank was forced out of AIG in 2005 by the NY Attorney General, Eliot Spitzer under allegations of fraudulent business practices, securities fraud, common law fraud and other violations of insurance and securities law.[35] The extent of Greenberg's culpability, who claims he was victimized by Spitzer, remains unclear. Hank successfully defended himself against criminal charges and has settled for peanuts allegations that he raided AIG to the tune of billions when he left AIG in 2005.[36]

Greenberg's reputation is rising, while Spitzer's remains in tatters. In 2008, Spitzer, then governor of New York, was forced to resign when he was caught purchasing services from a prostitute with the alleged use of campaign contributions.[37] Hank, who is in his eighties, is chock full of testosterone too. He's now raiding AIG's top executives, who, recall, just had their pay cut by 90 percent and are surely eager to jump ship. If AIG loses its top personnel and becomes a shell of its former self, which is even less able to cover its myriad debts, we, the people, will get stuck with an even larger bill for the ongoing AIG mess, which Hank created. The exodus of AIG talent is happening in real time; last week Robert Benmosche, AIG's current CEO, told AIG's Board that he was "done."[38]

Citigroup, which has already received $45 billion in taxpayer largess and can draw on another $300 billion under certain circumstances, is facing the same micro-management of its top salaries and a consequent talent drain that may cost taxpayers another fortune.[39] Indeed, in my nightmares I see Hank hiring Ken, Joe, Jimmy, Robert, Stan, Charles, and the rest of the financial rogue gallery recreating fundamentally fraudulent financial enterprises on an ongoing basis.

The other news on the economics scene is encouraging. Mervyn King, governor of the Bank of England, just gave a courageous and withering speech in favor of "Utility Banking," which is a different term for what I call Limited Purpose Banking.[40] Paul Volcker, former Chairman of the Federal Reserve, is expressing similar views and making it clear that he's being ignored by Obama's dream team of economists.[41]

Here are some of King's words:

To paraphrase a great wartime leader, never in the field of financial endeavour has so much money been owed by so few to so many. And, one might add, so far with little real reform. . . . The massive support extended to the banking sector around the world, while necessary to avert economic disaster, has created possibly the biggest moral hazard in history. The "too important to fail" problem is too important to ignore ... In other industries we separate those functions that are utility in nature—and are regulated—from those that can safely be left to the discipline of the market. There are those who claim that such proposals are impractical. It is hard to see why.... It is important that banks in receipt of public support are not encouraged to try to earn their way out of that support by resuming the very activities that got them into trouble.

And here are some of Volcker's:

The banks are there to serve the public, and that is what they should concentrate on. These other activities create conflicts of interest. They create risks, and if you try to control the risks with supervision, that just creates friction and difficulties (and ultimately fails).[42]

Some of the world's top finance economists have recently and independently come up with reforms that are very similar to LPB. For example, Anat Admati and Paul Pfleiderer, two of Stanford University's top financial economists,[43] have formulated a plan in which banks are broken into two parts. One part is 100 percent equity financed (can't borrow), has limited liability, and one part that's partly debt financed that has unlimited liability. This is equivalent to LPB, which has 100 percent equity financed mutual funds with limited liability, but permits banks that operate a unlimited liability proprietorships or partnerships to borrow with no limit. Most hedge funds would, presumably, go this route.

Douglas Diamond and a long list of other top finance economists who formed the Squam Lake Group are pushing a plan that entails transforming bank debt into equity when banks that are too big to fail start failing. This too sounds like a ban on debt finance of the type proposed under LPB.

If people like Admati, Pfeiderer, and Diamond, not to mention Mervyn King, who is an outstanding economist, are coming around to an LPB-type solution, the rest of the economics financial profession will soon be deriving this solution as well. In the end analysis, this is a problem of economic engineering. We economists now finally understand the interconnected problems of modern finance. We also understand that they won't be fixed by wishful thinking, and we recognize the extreme dangers of leaving the status quo in place. Whether one calls the solution Limited Purpose Banking or something else makes no difference. What matters is that LPB principles are applied in the reform and that we economists give credit where credit is due in describing this reform to the public, namely to our science, which points inexorably to this solution.

Chapter 8

Conclusion

"A financial system on the verge of collapse ..."
—President Barack Obama

Our financial system is in terrible shape and needs a fundamental overhaul, not an oil change. The system aids and abets financial malfeasance, particularly the leveraging of the American taxpayer. Most important, it leaves us at tremendous economic risk.

In reappointing Ben Bernanke chairman of the Federal Reserve, President Obama hailed Bernanke for bringing us back from the brink, saving us from a second Great Depression, and rescuing "a financial system on the verge of collapse."[1] The president is not one to exaggerate. His characterization of the dangers we faced and Bernanke's role in mitigating that danger is shared by most observers, myself included.

But what we don't know is whether the movie we've been watching—*It's a Horrible Mess*—is really over or just providing an intermission. What we do know is that we have the same pit in our stomachs—the same anxiety—we have after watching *It's a Wonderful Life*. It's the fear, to paraphrase President Bush, that "This sucker could easily blow."

Living under constant economic stress is no way to live. The fate of the world economy should not depend on Wall Street's "risk management" or on Uncle Sam's fortuitous choice of policymakers. Our retirements should not perpetually be on the verge of collapse. Our jobs should not continually be on the line. Our nation's finances should not forever be threatened. And our children should not be left to pick up the pieces.

If this means that the Dick Fulds, Jimmy Caynes, Anthony Mozilos, Stan O'Neals, Charles Princes, and Robert Rubins can't make fortunes gambling with our economic well-being, well, too bad. They'll have to make an honest and modest living like the rest of us. These people were the real rogue traders. They were not to be trusted in the past and are certainly not to be trusted in the future. Yet that's exactly what this administration and Congress is doing. They are restoring the same financial system, which has failed miserably and will do so again if given half a chance. And they are letting the same low- and high-class operators, the same rating companies, and more or less the same regulators lead us down the same primrose path.

Yes, there will be more regulations, more regulatory bodies, and more vigilant enforcement. But if the former head of the SEC, Arthur Levitt, can get conned by a Bernie Madoff and his ilk and if Levitt tells us point blank that regulators can't keep us safe, we should pay heed and enact the right financial fix before it's too late.

Limited Purpose Banking is the answer. This simple and easily implemented pass-through mutual fund system, with its built-in firewalls, would preclude financial crises of the type we're now experiencing. The system would rely on independent rating by the government, but permit private ratings as well. It would require full disclosure and provide maximum transparency. Most important, it would make clear that risk is ultimately born by people, not companies, and that people need, and have a right, to know what risks, including fiscal risks, they are facing. Finally, it would make clear what risks are, and are not, diversifiable. It would not pretend to insure the uninsurable or guarantee returns that can't be guaranteed. In short, the system would be honest, and, because of that, it would be safe—safe for ourselves and safe for our children.

Afterword

Fixing the Rest of Our Economic Mess

S aving our economy will require more than constructing an honest, safe, and efficient financial system. We also need modern, simple, and transparent tax, healthcare, and retirement saving systems to keep our nation from going broke, while meeting our paternalistic imperatives.

Let me briefly outline three proposals, one to address each of these challenges. These are proposals I've advanced on my own or with co-authors in various books and articles.[1] As you'll see, each plan starts with a clean slate, asking what we would do on taxes, healthcare, and retirement saving if we had nothing already in place and were able to put emotions and politics aside and view policy design simply as a question of economic engineering.

To my mind, tabula rasa is the only approach to take when you are starting with systems that are deeply flawed and financially extremely dangerous. I've already mentioned the huge fiscal gap facing our nation.

What I haven't discussed is the enormous inequities, inefficiencies, and complexities in our federal tax, Medicaid, Medicare, employer-based retirement saving, and Social Security systems. These programs rank among the top ten bureaucratic nightmares of the world.

Social Security, by itself, has 2,728 rules in its handbook and thousands upon thousands of rules in its Program Operating Manual System to explain the 2,728 rules.[2] These rules and the rules explaining the rules are written in a manner that is simply indecipherable to anyone not trained for years in the system's unique language. As a result, our nation's core retirement saving institution has been designed so that none of its hundreds of millions of participants can understand it.

And don't get me started on the federal tax system with its 17,000 pages of IRS code, or Medicaid, which has spent decades systematically locking low-income Americans into poverty by telling them if they earn too much money, they'll lose their own and then their children's healthcare benefits. Were Dickens alive today, he'd be writing *Oliver Twist* with a twist—the poor would be trapped in no-work houses, rather than workhouses.

Fixing Taxes: The Purple Tax

My ideal tax reform, which I'll initially call the *Demo Tax*, would replace all federal taxes (the FICA tax, the personal income tax, the corporate income tax, and the estate and gift tax), apart from excise taxes, with: (a) a one-time, 18 percent tax on wealth, (b) an ongoing 18 percent tax on wages, and (c) a demogrant.

I initially call this tax the DemoTax for three reasons. First, I think it will appeal to Democrats, because it's highly progressive in addition to being highly efficient. Second, *demos* is a Greek word meaning people. And this is a tax that should appeal to Republicans as well as Democrats. Indeed, if we can get Democrats to agree on the DemoTax, my guess is that Republicans will fall in line, too. In fact, as you'll see in a second, a whole army of Republicans has already signed onto it.

Getting Democrats and Republicans to agree agreeably—to agree to agree on something on which they do, in fact, agree would be a lovely and rare thing. Getting everyone behind a single tax reform would truly make this the *Demo Tax* or, if you like, the *People's Tax*.

Third, the DemoTax includes a *demo* grant—a fixed monthly payment to households based on their composition (number and ages of household members), not their income. Bill Gates gets the same size check as impoverished households with the same number and ages of family members.

This DemoTax sounds pretty left-wing, right? I'm proposing to tax wealth, lower taxes on labor, and send every household a monthly check. But if you are on the right wing, hang on. That army of supporters I just referenced is the FairTax movement, whose members are primarily right of center. The DemoTax, you see, is the FairTax with two important modifications, which ensure that the rich, particularly the superrich, can't avoid it and that the effective tax rate is just 18 percent rather than the 23 percent figure proposed in the FairTax.

For Democrats who don't like the sound of the FairTax, which so far has been championed primarily by Republicans, don't get queasy. The FairTax, you see, is the DemoTax in sheep's clothing. How often do you get Republicans pushing for a wealth tax, lowering taxes on workers, in part by eliminating the regressive FICA tax, and a demogrant!

And for you, Republicans who are getting queasy about advocating something that Democrats will like, hang on. The DemoTax is the FairTax in sheep's clothing. How often do you get Democrats pushing for something you think makes perfect sense and that also lowers marginal and average tax rates, while being revenue neutral!

The FairTax/DemoTax, or if you'd prefer, DemoTax/FairTax, would be implemented in the simplest way possible, namely by sending out a monthly check to each household and by having the tax collected at retail stores when people purchase goods and services. In other words, we'd implement this *BlueRedTax/RedBlueTax*—this *PurpleTax*—as a demogrant plus a tax paid at retail stores.

If you're a FairTax fan, think of the taxed collected at the stores as a federal retail sales tax. If you're are DemoTax fan, think of the tax collected at the stores as taxes levied on wages and wealth that are paid as workers spend their wages and as the rich spend their wealth.

I'm going to show you that you are free to think about the PurpleTax in either of these two different ways depending on what makes you most comfortable. If you are a supporter of the FairTax, think of the PurpleTax as a 22 percent retail sales tax, with an 18 percent effective rate. If you are a supporter of the DemoTax, think of the PurpleTax as an 18 percent tax levied on workers' wages and everyone's wealth, but that is conveyed to Uncle Sam when these monies are spent.

To keep everyone happy, the PurpleTax will be implemented by setting up two tax counters at retail stores. One will have a big red banner with the words FAIRTAX COUNTER, and one will have a big blue banner with the words DEMOTAX COUNTER. The FairTax counter will be situated after the checkout counter. The DemoTax counter will be placed before the checkout counter. To keep things simple in the example I now present, I assume there is no demogrant.

Implementation of the Purple Tax

Joe is a worker who earns $50,000 a year before his employer ships any of these earnings off to Uncle Sam as: (a) employer FICA payments, (b) employee FICA payments, and (c) federal income tax withholdings.

Joe is a rabid Republican and an avid fan of the FairTax. He also loves M&Ms, spending every cent he earns on those delectables. M&Ms sell for $1.00 per bag. So if he faced no taxes whatsoever, Joe could and would buy 50,000 bags of M&Ms and eat them at one sitting. But if we were to switch to the PurpleTax, with its 18 percent effective tax, Joe will only be able to consume 41,000 bags.

To see this, note that under the FairTax, Joe gets to keep everything he earns, which is $50,000. When he comes to the candy store with his pockets bulging with these funds, he first hands the checkout lady $41,000. Next, he proudly struts over to the FairTax counter where he pays $9,000 in taxes. Finally, he picks up his 41,000 bags.

Note that $9,000 is 22 percent of the $41,000, so the retail sales tax rate is, indeed, 22 percent. But $9,000 is just 18 percent of $50,000, so the effective FairTax rate, when measured in terms that are comparable to the way we measure FICA and income taxes, is only 18 percent.

John, Joe's uncle, is a rabid Democrat and also a devotee of M&Ms. John has $50 million, which he made selling liar mortgages to Fannie Mae and never getting caught. But he's feeling very guilty and wants to give back to society. So when John walks into the store, he happily proceeds to the DemoTax counter and forks over $9 million before proceeding to the checkout counter to pay his remaining $41 million and take delivery of 41 million bags of M&Ms.

This is 9 million bags fewer than John gets to consume under the current tax system. The reason is that under the current tax system, there is no tax on wealth.[3]

So rich John is worse off. How about relatively poor Joe? He's better off because under the current system, he pays about 30 percent of his $50,000 to Uncle Sam. This includes the 15.3 percent FICA tax (half of which is paid by his employer on his behalf) and a 12.7 percent federal income tax.[4]

Under the current tax system, Joe gets to consume 35,000 bags of M&Ms, whereas with the PurpleTax he consumes 41,000 bags. So poor Joe is better off and happier, and rich John is worse off, but less guilty, and thus happier.

But there's still one problem. John doesn't like paying taxes in stores. Doing so makes him feel like he's paying sales taxes, which he "knows" are the most regressive taxes in the world. John realizes that he's rich and has been made worse off and that Joe is poor and has been made better off, but this doesn't change his opinion.

John expresses his concern to the owners of Agreeable Treats, the candy store that he and Joe frequent. And since John is such a good customer, the store buys a building down the block to station the blue DemoTax counter. John is much relieved. He now has no sensation of paying a sales tax. Indeed, Agreeable Treats sets things up so that John can pay his taxes at any time and get a tax receipt so that whenever he buys his beloved M&Ms, he can do so without ever having to visit or even look at the hated FairTax counter.

(*Continued*)

(Continued)

Now, let's add back in the demogrant. First, let me point out that Uncle Sam has allowed Joe and John to receive their monthly check in different-colored envelopes with different names inscribed on them. Joe gets his check in a red envelope with the words "Tax Prebate" (the FairTax term) stamped across the top, and John gets his check in a blue envelope with the word "Demogrant" displayed. With the monthly check, Joe and John can each buy another 1,875 bags of M&Ms. This is meaningful to Joe, but peanuts to John.

The only real problem Joe and John have is getting together at holidays. They get into vicious M&M fights about whether the PurpleTax is really the FairTax or the DemoTax. This is all to the good, because everyone needs something meaningless to argue over.

If you are still with me, I'd implement the Purple Tax—a highly progressive-sounding tax reform with a tax that sounds highly regressive. Or, said the other way around, I'd implement a highly regressive-sounding tax reform with a tax that is highly progressive.

Looks can be deceiving and language is nothing if not flexible. The demogrant aside, we economists don't refer to the PurpleTax as the FairTax or the DemoTax. We call it a consumption tax. And we've known for years that a consumption tax can be implemented/described in a number of ways. Our mathematical models show us that taxing consumption is identical (isomorphic) to taxing what we use to pay for consumption, namely our existing wealth, plus our current and future wages. Hence, taxing consumption on an ongoing basis is equivalent to taxing wealth on a one-time basis and taxing wages as we earn them over time. Also note that the wealth tax hits home immediately. The minute the purple tax is signed into law, the rich will realize that their wealth can only purchase 82 percent of what used to be the case.

Since no one will be checking party credentials at the counters, as long as you go through one counter before leaving the store, you're all set. So if Republicans think Democrats are getting a break paying only 18 percent out of a larger amount and if Democrats think Republicans are getting a break paying 22 percent but on a smaller amount, they can switch counters and confirm that they end up with the same number of M&Ms either way.

Unlike the FairTax (proposed by FairTax.org), the PurpleTax would tax all of consumption, including the imputed rent on owner-occupied housing. This is a huge component of personal consumption, roughly 14 percent. It would also tax all educational consumption expenditures. As someone with over 30 years in the education industry, my view is that spending on education is primarily consumption, not investment. Finally, I would require Americans spending more than $5,000 outside of the country over the course of the year to pay the PurpleTax on all their foreign consumption expenditures.

These modifications to the FairTax will ensure that the rich don't sit in their mansions, enjoying their homes' consumption services while paying no taxes on those services, and don't escape taxation by earning their money in the United States and then spending it outside the country.

I don't want to take your time here with the mechanics of collecting the PurpleTax or the precise comparisons of its progressivity and efficiency features relative to the current tax system. My web site, www.kotlikoff.net, features a number of papers on the FairTax that pertain to the PurpleTax. My main purpose here is to signal that we can come up with a very low-rate, efficient, and transparent tax system to replace the current tax structure and that such a system will make all the difference in the world to our nation's future growth and revenue-generating capacity.

Fixing Healthcare:
Medicare Part C for All!

The PurpleTax will, I believe, generate a major increase in the present value of government revenue. But it won't eliminate the fiscal gap on its own. To do this we need to control our future healthcare, Social Security, defense, and other expenditures.

As I write, the administration and Congress are about to initiate another enormously expensive federal healthcare program to cover those now uninsured, and they are going to do so with no foolproof mechanism for limiting spending on Medicare and Medicaid—two programs that are fully capable of bankrupting the country on their own.

Let me outline what I would recommend, knowing full well that the new system will likely have been enacted by the time you read this, but also knowing that since the new system, coupled with the Medicare and Medicaid programs, is not affordable, healthcare reform will remain on the table.

We need to redesign the U.S. healthcare system from scratch, subject to two absolute requirements. First, we must provide all Americans with a first-rate, basic health insurance plan. Second, we must limit the costs of universal health insurance so that it doesn't drive the country broke.

The Medical Security System (MSS), which I proposed in *The Healthcare Fix* (MIT Press, 2007), delivers these goods. The MSS is very simple. Each American would receive a voucher each year. The amount of the voucher will equal the person's expected annual health-care costs that are covered under the MSS Basic Plan. Each person's voucher amount will be determined based on objective health indicators (e.g., blood tests, X-rays, MRI scans) reported via electronic medical records, using individual risk-adjustment software. Thus an 80-year-old, advanced diabetic male living in Miami might get a $70,000 voucher, whereas a perfectly healthy 14-year-old girl living in Kansas City might get a $3,500 voucher.

Each American would use his or her voucher to buy the basic plan from a health insurance company. Since health insurers would be compensated via the size of the voucher for taking on customers with preexisting conditions, they would have no incentive to cherry-pick. Nor would they be allowed to do so; no insurance company would be permitted to refuse coverage of anyone.

Those who can afford it would be free to buy supplemental insurance from the same insurance company from whom they purchase their basic plan. This eliminates cherry-picking (adverse selection) in the supplemental insurance market.

Insurance companies would, however, be free to offer their clients financial and other incentives to improve their health. Insurers would also be able to establish copays and deductibles. These incentives to properly use, but not overuse, the healthcare system would be subject to review by the independent panel of medical practitioners set up to oversee MSS.

This panel would also determine what the basic plan covers. It would do so subject to a strict budgetary ceiling, namely total MSS voucher payments would not be permitted to exceed 10 percent of GDP. Ten percent of U.S. GDP appears to suffice to finance basic healthcare, including nursing home care and prescription drug coverage, for the population. It is certainly a much larger share of GDP than is being spent on basic healthcare in other developed countries.

Once the vouchers are handed out, Uncle Sam is off the hook. The insurance industry and doctors, hospitals, and other private providers will be responsible for providing the basic plan based on the vouchers provided.

Since U.S. GDP will grow over time, total MSS expenditures will grow as well. Hence, the MSS panel will be able to add new medications, surgical procedures, new diagnostic technologies, and so on to the basic plan's coverage. But the panel will add these new coverages to the basic plan at a much slower pace than would occur under the current system. This will dramatically reduce the growth rate of federal healthcare spending, ensuring that the 10 percent ceiling on federal MSS expenditures relative to GDP is never violated.

How would we pay for MSS? With the Purple Tax, assuming it's enacted. Otherwise, we'd pay for MSS with federal and state government savings from closing down the new Healthcare Insurance Exchange (which I expect will be enacted), Medicare, and Medicaid and eliminating the federal income tax exclusion of insurance premiums for employer-provided healthcare benefits. Together these direct and indirect expenditures account for roughly 10 percent of GDP.

This healthcare fix will shave trillions off the government's long-term fiscal gap. And in providing all Americans with a basic health plan, we'll all be able to sleep at night. Those now uninsured will no longer face bankruptcy from an expensive illness. And those now insured will no longer have to fear the loss of coverage as a result of losing their job or switching jobs.

MSS achieves universal healthcare via universal health insurance. It doesn't nationalize the healthcare system. Instead, it maintains competitive provision and puts health insurers to work in generating the right incentive structure for people to improve or maintain their health, rather than cherry-picking healthcare winners and losers.

Finally, by handing the public their vouchers to spend on a health plan of their choosing, the MSS makes clear that the system is not free and that we all have a stake in ensuring it remain each year within its fixed 10-percent-share-of-GDP budget.

The Republicans will like this proposal, but the Democrats will be upset by the word "voucher." They shouldn't be. Every healthcare reform proposal includes some form of risk adjustment that keeps insurers from going broke because their clients are sicker than average. Recall that no insurer will be able to turn anyone down either directly or indirectly by charging premiums based on preexisting conditions. So if those who are sicker than average disproportionately sign up with a particular insurance company, the company will go broke if it's not compensated for the extra costs it will bear, on average. If it charges higher premiums to all its customers, it will lose them all to another company. The insurance companies, if they aren't compensated (penalized) for an unusually unhealthy (healthy) pool of customers, will try to make their plans as unattractive as possible to the sickest potential customers.

The only way to avoid these problems is to compensate insurance companies for taking on people with greater than average risks. And this can only be done by considering the objective health indicators of those being insured. If the risk adjustment is based on the care the patient actually received, the insurance companies will have an incentive to permit unlimited tests and doctor visits and pass the bill onto the government. So the risk adjustment needs to be ex-ante: "Here's what you get to cover Joe who has these and these objectively documented conditions." This ex-ante payment is, in effect, a voucher. But if Democrats prefer to provide the voucher using the words "Health Stamps," that works just as well.

To summarize, we need to provide ex-ante, individual-specific payments to insurers, no matter what they are called, to achieve two ends. To keep insurers from attempting to cherry-pick and to set a firm limit on what the government will pay. One path to achieving universal health insurance along these lines is for Republicans and Democrats to provide Medicare Part C for everyone. Under Medicare Part C, participants effectively get a voucher, which is individually risk adjusted, and use the voucher to buy a health insurance plan from an insurance company. Insurance companies participating in Medicare Part C include health maintenance organizations, or HMOs. They take the annual voucher and that's that. The government owes no more over the course of the year.

Under Medicare Part C, the vouchers aren't actually handed to the participants, who then give them to the insurance companies. Instead, they are effectively given straight to the insurance companies.[5] I think it would be much better to hand the public the vouchers directly so the public understands clearly that a great deal of money is being paid on their behalf and that they need to spend this "money" seriously in deciding which health plan to join.

Democrats like Howard Dean, former governor of Vermont, former presidential candidate, and former chairman of the Democratic Party, have been pushing for Medicare for All. And Republicans are particularly fond of Medicare Part C, which is their baby. So we can make both camps happy by adopting Medicare Part C for All; that is, by calling the Medical Security System "Medicare Part C for All" and making sure that Medicare Part C for All conforms with all the provisions of MSS.

Medicare Part C is called the Medicare Advantage Plan. It's a major part of Medicare. Indeed, some 10 million elderly are enrolled in a Medicare Advantage Plan, which represents one in four Medicare participants.[6]

And, yes, I know that Democrats feel that Medicare Part C has been too expensive because of the involvement of private insurance companies. But if we set up Medicare Part C for All with all the provisions of MSS, including a clear definition of coverages under the basic plan set by the MSS medical practitioners panel, electronic medical records, streamlined billing and insurance claim procedures, and tort reform that keeps doctors from practicing defensive medicine, we will turn basic plan health insurance into a homogenized product. At that point, competition will take over and provide the best basic healthcare to the American population that can be had for 10 percent of U.S. GDP.

Fixing Social Security and Retirement Accounts: The Personal Security System

The move from our current tax system to the PurpleTax will eliminate the federal income tax, and thus the tax breaks afforded 401(k), 403(b),

401(k) Roth, 403(b) Roth, regular IRAs, Roth IRAs, nondeductible IRAs, SEPs, Keogh Accounts, defined benefit pension plans, health savings accounts, and similar saving plans.

But these plans were set up to encourage saving, so won't eliminating them do the opposite? Not at all. These plans offset the disincentives to save arising under the corporate and personal income tax.[7] But the PurpleTax eliminates the federal corporate and personal income taxes as well as the federal estate and gift tax, and therefore eliminates all federal taxation of saving. Apart from state and city corporate and personal income taxes, households get to keep and spend all the interest, capital gains, dividends, and rents generated by investment of their savings.

Yes, we'll face a tax either before or after we check out at the store, but the PurpleTax is neutral as to when we spend our money. In contrast, the current system, in taxing not just our labor income but also the income we earn on our savings, encourages us to spend more today and less tomorrow (i.e., to save less). Thus, compared to the current system, the PurpleTax is much more saving-friendly.

In moving to the PurpleTax, we'll need to specify transition rules to deal with existing 401(k) and other tax-deferred savings accounts as well as defined benefit pensions, so that their owners can't avoid taxes they still owe under the current system. But once the PurpleTax is in place, saving in today's 401(k) retirement and similar accounts or saving done via defined benefit pension plans will afford no special tax breaks. As a result, these saving vehicles will go the way of the dinosaurs.

This is all for the good. These vehicles are highly inequitable, not to mention very costly to administer. Furthermore, the system leaves our employers with immense power to determine not just how much we pay in taxes, but also how we invest our saving.

Why would we want our bosses making these decisions? They are our employers, not our parents or our friends, and they don't necessarily have our best interests in mind. This is clear from the amount of employer-based stock that workers hold in their 401(k) plans. Investing with employers compounds the risk from labor earnings. If your employer's business fails, you not only lose your job, you also lose your savings. Yet many employers have forced their employees to hold their savings in the form of company stock. AIG's employees, Enron's employees, Bear Stearns' employees, Lehman's employees—there's a long list of workers who have lost their jobs and much of their life's savings thanks to their employers violating basic fiduciary standards, at least as economists would set such standards.

The fix then for our current tax-favored savings account system is simple—just enact the PurpleTax and let the old system wither on the vine. The fix for Social Security is also simple, namely: (a) freeze the current system in place so no additional benefits are accrued at the margin, and (b) replace it with a modern version of Social Security—the Personal Security System—that's simple, efficient, transparent, safe, and progressive.

Under this game plan, existing accrued Social Security benefits are paid as they come due. This means that current retirees, whose benefits have already come due, receive their current benefits on an ongoing basis. And current workers receive, in retirement, the benefits they've accrued to date. Freezing benefit accrual is easily implemented by simply filling in zeros in workers' Social Security earnings histories for each year after the date of the freeze.

Freezing Social Security will free us from a bureaucratic, underfinanced, inefficient, inequitable, and indecipherable 800-pound gorilla. But it won't free us from the need to force all Americans to save or to aid the poor in this endeavor. That's where the Personal Security System (PSS) comes in.

PSS is a personal, yet social, savings account system that features an 8 percent *compulsory* contribution rate. Spouses and legal partners would have half their 8 percent contribution allocated to their spouse's or partner's account. This way nonworking or low-earning spouses and partners have the same-size PSS account as the other spouse/partner.

The government makes matching contributions on behalf of the poor. The formula determining the PSS match can be as progressive as Congress wishes to make it. Hence, Social Security's current degree of progressivity could readily be emulated by the PSS.

All PSS contributions are invested at no cost by Uncle Sam in a global market-weighted index of stocks, bonds (including government bonds), and real estate investment trusts. Uncle Sam sets up one computer system (with lots of backups) to do all this investing electronically. He also guarantees that contributors' account balances at retirement equal at least what they contributed, adjusted for inflation. Thus the government guarantees a zero real return on workers' contributions. This guarantee entails the government providing minimal insurance, but will help us all sleep at night.

Between ages 57 and 67, each worker's account is gradually sold off by Uncle Sam on a daily basis at no cost to the PSS participant and used to purchase shares of a cohort-specific longevity mutual insurance fund managed at no cost by the government. Thus, Wall Street plays no role in this annuitization. Nor do private insurers. This is very different from typical privatization proposals, which rely on cherry-picking private insurance companies to provide longevity insurance to retirees.

In sum, the Personal Security System represents a modern version of Social Security, which the father of Social Security—Otto von Bismarck—would surely embrace were he reincarnated as an economist and asked to design a new, transparent, progressive, fully funded, low-cost, compulsory old-age saving and longevity insurance system from scratch.[8] The move to PSS also represents another means of reducing our nation's long-term fiscal gap by many trillions of dollars. The reason is the present value of accrued benefits is much lower than the present value of benefits projected under the current system.

Given the nature of Social Security benefit accrual, workers close to retirement will suffer minor reductions in their benefits, while those far away from retirement will suffer major reductions. On the other hand, younger workers will, thanks to the PurpleTax, be delighted to see the FICA tax go bye-bye even if it means giving up future benefits, much of which would not likely have been paid.

Removing the Fiscal and Economic Swords of Damocles

Coupled with limited purpose banking, the PurpleTax (which is a serious tax reform proposal notwithstanding its whimsical title), Medicare Part C for All, and the Personal Security System would do wonders for the economy. Each reform would complement the others, and selling them to the electorate as a joint package would be much easier than selling them individually.

The most important contribution of these policies would be to remove the fiscal and economic swords of Damocles that hang so dangerously over our children. We "adults" need to earn that title. For in the end analysis, our success is not measured by the quality or quantity of our material possessions. It's marked by the safety and security of our children. Their economic well-being is imperiled on many fronts. Business as usual won't keep them safe. These reforms are radical, but much safer than the status quo. We are at a turning point for our nation and our children, and we need at long last to seize the day and set our sights on their future, not our own.

Notes

Preface

1. My last job in Washington was in 1981 when I served as a senior economist for President Reagan's Council of Economic Advisors. Working in the Reagan administration, even at a junior level, suggests I'm a Republican. But I went to the Council for three reasons—the unique professional experience, a quixotic desire to interject sanity into economic policymaking, given what Carter had done and Reagan intended to do, and to get a date. I was at Yale at the time, and New Haven is tough duty for single male faculty.

2. Boston University economist Christophe Chamley and I first proposed limited purpose banking in a January 27, 2009, column published in the Financial Times Economists Forum (see http://people.bu.edu/kotlikoff/ newweb/LimitedPurposeBanking1-27-09.pdf). I subsequently discussed the proposal in singly-authored as well as co-authored (with Chamley, Columbia University economist Jeffrey Sachs, UCLA economist Edward Leamer, Ph.D., economist John Goodman, who is president of the National Center for Policy Analysis, Scott Burns, a nationally syndicated personal finance columnist, and Niall Ferguson, an economic historian at Harvard) articles, which appeared in the *New Republic*, Bloomberg.com, Forbes.com, FT.com, the *Dallas Morning News*, the *Boston Globe*, the *American Interest* and the *Financial Times*.

Chapter 1: It's a Horrible Mess

1. This description of banking practices by Goldman CEO Lloyd Blankfein may make the *Guinness Book of Records* for the chutzpah of all chutzpahs. www.dailyfinance.com/2009/11/09/goldman-sachs-is-doing-gods-work/.

2. http://thefinancebuff.com/2009/01/top-10-banks-in-united-states.html.

3. http://oversight.house.gov/documents/20081006125839.pdf.

4. www.bis.org/publ/otc_hy0905.htm.

5. "Fed's New Role as Lender Makes Some Uneasy," *New York Times,* June 13, 2009, pp. 1, 3.

6. Most of these bailouts are, it appears, coming in the form of lending on better-than-market terms, so from a immediate valuation perspective, they are losing propositions for U.S. taxpayers. Of course, there is always the chance the economy could turn around and make Uncle Sam's ostensibly bad investments look good.

7. "Print" refers to Uncle Sam either physically producing additional coin and currency or paying sellers for things it buys by creating, at the Federal Reserve, bank account balances for the sellers.

8. The Federal Reserve Bank of St. Louis keeps track of the monetary base. Its data series begins on January 1, 1959, recording a value of $50 billion. This is a statement about nominal, not real money creation; in other words, prices are a lot higher now than they were, for example, in 1909, so the amount of real goods and services the government can buy by printing a given amount of today is much less than it was in the past.

9. M1 is the sum of currency the public holds in its pockets or under its mattresses and its checking account (demand deposit) balances. When a dollar is injected into the system by Uncle Sam buying something, this $1 increase in the monetary base can lead to up to a $10 expansion of demand deposits and, thus, M1 if the bank getting the $1 deposit lends out 90 cents (in keeping with the Federal Reserve's 10 percent reserve requirement), and the party getting the 90 cent loan deposits this 90 cents in her bank, which leads her bank to keep 9 cents in reserve and lend out 81 cents, and on and on. The greater than dollar-for-dollar expansion of demand deposits and, thus, M1, via the lending process, of monetary base injections is called the M1 money multiplier. As shown at http://research.stlouisfed.org/fred2/data/MULT.txt, the M1 money multiplier was roughly 1.6 at the beginning of the current crisis. As of early June 2009 it had fallen to .9, indicating that the banks had severely contracted their lending.

10. As discussed below, no mutual fund would be able to take open short positions that obligate the fund to payments that go beyond the value of the fund's assets. That is, mutual funds can lose all their value, but they cannot impose losses on

third parties. Hence, hedge funds wishing to short securities would need to operate with unlimited liability.

11. The Bank of International Settlements (BIS) defines the financial sector very broadly (see www.bis.org/img/speeches/sp081119_g3.gif), placing the financial sector's share of GDP at close to 30 percent. I'd opt for a narrower definition, which places the share closer to 20 percent.

12. Wendy Kaufman, "Decline in U.S. Exports Hurts Jobs at Home," April 4, 2009, National Public Radio.

13. Department of Agriculture Report, September 4, 2009.

14. www.nydailynews.com/real_estate/2009/04/16/2009-04-16_us_home_foreclosures_jump_24_in_first_quarter.html.

15. www.hudclips.org/.

16. http://business.theage.com.au/business/world-business/us-housing-foreclosures-hit-record-20090417-a954.html.

17. Raising equity means selling stock of (ownership claims to) a company.

18. http://news.bbc.co.uk/2/hi/business/8016364.stm.

19. www.dailymarkets.com/economy/2009/03/09/markets-continue-to-decline-as-world-bank-predicts-that-global-gdp-may-contract-for-first-time-since-wwii/.

20. http://uk.biz.yahoo.com/29052009/323/instant-view-3-swedish-q1-gdp-posts-record-fall.htm.

21. www.npr.org/templates/story/story.php?storyId=103217192.

22. The Obama administration ably helped move Chrysler into Fiat's hands immediately after it declared bankruptcy.

23. www.nytimes.com/2009/04/16/business/16air.html and "Airlines, Already Suffering in the Downturn, Are Bracing for Further Woes," *New York Times,* July 14, 2009, p. B7.

24. Energy Information Commission, www.eia.doe.gov.

25. http://online.wsj.com/article/SB123284444303813147.html.

26. www.latimes.com/business/la-fi-caljobs18-2009apr18,1,4300050.story.

27. http://business.smh.com.au/business/us-housing-foreclosures-leap-81-20090116-7icz.html.

28. www.usatoday.com/news/nation/2009-01-11-lotterysales_N.htm.

29. www.nj.com/news/index.ssf/2009/01/atlantic_city_casino_revenue_d.html.

30. www.bloodhorse.com/horse-racing/articles/50592/kentucky-derby-total-handle-declines-53.

31. www.investmentpostcards.com/2009/01/03/stock-market-performance-round-up-torrid-2008-ends-with-guarded-hope/.

32. These figures are based on the Case-Shiller Index. The Federal Housing Finance Agency, which covers small as well as large cities and weights house price changes equally regardless of the value of the house shows only a 10.5 percent decline in house prices. www2.standardandpoors.com/portal/site/sp/en/us/page.topic/indices_csmahp/0,0,0,0,0,0,0,0,0,0,1,1,0,0,0,0,0.html.

33. www.businessinsider.com/henry-blodget-housing-market-2009-4.

34. www.globalresearch.ca/index.php?context=viewArticle&code=20090613&articleId=13961.

35. The decline in net wealth may be overstated if the decline in house values are those reported by the Federal Housing Finance Agency as opposed to the Case-Shiller Index. www.ritholtz.com/blog/2009/08/1-in-8-mortgages-behind and www.nytimes.com/2009/07/05/opinion/05rich.html.

36. Tom Barkley, "New Jobless Claims Rise as Labor Woes Continue," *Wall Street Journal,* August 21, 2009, p. A4.

37. www.bls.gov/web/laumstrk.htm.

38. Robin Sidel, "In New Phase of Crisis Securities Sink Banks," *Wall Street Journal,* August 21, 2009, pp. A1, A10. www.fdic.gov/bank/individual/failed/banklist.html.

39. www.businessweek.com/magazine/content/06_37/b4000001.htm.

40. www.smartmoney.com/Personal-Finance/Insurance/How-Safe-Are-FDIC-Insured-Bank-Accounts/.

41. www3.fdic.gov/idasp/, Gretchen Morgenson, "What the Stress Test Didn't Predict," *New York Times,* SundayBusiness, August 23, 2009, p. 1.

42. Ibid.

43. See Michael Pomerleano, "Geithner and Summers Need to Address the Banking Problems Square on," http://blogs.ft.com/economistsforum/2009/04/geithner-and-summers-need-to-address-the-banking-problems-square-on/.

44. www.cbpp.org/cms/index.cfm?fa=view&id=2231.

45. Leslie Eaton, Ryan Knutson, and Philip Shishkin, "States Shut Down to Save Cash," *Wall Street Journal,* September 4, 2009, p. 1.

46. www.cnn.com/2009/POLITICS/07/28/states.budget.crunch/index.html.

47. www.csmonitor.com/2009/0508/p02s04-usgn.html and Stephanie Simon, "Cash-Strapped California's IOUs: Just the Latest Sub for Dollars," *Wall Street Journal,* July 25-26, 2009, p. 1.

48. Ibid.

49. http://latimesblogs.latimes.com/money_co/2009/07/the-staff-of-the-securities-and-exchange-commission-has-issued-guidance-that-registered-warrants-also-known-as-ious-being-i.html.

50. www.lubbockonline.com/stories/071909/bus_465634882.shtml.

51. Ibid.

52. "Sunspot equilibria" is the term coined by economists Karl Shell and David Case in their seminal work showing the potential of economies to exhibit multiple equilibria, with the choice of equilibria (high or low levels of economic activity) being mathematically up for grabs, determined, as it were, by the occurrence of a sunspot.

53. www.dvrbs.com/camden/CamdenNJ-Kotlikoff.htm.

54. en.wikipedia.org/wiki/Modigliani-Miller_theorem.

55. Cerberus Capital Management is the latest hedge fund to go. It made a big bet on Chrysler and lost big time. Now its investors want their money back. The fund is highly secretive (see dealbook.blogs.nytimes.com/2009/08/28/ investors-flock-to-leave-cerberus-funds/?ref=business) and didn't expect anyone to find out what it was doing with their money. As Stephen Feinberg, the head of Cerberus, stated in a letter to his investors explaining his losers, "We never expected to receive the publicity surrounding those investments."

56. Naval.Technology.com, Net Resources International, a division of SPG Media Limited.

57. www.success-and-culture.net/articles/percapitaincome.shtml.

58. Jonathan Weisman and Deborah Solomon, "Decade of Debt: $9 Trillion," *Wall Street Journal,* August 26, 2009, p. 1.

59. Ibid.

60. Economist Perry Mehrling of Barnard College, Columbia University, has a fascinating new book called *The New Lombard Street*, which, among many other things, clarifies this government insurance role.

61. www.nytimes.com/interactive/2009/02/04/business/20090205-bailout- totals-graphic.htm.

62. The government could simply have provided explicit guarantees on these securities (i.e., it could have simply insured their full payment) and then had these government-sponsored enterprises (GSEs) sell their new healthy assets (insured toxics assets = healthy assets) to the market. This would have given the GSEs the same amount of money for their toxics, and, if you work through the cash flows, left the government in the same boat, in each state of nature, as well. So, even this direct outlay of $1.5 trillion can be viewed as entailing insurance provision.

63. As discussed below, this policy has yet to be implemented.

64. Lawrence G. McDonald and Patrick Robinson, *A Colossal Failure of Common Sense,* New York: Crown Business, 2009, p. 323.

65. Ibid, p. 298.

66. http://money.cnn.com/2008/09/15/news/companies/lehman_endofwallstreet_tully.fortune/index.htm. By some estimates, Lehman was leveraged 44 to 1. McDonald, op. cit., p. 287.

67. Ibid, p. 310.

68. Charles W. Calomiris. oversight.house.gov/documents/20081209145551.pdf.

69. Ibid, p. 2.

70. Nobel Laureate, economics professor, and *New York Times* columnist Paul Krugman wrote a column on July 14, 2008 ("Fannie, Freddie, and You") claiming that neither Fannie nor Freddie participated in subprime lending at all. Krugman columns are often marked by such "facts," reflecting what I believe to be sloppiness as opposed to any intention to deceive, but this was a real whopper. But Krugman was hardly alone. Most academic economists, including myself and Charles Calomiris, were astounded to learn what Fannie, Freddie, Ginnie, the Federal Home Loan Banks, and the other housing agencies were doing.

71. www.bis.org/publ/otc_hy0905.htm.

72. www.time.com/time/business/article/0,8599,1723152,00.html.

73. More precisely, what these companies really want is to conceal their positions from others, lest they be front run in the same manner as they, themselves, front run those whose securities they trade.

74. blogs.reuters.com/felix-salmon/2009/07/27/was-the-aig-bailout-a-goldman-bailout-by-proxy/.

75. I personally like and trust Hank Paulson, not that I know him very well. But his negotiations with Goldman were hardly disinterested. He appears to have held millions in Goldman stock in a blind trust designated for his children. www.huffingtonpost.com/2008/09/22/paulsons-conflicts-of-int_n_128476.html.

76. One important aspect of this freezing due to counterparty risk is that gross, rather than simply net positions, suddenly became important. Party G might have held two ostensibly offsetting securities—a CDS that it sold and a CDS that it bought on, say, IBM defaulting on its debt. But if the CDS it sold (insurance it provided against IBM defaulting) was sold to Party K and the CDS that it bought was from Party Z (insurance it purchased against IBM default), Party G, as well as potential lenders to Party G, suddenly had to worry if Party Z would pay up to Party G in the event that Party G had to pay off Party K.

Chapter 2: The Big Con: Financial Malfeasance, American Style

1. Lawrence G. McDonald and Patrick Robinson, *A Colossal Failure of Common Sense,* New York: Crown Business, 2009, p. 300.

2. www.time.com/time/specials/packages/completelist/0,29569,1877351,00. html.

3. Short selling refers to borrowing a security (e.g., a share of Microsoft) and selling it. The short seller is exposed because when it comes time to return the share of Microsoft stock (and the interest charge for borrowing it), the short seller needs to go into the market and purchase the share at the prevailing price. If the price went down, the short seller makes a profit. If it goes up, the short seller makes a loss. Naked short selling is when the short seller sells a share of Microsoft without having first borrowed it. He has to come up with the stock that he's sold at some point, but the naked short seller is saying to the buyer, "Trust me, I'll get you the stock I just sold you." In this case, the short seller and the stock buyer are both gambling on the short seller's ability to deliver the stock. So the naked short seller may arguably be viewed as engaged in more gambling in the course of her short selling.

4. http://oversight.house.gov/documents/20081006125839.pdf.

5. Kate Kelly, "Bear CEO's Handling of Crisis Raises Issues," *Wall Street Journal,* November 1, 2007.

6. JPMorgan agreed to revise its purchase price to $10 per share after realizing it had unintentionally entered into an agreement that left it very badly exposed in some circumstances.

7. en.wikipedia.org/wiki/James_Cayne.

8. http://uncyclopedia.wikia.com/wiki/George_Bailey.

9. McDonald and Robinson, p. 229.

10. Risk analysts refer to this as "operational risk." There are other, less polite terms I could suggest.

11. www.time.com/time/specials/packages/article/0,28804,1877351_1877350_ 1877344,00.html.

12. www.forbes.com/2008/12/05/merrill-lynch-oneal-biz-wall-cz_mc_ 1205merrill.html?partner=contextstory. I don't know many people on Wall Street, but I do know Win Smith, having spent some time with him when I was helping the Bolivian government find bidders for its oil company. Merrill would have done extremely well to have had Win at its helm in the past decade.

13. Louise Story, "Judge Attacks Merrill Pre-Merger Bonuses," *New York Times,* August 11, 2009, p. B1.

14. Ibid.

15. Louise Story, "Scrutiny for S.E.C. in Merrill Bonuses," *New York Times,* August 26, 2009, pp. B1, B5.

16. www.nytimes.com/2009/09/15/business/15bank.html?_r=1&hp.

17. www.newsweek.com/id/171243.

18. www.nytimes.com/2009/01/10/business/10rubin.html.

19. www.rollingstone.com/politics/story/26793903/the_big_takeover/print.

20. They each don't necessarily need to invest the same amount.

21. www.insurancejournal.com/news/national/2008/09/15/93707.htm.

22. http://seattletimes.nwsource.com/html/businesstechnology/2008911761_ilfc24.html?syndication=rss.

23. www.nytimes.com/2008/09/28/business/28melt.html?ex=1380340800&en=39f686dd31af8cbd&ei=5124&partner=permalink&exprod=permalink.

24. In the six months before it went belly up, AIG's CEO and Directors had neither a Chief Financial Officer nor a Chief Risk Officer in place. http://www.rollingstone.com/politics/story/26793903/the_big_takeover/print.

25. http://articles.moneycentral.msn.com/Investing/Extra/was-aig-watchdog-not-up-to-the-job.aspx.

26. www.washingtonpost.com/wp-dyn/content/article/2008/11/22/AR2008112202213_5.html?sid=ST2008122202386.

27. Ibid.

28. http://industry.bnet.com/financial-services/1000644/did-aig-find-the-dumbest-regulator-in-town/.

29. www.rollingstone.com/politics/story/26793903/the_big_takeover/print.

30. www.washingtonpost.com/wp-dyn/content/article/2008/11/22/AR2008112202213.html.

31. Connie Bruck, "Angelo's Ashes," *New Yorker,* June 29, 2009.

32. www.cbsnews.com/stories/2009/07/31/eveningnews/main5202115.shtml.

33. www.sandiegoreader.com/weblogs/financial-crime-politics/2009/jun/04/countrywides-ex-chief-mozilo-charged-with-fraud/.

34. Ibid.

35. http://online.wsj.com/article_print/SB12087381317152991.html.

36. http://projects.nytimes.com/executive_compensation?ref=business.

37. http://seekingalpha.com/article/156141-larry-summers-potential-conflict-of-interest.

38. http://bartelby.org/124/pres49.html.

39. http://people.bu.edu/kotlikoff/newweb/DallasMorningNews9-28-08.pdf.

40. www.mondaq.com/article.asp?articleid=84204.

41. www.investmentnews.com/article/20081110/REG/811109984.

42. www.bloomberg.com/apps/news?pid=newsarchive&sid=avZf2jYScvuk.

43. Part of the reason the SEC didn't investigate Madoff more carefully was that Madoff had a hedge fund. Hedge funds are formally and actually carve-outs

from the 1940 Investment Company Act. They do not sell registered securities, they are not regulated by the SEC, and they can only sell interests to rich people. And they are not allowed to advertise generally. Their offering documents generally allow the fund to do anything it deems likely to make money and provides for no disclosure of holdings to investors. The SEC does random inspections of mutual funds (registered and sold to ordinary folks), but not hedge funds. It does not even inspect hedge funds for inappropriate customers. Hedge fund accounting is a matter of contract between general partners and their investors, and is not governed by GAAP or any SEC rules. The only reason the SEC was so often in Madoff's offices was its interest in his off-NYSE trading operation, which did trades for ordinary folks routed to them by brokers. www.washingtonpost.com/wp-dyn/content/article/2008/12/15/AR2008121502971.html.

44. www.nytimes.com/2009/10/31/business/31sec.html?hp.

45. www.nytimes.com/2009/09/03/business/03madoff.html?_r=1&ref=business.

46. Ibid.

47. Just to be clear, this is not a legal definition. This is an economics definition or at least one to which I believe most economists would subscribe.

48. www.reuters.com/article/newsOne/idUSN0235590020090402.

49. The practice of the Fed and Treasury having a handful of top officials spending tens, if not hundreds of billions of taxpayers' dollars in a matter of days or hours, without consulting outside experts on the values of what they are buying, let alone, in the Fed's case, with its own board, let alone with Congress, raises very serious questions of fiduciary responsibility and legality.

50. Bob Herbert, "Chutzpah on Steroids," www.nytimes.com/2009/07/14/opinion/14herbert.html?_r=1.

51. www.mrrc.isr.umich.edu/publications/Papers/pdf/wp093.pdf.

52. Jagadeesh Gokhale and Kent Smetters headed up the Treasury team that generated this fiscal gap analysis.

53. http://people.bu.edu/kotlikoff/Who%20is%20%20going%20Broke,%20August%2029,%202006.pdf.

54. See www.ssa.gov/OACT/TR/2009/IV_LRest.html#267012 and divide the 3.4 percent figure reported in the table by the system's current 12.4 percent tax rate.

55. Alexander Blocker, Steven Ross, and Laurence J. Kotlikoff, "The True Cost of Social Security," mimeo, Boston University, March 2009, posted at http://people.bu.edu/kotlikoff/newweb/TrueCostofSocSecurity3-29-09.pdf.

56. Much of this understatement, incidentally, arises from Social Security's failure to properly risk-adjust its safe/sure benefit obligations to current retirees. When a benefit obligation is safe (a sure thing), risk adjustment simply means

discounting at the prevailing risk-free discount rate. In the United States, the risk-free discount rate is given by the term structure of yields on U.S. Treasury Inflation Protected (Indexed) Securities (bonds), also known at TIPS. Social Security makes no use of these yields in its valuations. Instead, it uses the same arbitrarily chosen real rate to discount its safe/sure obligations to current retirees as well as its (a) unsafe/unsure tax receipts payable by current and future workers, and (b) its unsafe/unsure benefits payable to these workers. The discount rate that Social Security is now using and has been using exceeds the real yield on TIPS of all maturities. There is a related study by John Geanakoplos and Steven Zeldes (http://cowles.econ.yale.edu/P/cd/d17a/d1711.pdf), which suggests that risk adjusting Social Security's liabilities could lead to a smaller rather than larger measure. But their analysis, notwithstanding some quite important methodological contributions to this nascent literature, undervalues the safe liabilities of Social Security (e.g., current and future benefits being paid to current retirees) by failing to discount them at the appropriate risk-free TIPS maturity structure.

57. www.ssa.gov/OACT/TR/2009/IV_LRest.html#267012.

Chapter 3: Uncle Sam's Dangerous Medicine

1. www.financialstability.gov/docs/regs/FinalReport_web.pdf.

2. Joe Nocera, "A Financial Overhaul Plan, But Only a Hint of Roosevelt," *New York Times,* June 18, 2009, p. 1.

3. http://baselinescenario.com/2009/06/18/too-big-to-fail-politically and www .nytimes.com/2009/06/17/business/17regulate.html?_r=1.

4. The Office of Thrift Supervision is slated to be eliminated, apparently due to its failure to properly regulate AIG.

5. www.nakedcapitalism.com/2009/04/guest-post-fdics-insurance-commitments .html.

6. The assumption here is that people would run on their FDIC-insured money market accounts as well. If banks stopped trusting banks, as they are wont to do in periods of financial crises, the use of credit and debit cards for transaction purposes could break down and make cash king with respect to buying things. In this case, Uncle Sam would literally need to print up 24 trillion dollars.

7. Some economists would disagree, claiming that moving money from our banks to our pockets wouldn't increase the money supply and would not, therefore, produce inflation. But hyperinflations are governed largely by people's fears that prices are going to skyrocket because the government's finances are out of control. This fear, rather than consideration of the precise size of M1, leads people to stop selling (swapping) real goods and services (hot dogs, sofas, cars, massages) except at very high prices (for huge amounts of money). Money

becomes a hot potato, prices and interest rates soar, and the economy panics and tanks. As revenues fall and borrowing becomes difficult, governments are forced to print more money. Hence, prophesies of hyperinflation can be self-fulfilling.

8. en.wikipedia.org/wiki/Argentine_economic_crisis_(1999%E2%80%932002).

9. Ibid.

10. en.wikipedia.org/wiki/Diamond-Dybvig_model.

11. See note 13 and www.fdic.gov/about/strategic/corporate/cfo_report_4qtr_08/balance.html.

12. Note that money market mutual funds aren't the same as money market deposit accounts issued by commercial banks. Such accounts are insured by the FDIC.

13. www.treas.gov/press/releases/hp1147.htm.

14. www.usatoday.com/money/perfi/basics/2008-09-16-damage_N.htm.

15. On dozens of occasions, money market funds have broken the buck, but their sponsors have topped up the funds with their own money to keep the net asset valuation at $1 and the fact that the buck had been broken out of the newspapers.

16. www.treasury.gov/press/releases/hp1147.htm.

17. www.moneymorning.com/2009/06/03/china-dollar-debt/.

18. www.atimes.com/atimes/Global_Economy/JI10Dj05.html.

19. Keith Bradsher, "China Moves to Beat Back a Tire Tariff," *New York Times,* September 14, 2009, p. A1.

20. www.wto.org/english/news_e/pres09_e/pr554_e.htm.

21. *Böse* is pronounced "bersa."

22. www.thedeal.com/dealscape/2009/05/aigs_cds_unwind_slows_down.php.

23. www.cnbc.com/id/27719011/.

24. www.aig.com/aigweb/internet/en/files/AIG%20Systemic%20Risk2_tcm385-152209.pdf.

25. www.annuityadvantage.com/stateguarantee.htm.

26. In the case of complete economic meltdown, the PBGC would have liabilities that the government could simply not cover in real terms. That is, the PBGC represents another case of insuring the uninsurable.

27. www.cleveland.com/business/index.ssf/2009/05/charles_millard_the_former_hea.html.

28. www.boston.com/news/nation/washington/articles/2009/05/29/labor_chief_wants_pension_insurer_on_less_risky_path/, http://network.nationalpost.com/np/blogs/wealthyboomer/archive/2009/06/15/zvi-bodie-debunks-stocks-for-the-long-run-on-pbs.aspx.

29. Reinvestment risk can be avoided by buying zero coupon Treasuries, and mortality risk can be hedged, albeit imperfectly, via puts on insurance companies' selling annuities.

30. The SEC has recently put an end to this practice with respect to all public companies by requiring that their pension liabilities be valued using AA corporate bond rates, which are lower than the actuaries were using and thus show larger liabilities.

31. http://norris.blogs.nytimes.com/2009/05/15/in-praise-of-slow-bureaucracy/.

32. www.tradingmarkets.com/.site/news/Stock%20News/2454150/.

33. Ibid.

34. www.pbgc.gov/media/news-archive/testimony/tm16758.html.

35. Prior to Goldman's move, the Fed was providing it temporary access to the discount window.

36. It's a wash insofar as it doesn't change the market value of the government's net wealth. But it does change the government's portfolio, and thus its risk exposure. Indeed, it simply represents leveraging by the government.

37. http://people.bu.edu/kotlikoff/newweb/Kotlikoff-Sachs%204-5-09.pdf.

38. http://blogs.ft.com/economistsforum/2009/04/the-geithner-summers-plan-is-worse-than-you-think/ and this contribution by Michael Spence http://blogs.ft.com/economistsforum/2009/04/the-geithner-plan-criticisms-are-off-the-mark/ that offers and alternative view.

39. http://people.bu.edu/kotlikoff/newweb/scrap_the_summers_geithner_plan.pdf.

40. www.treas.gov/press/releases/tg65.htm.

41. http://seekingalpha.com/article/141223-fdic-cracking-down-on-ppip-none-of-those-tricky-asset-sales-thank-you.

42. "Mr. Geithner is expected to propose that all banks maintain higher capital levels, with a big part in common stock. But so-called systemically important institutions—perhaps two dozen, mostly big banks, plus a handful of other financial institutions—would be held to even tougher standards. He is also expected to propose that institutions that engage in risky activities, like derivatives and proprietary trading, hold a larger buffer to guard against an industry-wide shock." www.nytimes.com/2009/09/03/business/03bank.html?em.

43. en.wikipedia.org/wiki/Enron.

44. www.icahnreport.com/report/2008/10/100-million-rea.html.

45. http://oversight.house.gov/documents/20081006125839.pdf.

46. The definition of Tier 1 capital that is used for purposes of meeting capital requirements incorporating not just owners' equity, but also bank reserves. But I'm ignoring bank reserves to keep things simple.

47. www.bis.org/publ/otc_hy0905.htm.

48. Not being an expert on financial history, I may be ignoring ways in which combinations of securities in existence at the time could have been used to approximate the payoffs of many modern derivatives.

49. www.nytimes.com/2009/06/11/business/11pay.html.

50. www.nytimes.com/2009/09/03/business/03bank.html?em.

51. http://blogs.wsj.com/deals/2009/07/30/wall-street-compensation-no-clear-rhyme-or-reason/.

52. www.marketwatch.com/story/bank-pay-unmoored-from-performance-cuomo-says-2009-07-30.

53. Ibid.

54. In Lehman's case, the 10-member board consisted of four members over age 75. Nine were retired; one was a theatre producer; one was an admiral; and only two had direct experience in the financial services industry. If there was ever a board picked to be a rubber stamp, it was Lehman's. http://blogs.wsj.com/deals/2008/09/15/where-was-lehmans-board/.

55. www.marketwatch.com/story/house-begins-debate-on-controversial-say-on-pay-2009-07-31.

56. Ibid.

Chapter 4: "This Sucker Could Go Down"

1. www.nytimes.com/2008/09/26/business/26bailout.html?scp=1&sq=this%20sucker%20could%20go%20down&st=cse. The president's full statement was "If money isn't loosened up, this sucker could go down." For a description of TARP.

2. http://afp.google.com/article/ALeqM5iFZoKx_qR_tpP1O-dGH0vh_zPWwg; www.cnn.com/2008/POLITICS/09/24/campaign.wrap/index.html.

3. The market crashed by 23 percent on October 19, 1987, but recovered later in the week.

4. www.reuters.com/article/newsOne/idUSTRE48O0KW20080925.

5. www.asksam.com/ebooks/releases.asp?file=Obama-Speeches.ask&dn=Confronting%20an%20Economic%20Crisis.

6. www.rvindustrynews.com/News/tabid/16941/ctl/ArticleView/mid/38805/articleId/3180/Obama-compares-economy-to-Great-Depression-during-Elkhart-trip.aspx.

7. www.pbs.org/moyers/journal/blog/2009/04/.

8. Apart from Keynes, himself, the economists who have made the significant contributions to our understanding of multiple equilibria and coordination failure include Axel Leijonhufvud, Karl Schell, David Cass, Peter Diamond, Guillermo Calvo, Enrique Mendoza, Nobuhiro Kiyotaki, Christophe Chamley, Roger Farmer, Costas Azariadis, Douglas Gale, Marty Weitzman, Bengt Holmstrom, Oliver Hart, Russell Cooper, Andrew John, Abhijit Banerjee, Robert Shiller, Sushil Bikchandani, David Hirschleifter, Evo Welch, and Markus Brunnermeier.

9. Actually, any price will do in clearing this market. Alex the buyer can hand Alex the seller, say, 50 grains of sand in exchange for the fish, which Alex the seller can then turn around and give back to Alex the buyer so he can purchase the fish.

10. http://gasbuddy.com/gb_retail_price_chart.aspx.

Chapter 5: Limited Purpose Banking

1. David Enrich, and Damian Paletta, "Financial Reform Falters as Shock of '08 Fades," *Wall Street Journal,* September 9, 2009, pp. A1, A20.

2. Ibid.

3. Andrew Ross Sorkin, "A Breakdown on Handling Big Failures, *New York Times,* September 8, 2009, p. B1.

4. www.nytimes.com/2009/09/06/business/06insurance.html.

5. www.atimes.com/atimes/Global_Economy/JI17Dj03.html; http://papers .ssrn.com/sol3/Delivery.cfm/99041603.pdf?abstractid=160989&mirid=1; http://en.wikipedia.org/wiki/Narrow_banking; http://www.imes.boj.or.jp/ english/publication/mes/2000/me18-1-4.pdf.

6. www.answers.com/topic/irving-fisher#Biography.

7. Fisher's optimistic assessment of the stock market a few days before its collapse in 1929 undermined his credibility from that point forward.

8. See Harvard economist and law professor Steven Shavell's seminal article on moral hazard and insurance: http://www.law.harvard.edu/faculty/shavell/ pdf/92_Quart_J_Econ_541.pdf.

9. The increase in real wages in the early thirties was modest and may reflect a change in the composition of the employed workforce, with the most productive workers, earning higher real wages, being retained, and the least productive workers being laid off.

10. www.time.com/time/business/article/0,8599,1909115,00.html.

11. http://en.wikipedia.org/wiki/Long-Term_Capital_Management.

12. www.bloggingstocks.com/2009/07/08/john-meriwether-closes-anothe-hedge-fund-after-steep-losses/.

13. http://news.bbc.co.uk/2/hi/americas/8016909.stm; http://www.thaindian.com/newsportal/health1/swine-flu-kills-more-young-middle-aged-people-study_100241457.html.

14. http://en.wikipedia.org/wiki/Swine_flu#1918_pandemic_in_humans.

15. http://virus.stanford.edu/uda/.

16. www.acli.com/NR/rdonlyres/66E129A1-58EA-4AF2-BC38-F568FD185762/16409/FB0708LifeInsurance1.pdf. See Table 7.1.

17. www.acli.com/NR/rdonlyres/66E129A1-58EA-4AF2-BC38-F568FD185762/16405/FB0308Liabilitie1.pdf, Table 3.2.

18. This 5.6 percent figure is the ratio of $1.1 trillion in reserves to the $19.5 trillion in face value life insurance obligations.

19. As indicated above, the cash surrender values for life insurance, annuities, and GICs appear to total roughly $3 trillion.

20. www.insuranceheadlines.com/Health-Insurance/5840.html.

21. I say this from personal experience. My own small personal financial planning software company, Economic Security Planning, Inc., uses Paypal to process transactions, and it often takes Paypal a couple of days to electronically transfer money from our Paypal account to our business checking account, which is with Bank of America. Paypal is, perhaps, the largest processor of online transactions and B of A is one of nation's largest banks, so go figure. Part of this, presumably, is that Paypal is taking its good old time to get our money to us in order to enjoy the float (earn interest on our balances).

22. http://74.125.113.132/search?q=cache:_RpTIJLUWFQJ:www.fdic.gov/regulations/examinations/supervisory/insights/sisum09/si_sum09.pdf+FDIC+bank+supervision+government+support+for+financial+assets&cd=2&hl=en&ct=clnk&gl=us&client=safari.

23. Before Captain Cook arrived in Australia, black swans had never been observed. Hence, everyone in Europe was 100 percent sure that all swans were white. Nassim Taleb's book *The Black Swan: The Impact of the Highly Improbable* is well worth reading in this regard.

24. http://en.wikipedia.org/wiki/Tontine.

25. Stiles, T. J., *The First Tycoon: The Epic and Life of Cornelius Vanderbilt,* Alfred A. Knopf, New York 2009, p. 19.

26. http://en.wikipedia.org/wiki/Mutual_fund.

27. http://en.wikipedia.org/wiki/Parimutuel_betting.

28. By the way, *King of Hearts* is a must-see movie, which ran for five years straight at the Central Square Cinema in Cambridge, Massachusetts. Those were the days, my friend.

29. www.bloomberg.com/apps/news?pid=newsarchive&sid=alPmYvSgJAF0.

30. Okay, but why not just apply Glass-Steagall to all financial companies? In other words, don't let any operate differently from commercial banks. This policy, it seems, translates into restricting what financial assets are sold in the market place. It suggests we can go back to the days of Bailey Savings & Loan, which we can't.

Chapter 6: Getting from Here to There

1. http://ici.org/pdf/fm-v18n5.pdf; www.federalreserve.gov/releases/z1/Current/z1r-5.pdf.

2. www.federalreserve.gov/releases/z1/Current/z1r-5.pdf.

3. http://news.bbc.co.uk/2/hi/business/1251019.stm.

4. www.ici.org/pdf/fm-v18n5.pdf.

5. www.nytimes.com/2009/07/14/opinion/14herbert.html?_r=1.

6. http://research.stlouisfed.org/fred2/data/TOTRESNS.txt.

7. Ibid.

8. This is the requirement for large depository institutions.

9. In moving checking account deposits into cash mutual fund shares, the banks eliminate a liability from their balance sheets. But in transferring reserves of equal size into the cash mutual funds to fully back the newly issued shares, the banks also eliminate an asset of equal magnitude. Hence, setting up the cash mutual funds doesn't change the bank's net worth, and income flowing from that net worth would fund the dividend payments or repurchases of bank shares.

10. See Zvi Bodie and Robert C. Merton, "On the Management of Financial Guarantees," http://findarticles.com/p/articles/mi_m4130/is_n4_v21/ai_13928778/ to understand the degree to which managing these risks can and cannot limit banks' exposures.

11. http://en.wikipedia.org/wiki/Rogue_trader.

12. Ibid.

13. http://en.wikipedia.org/wiki/Soci%C3%A9t%C3%A9_G%C3%A9n%C3%A9rale#.2411_billion_bailout_from_United_States_taxpayers.

Chapter 7: What About?

1. http://blogs.ft.com/economistsforum/.

2. This space allocation problem is referred to as the "tragedy of the commons." It arises whenever there is a commodity of real value, in this case, prominent FT web posting space, that's available for free, first come, first serve. The commons refers to unfenced pastureland, which English farmers collectively overgrazed because it was free to do so. Here we have economists literally talking over each other (one positing placed over another) because they are free to do so.

3. In the current system, lenders also put money in mutual funds, which give it to borrowers. For example, Fidelity Investment's web site lists over 40 bond funds available for purchase.

4. The Treasury doesn't auction off new bills and bonds every day, and in recent years hasn't issued new 30-year TIPS, but appears to be considering doing so in the near future.

5. www.chartingstocks.net/2008/12/campbells-soup-safer-credit-risk-than-us-government/.

6. www.forbes.com/2009/04/16/government-debt-credit-default-swaps-business-washington-default.html.

7. www.chartingstocks.net/2008/12/campbells-soup-safer-credit-risk-than-us-government/.

8. Inflation caused by printing money to pay government bills is an implicit tax because it reduces the real purchasing power of our nominal assets. Economists call the inflation tax seignorage.

9. Life insurance companies charge higher premiums for those in worse medical shape as documented by medical checkups and histories. Such underwriting can be accommodated under LPB by simply establishing separate mutual funds for those with different medical statuses.

10. A big problem here is that if the same, but very high price is charged to all, only those in most need of insurance will buy it, which then justifies the high price. Compelling insurance purchase by everyone in the relevant pool alleviates this problem. This is supposed to happen with the proposed Health Exchange, but the proof is in the pudding.

11. http://people.bu.edu/kotlikoff/newweb/FinallySystemRiskInsurance.pdf; http://people.bu.edu/kotlikoff/New%20Kotlikoff%20Web%20Page/Bagehot%20plus%20RFC%20the%20right%20financial%20fix.pdf; http://people.bu.edu/kotlikoff/newweb/DisInsAnswerFT101008.pdf; http://people.bu.edu/kotlikoff/newweb/Recapitalisingnotenough10_26_08.pdf.

12. James B. Stewart, "Eight Days," *New Republic,* September 21, 2009, pp. 58–81.

13. http://en.wikipedia.org/wiki/2008%E2%80%932009_Icelandic_financial_crisis.

14. http://research.stlouisfed.org/msi/.

15. Money connotes three things to economists—a means of payment, a store of value, and a unit of account. There are lots of things, including old baseball cards, which represent a store of value, but they aren't a very good unit of account. We don't price baseball tickets in baseball cards. We don't say, "Seat 15 in row 4 section 26 at Fenway Park costs 2,173 baseball cards from 1944, and no Yankees, please." So baseball cards aren't a standard measure of money. They are also a tough thing to use to buy lunch, meaning they are hard to quickly swap for other things. But they aren't impossible to swap, which means they could serve as a means of payment were push to come to shove. Over the centuries, all manner of things have been used as money, including cigarettes, large stones, and seashells.

16. www.nytimes.com/2009/11/20/business/20mortgage.html?ref=business.

17. robertreich.blogspot.com/, October 2, 2009.

18. research.stlouisfed.org/fred2/series/UEMPMED.

19. Greenhouse, Steven, "65 and Up and Looking for Work," *New York Times*, October 23, 2009.

20. www.nytimes.com/2009/11/07/business/economy/07econ.html.

21. money.cnn.com/2009/11/11/news/economy/states_economies/index.htm.

22. www.nytimes.com/2009/11/11/opinion/11dowd.html.

23. money.cnn.com/2009/10/30/news/economy/fbop_failure/index.htm?postversion=2009103023.

24. Dach, Eric, "Small Banks Fail At Growing Rate, Straining F. D. I.C.," *New York Times*, October 11, 2009.

25. www.msnbc.msn.com/id/33236758/ns/business-the_new_york_times/.

26. www.forbes.com/2009/10/12/dollar-reserves-central-markets-currencies-bank.html.

27. Anderson, Jenny, "Debt Market Paralysis Deepens Credit Drought," *New York Times*, October 6, 2009. www.nytimes.com/2009/10/07/business/economy/07shadow.html?scp=24&sq=wednesday,%20october%207,%202009&st=cse.

28. www.nytimes.com/2009/10/31/business/31aig.html?hp.

29. abcnews.go.com/Business/Politics/story?id=8140184&page=1&page=1.

30. www.huffingtonpost.com/2009/10/22/white-house-waves-off-dir_n_330270.html.

31. Morgenson, Gretchen, "When Bond Ratings Get Stale," *New York Times*, Sunday Business, pp. 1, 6. October 11, 2009.

32. www.nytimes.com/2009/10/22/business/22pay.html?_r=1&hp.

33. www.nytimes.com/2009/10/24/business/economy/24fed.html?ref=business.

34. www.nytimes.com/2009/10/27/business/27aig.html?_r=3&ref=business.

35. en.wikipedia.org/wiki/Maurice_R._Greenberg.

36. www.businessweek.com/magazine/content/06_13/b3977081.htm.

37. en.wikipedia.org/wiki/Eliot_Spitzer.

38. money.cnn.com/2009/11/11/news/companies/Benmosche_AIG/index.htm.

39. www.nytimes.com/2009/11/01/business/economy/01citi.html?scp=3&sq=citigroup&st=Search.

40. www.telegraph.co.uk/finance/economics/6394077/Mervyn-King-on-banks-the-key-quotes-from-his-October-20-speech.html.

41. www.nytimes.com/2009/10/21/business/21volcker.html?_r=2&hp. As indicated above, Volcker seeks to fence off good from bad banks via modern version of Glass-Steagall, which I don't feel goes far enough.

42. Ibid.

43. Admati, Anat and Paul Pfeiderer, "Increased Liability Equity," draft October 8, 2009, mimeo, Stanford University.

Chapter 8: Conclusion

1. Andrews, Edmund, "Obama's 2nd-Term Challenge Will Be to Undo First-Term Steps," *New York Times*, August 26, 2009, p. A4.

Afterword

1. See, for example, my book (co-authored with Scott Burns), *The Coming Generational Storm,* published by MIT Press in hardback in 2004 and paper back in 2005, and my book *The Healthcare Fix,* published by MIT Press in 2007.

2. www.ssa.gov/OP_Home/handbook/handbook-toc.html.

3. There is no direct taxation of wealth in our current tax system, but there are capital income taxes. In John's case, he can avoid all capital income taxation by spending his wealth immediately. Were he to live forever and live off the income on his wealth, he'd likely invest it in growth stocks and earn his capital income in the form of deferred capital gains, whose effective tax rate would likely run around 10 percent. This is the maximum degree of taxation that John would likely face under our current system. An 18 percent tax is clearly higher than either a 0 percent tax or a 10 percent tax.

4. This is an assumed average rate, not a marginal rate.

5. www.cms.hhs.gov/apps/media/press/factsheet.asp?Counter=3437&intNumPerPage=10&checkDate=&checkKey=&srchType=1&numDays=3500&srchOpt=0&srchData=&keywordType=All&chkNewsType=6&intPage=&showAll=&pYear=&year=&desc=false&cboOrder=date.

6. www.tampabay.com/news/health/medicare-advantage-sees-rapid-growth-but-draws-fire-in-health-care-debate/1039264.

7. The impact of the corporate income tax on the after-tax return to saving, and thus the incentive to save, depends on the degree of international capital mobility. If American savers can earn the same amount investing in foreign as they can in domestic assets, they can avoid getting burnt by an increase in the U.S. corporate tax by simply investing abroad. This doesn't work for individual income taxes, since the personal income tax taxes asset income earned worldwide.

8. www.absoluteastronomy.com/topics/Otto_von_Bismarck.

About the Author

Laurence J. Kotlikoff is a William Fairfield Warren Professor at Boston University, a professor of Economics at Boston University, a research associate of the National Bureau of Economic Research, a fellow of the Econometric Society, and the president of Economic Security Planning, Inc., a company that markets economics-based financial planning software to the public.

Professor Kotlikoff received his B.A. in Economics from the University of Pennsylvania in 1973 and his Ph.D. in Economics from Harvard University in 1977. Prior to joining Boston University, Professor Kotlikoff served on the faculties of UCLA and Yale. In 1981–1982 Professor Kotlikoff was a Senior Economist with the President's Council of Economic Advisers. Professor Kotlikoff has served as a consultant to the Office of Management and Budget, the U.S. Department of Education, the U.S. Department of Labor, the Joint Committee on Taxation, the Commonwealth of Massachusetts, the International Monetary Fund, the World Bank, the Harvard Institute for International Development, the OECD, and the governments of Sweden, Norway, Italy, Japan, Great Britain, Russia, Ukraine, Bolivia, Bulgaria, New Zealand, and China. He has also consulted for the American Council of Life

Insurance, Merrill Lynch, Fidelity Investments, AT&T, AON, Teva, and other major U.S. corporations.

Professor Kotlikoff has provided expert testimony on numerous occasions to the Senate Finance Committee, the House Ways and Means Committee, the Joint Economic Committee, and other congressional committees. Professor Kotlikoff is author or co-author of 13 books and hundreds of professional journal articles. His most recent books are *Spend 'Til the End* (co-authored with Scott Burns) and *The Healthcare Fix*.

Professor Kotlikoff publishes extensively in newspapers, magazines, and on the web on issues of macroeconomics, deficits, generational accounting, the tax structure, social security, health reform, pensions, saving, insurance, international trade, and personal finance. He is also a frequent guest on radio and television shows focused on the economy's performance and policies.

Index